The Canterbury and York Society

GENERAL EDITOR: DR P. HOSKIN

ISSN 0262–995X

DIOCESE OF COVENTRY AND LICHFIELD

CANTERBURY AND YORK SOCIETY VOL. XCVIII

The Register of

William Bothe

BISHOP OF COVENTRY AND LICHFIELD

1447–1452

EDITED BY

† JOHN CONDLIFFE BATES

The Canterbury and York Society

The Boydell Press

2008

First published 2008

A Canterbury and York Society publication
published by The Boydell Press
an imprint of Boydell & Brewer Ltd
PO Box 9, Woodbridge, Suffolk IP12 3DF, UK
and of Boydell & Brewer Inc.
668 Mt Hope Avenue, Rochester, NY 14620, USA
website: www.boydellandbrewer.com

ISBN 978-0-907239-70-3

A CIP catalogue record for this book is available
from the British Library

Details of previous volumes are available from Boydell & Brewer Ltd

This publication is printed on acid-free paper

Typeset by Pru Harrison, Hacheston, Suffolk
Printed in Great Britain by
Antony Rowe Ltd, Chippenham, Wiltshire

CONTENTS

PREFACE

An edition of the register of William Bothe, bishop of Coventry and Lichfield, was prepared by John Bates for his M.Phil. thesis at the University of Nottingham under the supervision of Professor Robin Storey and was submitted in 1981. Mr Bates was in the process of preparing this volume for publication by the Canterbury and York Society at the time of his sudden death in March 2005. At this point the files, including the majority of the index, were all but complete and very little additional work has been undertaken by the General Editor to complete the volume. The Society are grateful to Mr Bates' family for allowing the proposed publication of this volume to continue. This register is published by the kind permission of the Diocesan Registrar at Lichfield.

ABBREVIATIONS OF SOURCES

Axon, 'The family of Bothe' Ernest Axon, 'The family of Bothe (Booth) and the church in the 15th and 16th centuries', *Trans. Lancs. & Ches. Antiq. Soc.* 53 (1943)

BIHR *Bulletin of the Institute of Historical Research*

Boothroyd, *Pontefract* Benjamin Boothroyd, *The history of the ancient borough of Pontefract, containing an interesting account of its castle, and the three different sieges sustained during the Civil War, with notes and pedigrees, of some of the most distinguished royalists and parliamentarians, chiefly drawn from manuscripts never before published* (Pontefract, 1807)

Burke, *Extinct Peerages* J.B. Burke, *A Genealogical History of the Dormant, Abeyant, Forfeited and Extinct Peerages of the British Empire* (London, 1883)

CCR *Calendar of the Close Rolls preserved in the Public Record Office* (London, 1902–)

CPL *Calendar of entries in the Papal Register relating to Great Britain and Ireland*, ed. W.H. Bliss *et al.* (London, 1893–)

CPR *Calendar of Patent Rolls* (London, 1891–)

Dictionary of National Biography [old version] *Dictionary of National Biography*, ed. L. Stephen and E. Lee (new edn in 22 vols, London 1908–9, repr. 1921–2)

DKR *Deputy Keeper of the Public Records Reports*

Dugdale, *Monasticon* William Dugdale, *Monasticon Anglicanum*, ed. J. Caley, H. Ellis and B. Bandinel (6 vols in 8, London, 1817–30)

Eakwaker, *East Cheshire* J.P. Eakwaker, *East Cheshire past and present, or a History of the Hundred of Macclesfield in the county palatine of Chester from original records* (2 vols, London, 187–80)

Emden A.B. Emden, *A Biographical Register of the University of Oxford, A.D. 1501–1540* (3 vols, Oxford, 1957–9)

Emden, *Cambridge* A.B. Emden, *A Biographical Register of the University of Cambridge to 1500* (Cambridge, 1963)

Fasti J. Le Neve, *Fasti Ecclesiae Anglicanae 1300–1541* (12 vols, London, 1962–7)

Gascoigne, *Loci* Thomas Gascoigne, *Loci e Libro Veritatum*, ed. J.E.T. Rogers (Oxford, 1881)

Handbook of British Chronology *Handbook of British Chronology*, ed. E.B. Fryde, D.E. Greenway, S. Porter and I. Roy (Royal Historical Society Guides and Handbooks 2, 3rd edn, 1985)

Harvey, *Cade's Rebellion* I.M.W. Harvey, *Jack Cade's Rebellion of 1450* (Oxford, 1991)

Heads of Religious Houses	*Heads of Religious Houses in England and Wales*, ed. D. Knowles, C.N.L. Brooke, D.M. Smith and V. London (London, 1972–)
Magnum Registrum Album	*Magnum Registrum Album*, ed. H.E. Savage (Staffordshire Historical Collections, 1924)
Myers, 'The house-hold of Queen Margaret of Anjou'	Myers, 'The household of Queen Margaret of Anjou', *Bulletin of the John Rylands Library* 40 (1957–8)
Ormerod, *Chester*	G. Ormerod, *The History of the County Palatine and City of Chester* (3 vols, London, 1875–82)
The Parliament Rolls of Medieval England	*The Parliament Rolls of Medieval England*, ed. C. Given-Wilson *et al.*, CD-ROM, Scholarly Digital Editions (Leicester, 2005); print edition Boydell & Brewer
Reg. Catterick	R.N. Swanson, *The Register of John Catterick, Bishop of Coventry and Lichfield, 1414–1418* (Canterbury and York Society 71, 1991)
Reg. Chichele	*The Register of Henry Chichele, 1414–1443*, ed. E.F. Jacob (4 vols, Canterbury and York Society, 1937–47)
Reg. Langley	*The Register of Thomas Langley, Bishop of Durham 1406–1437*, ed. R.L. Storey (5 vols, Canterbury and York Society, 1949–62)
Registrum Sacrum Anglicanum	W. Stubbs, *Registrum Sacrum Anglicanum* (2nd edn, London, 1897)
RS	Rolls Series
Swanson, 'Lichfield Chapter Acts'	R. Swanson, 'Lichfield Chapter Acts', *Collections for a History of Staffordshire* (Staffordshire History Society 13, 1988)
Thompson, *The English Clergy*	A.H. Thompson, *The English Clergy and their Organisation in the Later Middle Ages* (Oxford, 1947)
Trans. Lancs. & Ches. Antiq. Soc.	*Transactions of the Lancashire and Cheshire Antiquarian Society*
TRHS	*Transactions of the Royal Historical Society*
Valor ecclesiasticus	*Valor ecclesiasticus temp. Henr. VIII. Auctoritate regia institutus* (6 vols, London, 1810–1834)
VCH	*Victoria County History*
Venn	*Alumni Cantabrigiensis* (4 vols, Cambridge, 1922–7)

GENERAL ABBREVIATIONS

archdn	archdeacon
B.A.	Bachelor of Arts
B.C.L.	Bachelor of Civil Law
B.Cn.L.	Bachelor of Canon Law
B. Dec.	Bachelor of Decrees
Br.	Brother
B.Th.	Bachelor of Theology
D.C. and Can. L.	Doctor of Civil and Canon Law
D.D.	Doctor of Divinity
D. Dec.	Doctor of Decrees
dioc.	diocese
ed.	edited
edn	edition
fo., fos	folio, folios
Ind. Archdn	Induction of archdeacon
Ind.	induction
L. Dec.	Licenciate in Decrees
Leg.	Licenciate in Law
lett. dim./l.d.	letters dimissory
Lic.	Licenciate
LL.B.	Bachelor of Law
LL.D.	Doctor of Law
M.A.	Master of Arts
M.D.	Doctor of Medicine
Mr	Magister
n.s.	new series
O.Carm.	Carmalite
O.Carth.	Carthusian
O.Clun.	Cluniac
O.E.S.A.	Augustinian friar
O.F.M.	Order of Friars Minor
O.P.	Dominican
O.Prem.	Premonstratensian
O.S.A.	Order of St Augustine
O.S.B.	Order of St Benedict
RR	Registrar
S.T.P.	Professor of Sacred Theology
t.	title
TNA	The National Archives

INTRODUCTION

THE BISHOP

William Bothe (?1390–1464), sometimes Bathe, Both, Bouthe, or Buth, was the first of what has been described as a virtual episcopal dynasty.[1] He was also, if Thomas Gascoigne was correct, the first common lawyer of his day to become a bishop.[2] His half-brother Laurence was successively bishop of Durham (1457–1476) and archbishop of York (1476–1480).[3] John Bothe, a nephew, became bishop of Exeter (1465–1478),[4] while Charles Bothe, a great nephew, was bishop of Hereford (1516–1535).[5] In addition to these prelates other members of the Bothe family achieved high office in the church.[6]

William Bothe was probably the third or fourth son of John Bothe of Barton-upon-Irwell, Lancashire, and his wife Joan, daughter of Sir Henry Trafford of Trafford, Lancashire.[7] As the eldest son, Thomas, was over forty when he inherited the family estate in 1422, and William's younger brother Robert is said to have been born in 1400,[8] William may well have been born about 1390, as A.F. Pollard asserted.[9] Although at his death John Bothe possessed property worth more than £60 p.a., which at that time more than justified compulsory knighthood, there is no formal evidence that he was knighted, even though he is named 'Sir John' in some pedigrees.[10] It is the knightly birth on his mother's side that is referred to in

---

[1]   A. Compton Reeves, 'William Bothe, bishop of Coventry and Lichfield 1447–1452', *Midland History* 3 (1972), 11–29.

[2]   Gascoigne, *Loci*, 48.

[3]   Emden i, 78–9. Laurence Bothe was also chancellor to Queen Margaret, 1452, keeper of the privy seal, and chancellor of England.

[4]   He was secretary of King Edward IV (1462–65), chancellor of Cambridge University (1463–4), and bishop of Exeter (1465–78): *ibid.*, 77–8.

[5]   For the life of Charles Bothe see D.G. Newcombe, 'Booth, Charles (*d.* 1535)', *Oxford Dictionary of National Biography* (Oxford University Press, 2004). According to Axon, 'The family of Bothe', 76–8, he received his LL.B. at Oxford University in 1484–5, but he is not included in A.B. Emden, *A Biographical Register of the University of Oxford to 1500* (3 vols, Oxford, 1957–59).

[6]   Axon, 'The family of Bothe'.

[7]   Axon, 'The family of Bothe'. Other references are in *Lincolnshire Pedigrees*, vol. 1, ed. A.R. Madison (Harleian Society 52, 1902); Ormerod, *Chester* ii, 17; Eakwaker, *East Cheshire, passim*; Burke, *Extinct Peerages*, 59–61; Thompson, *The English clergy*, 25, 42, and n. The Bothe family acquired the manor of Barton-upon-Irwell towards the end of the thirteenth century, apparently through the marriage of John of the Bothe with Loretta, daughter of John Grelley: *VCH Lancashire* iv, 366. The Traffords were neighbours of the Bothes.

[8]   Axon, 'The family of Bothe', 35.

[9]   *Dictionary of National Biography*, vol. xxii (supp.) (London, 1922), 235.

[10]   *Ibid.*

William Bothe's subsequent papal dispensations.[11] Of John Bothe's other sons, Robert married Douce or Dulcie Venables, younger daughter of Sir William de Venables of Bollin, Cheshire, and thereby became one of the lords of the manor of Wilmslow, Cheshire. He later acquired half the manors of Dunham Massey and Altrincham, Cheshire. He and his son William became sheriffs of Cheshire *conjunctim vel divisim* for both their lives in 1443, an appointment cancelled in 1462.[12] Several of their sons became clergymen and are mentioned in William Bothe's register.[13] Another son, Roger, received from William Radclyff, treasurer of Lichfield cathedral, a lease for three lives on the prebendal estates of Sawley, which were annexed to the treasurership, and established a third branch of the family in Derbyshire.[14] There were two others sons of John Bothe's marriage to Joan Trafford. Richard, a co-founder of the chantry of St Katherine in Eccles parish church, and of the chantry of Jesus and the Blessed Virgin Mary in the same church,[15] is said to have married a Suffolk heiress and to have left issue.[16] A man of this name is recorded as a justice of the peace and sheriff of Essex.[17] Of John Bothe nothing seems to be known beyond the inclusion of his name among those of the Bothe family inscribed on the tablets suspended above the altars of the two chantries at Eccles.[18] Laurence Bothe was a natural son of John Bothe and an unknown woman.[19] At some time he received a papal dispensation for bastardy. Although now lost, it is mentioned in another of 1442 for plurality, which excused him from mentioning his illegitimacy in any future graces.[20] In addition to his sons, John Bothe had at least five daughters who married into Lancashire and Cheshire families of their own rank – Byron, Weever, Radclyff, Southworth, and Clyfton – and who appear among the twenty-five names inscribed on the tablets above the altars in the two chantries in Eccles parish church.[21]

William Bothe's family background is perhaps better described as 'country gentry'[22] rather than 'aristocratic'.[23] Although he had served Richard II, John

---

[11] *CPL* vii, 459: 'of knightly birth on his mother's side'. *CPL* viii, 324, 448–9, 634–5, contain further dispensations for pluralism.
[12] Eakwaker, *East Cheshire*, 53, citing Sir Peter Leycester, *Historical Antiquities of Bucklow Hundred*, 244.
[13] **192** (Peter Bothe, rector of Northenden); **210** (John Bothe, rector of Thornton in the Moors); **223** (Edmund Bothe, rector of Thornton in the Moors).
[14] Roger Bothe received the lease from Mr William Radclyff, treasurer of Lichfield in succession to Mr George Radclyff (**135**). He was granted a papal indult to farm the prebend on 27 February 1451 (*CPL* x, 125). See also Ormerod, *Chester* ii, 380.
[15] **314, 315**.
[16] Axon, 'The family of Bothe', 36, again with unknown authority.
[17] *CPR 1452–61*, 263, 283, as sheriff; *ibid.*, 678, as J.P.
[18] **314, 315**.
[19] Burke, *Extinct Peerages*, 59–61, mistakenly makes him the child of John Bothe's second marriage, to Maude Savage; Thompson, *The English Clergy*, 42, mistakenly has him as the son of John Bothe's first marriage.
[20] *CPL* ix, 258–9; *ibid.* x, 338. For his birth see also Gascoigne, *Loci*, 194; *CPL* x, 125.
[21] **314, 315**.
[22] Thompson, *The English Clergy*, 42.
[23] L.R. Betcherman, 'The making of bishops in the Lancastrian Period', *Speculum* 12 (1966), 379–419.

Bothe was soon reconciled to the new government of Henry IV and served it loyally. In 1402 he was appointed to the commission to assure the king's lieges of Lancashire of the good intention of the government to maintain the common-wealth and resist those who cast doubt upon the king's policies and preached lies.[24] In the same year he was one of the fifteen commissioners of array appointed for Lancashire in connection with Henry IV's campaign against Glendower from Shrewsbury.[25] He was commissioned with five others to assemble the knights, esquires, yeomen, and other fencibles of Lancashire to meet the king on the occasion of Northumberland's insurrection.[26] A justice of the peace for Lancashire,[27] he was elected as a member for Lancashire in the parliaments of 1411 and 1420.[28] His son and heir Thomas was a member of a commission appointed by the Prince of Wales in 1401 to collect a subsidy in the hundred of Eddisbury, Cheshire.[29] John Bothe's services to the Henry IV could only have helped the family fortunes, and must have been a factor in the rise of the episcopal dynasty.

Despite some wrongful attributions,[30] William Bothe attended neither of the universities: only John Benet's chronicle calls him 'master', the title accorded normally to graduates.[31] It has been said that Bothe studied law at Gray's Inn prior to taking holy orders.[32] The anonymous historian of York who wrote Bothe's obituary certainly mentions his long association with Gray's Inn;[33] while Gascoigne refers scathingly to Bothe's background as 'a greedy common lawyer'.[34] Unfortunately, loss of the Gray's Inn records means that any association cannot be proved; though it is clear that he was a lawyer.[35]

Bothe's ecclesiastical preferment makes a formidable list. Although there is no record of his institution, he held the family rectory of Wilmslow, Cheshire, which

---

[24] *CPR 1401–5*, 130.

[25] *DKR* xxxiii, xl, 531. Sir John Massey of Tatton, Cheshire, who had custody of the lands of Sir William Venables, was killed at Shrewsbury, 1403. The Venables wardship was then granted to Sir Ralph and Oliver Staveley and John Bothe, and in 1410 Douce Venables was married into the Bothe family: J.S. Roskell, *The Knights of the Shire for the County Palatine of Lancaster 1377–1460* (Chetham Society, n.s. 96, 1937), 119–23.

[26] *CPR 1405–08*, 66.

[27] *DKR* xxxvii, App. i, 174.

[28] With Sir John de Assheton, Bothe was elected as knight of the shire for Lancashire in the county court held at Lancaster on 19 October 1411. Parliament met at Westminster on 3 November 1411. He was also returned as knight of the shire to the parliament of 2 November 1420: TNA, C 219/10.

[29] *DKR* xxxvi, App. ii, 43.

[30] *Fasti* iii, 600 (this is really a reference to John Bothe: see Axon, 'The family of Bothe', 63–4; Venn i, 205). See Emden, *Cambridge*, 73.

[31] The Chronicle of John Benet, published in Royal Historical Society, Camden Fourth Series, Camden Miscellany xxiv, 1972. Professor Storey kindly gave me a copy of his translation of Benet's chronicle.

[32] T. Fuller, *The Worthies of England* (London, 1840), 69; T. Harwood, *The History of Lichfield* (Gloucester, 1806), 144.

[33] *The Historians of the Church of York and its Archbishops*, ed. J. Raine (RS, 1879–94), ii, 487; iii, 331–3, 334–5.

[34] Gascoigne, *Loci*, 175.

[35] E.W. Ives, 'The common lawyer in pre-Reformation England', *TRHS*, 5th series 5, 18 (1968), 159 and note, lists the gaps in the records of the Inns of court.

he resigned in July 1418.[36] In 1416 Bothe received the prebend of Oxton and Cropwell (*secunda pars*) in Southwell Minster by exchange, resigning in 1422.[37] He held the prebend of Dunholme (alias Newport and Dunham) in Lincoln cathedral for a short while in 1420.[38] From 1420 to 1421 he was sub-dean and first canon of St Paul's cathedral.[39] He was prebendary of Consumpta per Mare in Walton le Soken parish church, Essex, from 1421 to 1423.[40] On 21 December 1421 he was presented by the king (patron as holder of the temporalities of the see of London *sede vacante* following the death of Richard Clifford) to the rectory of Hackney.[41] It was during 1421 that Bothe was ordained in St Paul's cathedral. He became acolyte and subdeacon on 17 May 1421, being described as a canon of Lincoln and giving his own benefice as his title.[42] Defects in the Canterbury ordination lists mean that details of Bothe's advancement to the diaconate are lost. He became a priest on 21 December 1421, under letters dimissory, with his title provided by a canonry of London.[43] Bothe kept Hackney until he exchanged it for the rectory of Leigh, Lancashire, to which he was presented by William, lord of Lovell and Holland, being represented at his institution by his brother Thomas as his proctor.[44] He held Leigh until his consecration in 1447, and in 1450 approved its appropriation to Arbury priory.[45] From 1429 until 1441 he was archdeacon of Middlesex.[46] He also held the prebend of Cherdstock in Salisbury cathedral from 1432 to 1441 when he exchanged it for the second of his Lancashire rectories, Prescot, to which he was presented by the king as duke of Lancaster, again being instituted by proxy.[47] He held Prescot until his consecration and shortly afterwards sanctioned its appropriation to King's College, Cambridge.[48] In 1434 he acquired the prebend of Langford Ecclesia in Salisbury cathedral,[49] and the next year was appointed master or warden of the hospital of St Nicholas, Pontefract. He resigned the hospital in 1438, receiving an annual pension of £40 on its annexation to Nostell priory.[50] He was prebendary of Chamberlainwood in St Paul's cathedral

---

[36] Eakwaker, *East Cheshire*, 88; *Reg. Catterick*, no. 166. Wilmslow rectory was assessed at 85 marks in 1379: M.J. Bennett, 'The Lancashire and Cheshire clergy, 1379', *Trans. Lancs. & Ches. Antiq. Soc.* 124 (1972), 7.

[37] *Fasti* iii, 450. He resigned before 12 February 1422, exchanging with John Rider for the rectory of Hackney. *CPR 1416–22*, 407.

[38] *Fasti* i, 62.

[39] *Novum Repertorium Parochiale Londinense*, ed. G. Hennessy (London, 1898), 8, 13, 20, 61, 177.

[40] *Ibid.*, 32.

[41] *CPR 1416–22*, 207.

[42] *Reg. Chichele* iv, for acolyte and subdeacon orders, nos 343, 349.

[43] *Ibid.* iv, 392.

[44] Lichfield Record Office, B/A/1/9 (Register of William Heyworth), fo. 115v.

[45] He was succeeded at Leigh by William Catton, prior of Arbury, on 13 July 1447 (**187**). For appropriation see **283**.

[46] *Fasti* v, 12.

[47] *Fasti* iii, 40. He exchanged with Stephen Wilton, D.D. (Lichfield Record Office, B/A/1/9 (Register of William Heyworth), fos 125–v).

[48] **281**.

[49] *Fasti* iii, 74.

[50] There are conflicting authorities here; see Boothroyd, *Pontefract*, 380, and *VCH Yorks.* iii, 320. Following Nostell's petition the hospital was to be annexed to the priory on the death or

from 1443 to 1447.[51] In 1438 he obtained a twenty-year lease on lands in Essex belonging to the convent of St Osyth for a rent of one red rose at midsummer.[52] Several papal dispensations for pluralism cover the years when Bothe was garnering his benefices.[53] Despite some uncertainties, Bothe may have been among the first fellows of Manchester college.[54] The college was founded by the de la Warres, the former feudal overlords of the Bothes;[55] the first master, John Huntyngton was clearly a friend of Bothe and appointed him as supervisor of his will and protector of his executors.[56] One estimate values Bothe's various preferments in 1432 at £176 16s 8d.[57] Bothe was obviously well-regarded by William Gray, bishop of Lincoln, who left him £20 in his will in 1436.[58] He was one of three canons of St Paul's suggested to the archbishop as suitable for appointment as keeper of the spiritualities during the vacancy of London in 1436 after the death of Robert Fitzhugh, but was not chosen.[59] He was an envoy of Canterbury convocation to the archbishop of York in 1439.[60]

The accumulation of such revenues argues that Bothe was in favour, and engaged in some form of royal service whose precise nature is obscure, which perhaps began in the reign of Henry IV. The first reference to Bothe as 'king's clerk' occurs in 1447.[61] His family background was probably a considerable advantage to him, but it is also likely that he had the help of Thomas Langley.

In 1445 King Henry VI married Margaret of Anjou, and shortly afterwards Bothe is referred to as her chancellor.[62] By this time he had clearly gained the confidence of William de la Pole, earl (later duke) of Suffolk. Bothe continued to act as the queen's chancellor after his consecration, until at least 1449.[63] He was

resignation of William Bothe, the present warden: *CPR 1436–41*, 90. The pension was payable in St Paul's cathedral: *CCR 1435–41*, 177.

[51] *Fasti* v, 29.

[52] *CCR 1435–41*, 188–9.

[53] *CPL* vii, 459; *ibid.* viii, 324, 448–9, 634–5.

[54] F.R. Raines, *The Fellows of the Collegiate Church of Manchester* (Chetham Society, n.s. 21, 1891), 21, 23; Axon, 'The family of Bothe', 38.

[55] *CPR 1416–22*, 366.

[56] 'The will of Sir John Huntyngton, 1458', trans. J.P. Eakwaker, *Trans. Lancs. & Ches. Antiq. Soc.* 3 (1885), 144–61.

[57] Axon, 'The family of Bothe', 38. Several references in the Calendar of Close Rolls refer to Bothe's lands in Lancashire. See *CCR 1419–22*, 255: memorandum of mainprize under pain of £40 15s 9¾d made in chancery in 1422 by William Bothe, rector of Hackney, to send troops to the King in France, with a covenant that the money shall be levied on, *inter alia*, the parson's lands in Lancashire. *CCR 1422–29*, 303, and *CCR 1429–35*, 243, which refers to recognizances entered into by Laurence Warrene to keep the peace towards William de Bothe, clerk, his servants and tenants in Withington, and towards Seth de Worsley and Margaret his wife, his tenants and servants.

[58] *Reg. Chichele* ii, no. 28.

[59] *Ibid.* i, 115.

[60] *Ibid.* iii, 284.

[61] *CPR 1446–52*, 55.

[62] *Ibid.*

[63] *Letters of Queen Margaret of Anjou and Bishop Bekynton and others*, ed. C. Munro, Camden Society lxxxvi, 1863), 156; Myers, 'The household of Queen Margaret of Anjou', 90.

followed in the office by his half-brother Laurence, who is first identified as chancellor to the queen in 1452.[64] The office was worth £40 p.a.[65]

The opportunity to promote Bothe to a bishopric came on the death of William Heyworth in March 1447. He was provided by Pope Nicholas V on 26 April 1447;[66] as he had been granted the temporalities on 29 March 1447 this was clearly in accord with royal wishes.[67] The formality of an election was followed, with the dean and chapter of Lichfield requesting a licence to elect on 21 April, which was granted a week later.[68] Although archbishop Stafford's register records the date of Bothe's profession at Croydon as 2 May 1447, a more likely date would be 2 June.[69] This would appear to be confirmed by the restoration of the temporalities on 3 June.[70] Bothe was consecrated in St Paul's cathedral on 9 July 1447 by the bishops of London, Bath, Norwich and St Asaph.[71]

Bothe remained in London for a short while after his consecration, performing an institution there on 28 July.[72] He then began what, in the absence of mandates, can be described as an informal visitation of his diocese, which lasted for ten weeks. On 4 August 1447 he was at Coleshill, Warwickshire,[73] and on 20 September visited his erstwhile rectory of Wilmslow.[74] He no doubt visited his brother Sir Robert at this time. He visited his cathedral cities of Lichfield and Coventry, and on 2 October 1447 exercised his right of visitation of Lichfield cathedral.[75] There is no firm evidence of the date of Bothe's enthronement, but it is highly probable that it took place on 2 October, to coincide with the visitation. The tour of inspection allowed Bothe the opportunity to take stock of his diocese, and he made a number of appointments that were to last throughout his episcopate, including the suffragan and the sequestrator and commissary general.[76] On 11 October, as he was about to leave his diocese to return to London, he appointed Mr George Radclyff, D. Dec., as his vicar general, renewing his commission annually until 1452 and his translation to York.[77]

The visitation of Lichfield cathedral was sufficiently thorough to cause Bothe to question the title of Mr Roger Walle, archdeacon of Coventry, to hold the hospital of St Andrew, Denwall in Wirral, and the rectory of Burton in Wirral, annexed to the hospital, with his archdeaconry. The matter was resolved by an episcopal

---

[64] *CPL* x, 125, 241, 516.

[65] Myers, 'The household of Queen Margaret of Anjou', 92, 93.

[66] *Fasti* x, 2.

[67] *CPL* x, 296.

[68] *CPR 1446–52*, 55; TNA, C 84/46/48; *CPR 1446–52*, 53.

[69] Lambeth Palace Library, Reg. Stafford, fo. 26v; see also I.J. Churchill, *Canterbury Administration* (2 vols, London, 1933), i, 270 and note.

[70] *CPR 1446–52*, 54, shows Stafford at Croydon on 1 June 1447. *Ibid.*, 55, has the temporalities restored on 3 June. It was usual for the restoration to occur on the day after profession of obedience.

[71] **10**. See also *Registrum Sacrum Anglicanum*, 89.

[72] **188**.

[73] **12.**

[74] **189**.

[75] **312**.

[76] **316, 240**.

[77] **11, 286, 290, 291, 294, 295, 299.**

declaration that the offices were compatible.[78] He also issued a monition to the dean and chapter for the repair of the clerical houses in the close at Lichfield.[79]

The medieval diocese of Coventry and Lichfield covered an enormous area, embracing the whole of the counties of Stafford, Chester and Derby, half of Shropshire, much of Warwickshire, a part of Flintshire, and that part of Lancashire lying south of the Ribble. The see had been moved from Lichfield to Chester in 1075, but the diocese was still frequently referred to as Chester.[80]

The diocese was divided into five archdeaconries: Coventry, Stafford, Derby, Salop and Chester.[81] It was, for an English diocese, relatively poor. According to the *Valor ecclesiasticus* of 1535 the spiritual and temporal revenues of thirteen English sees exceeded those of Lichfield, and only Rochester and Chichester received less.[82] The 1535 survey shows that the net income was £703 from a total of £796;[83] while the receiver general's account for 1464–5 shows that a gross income of £921 left a net total of only £359.[84] Out of this the bishop had to support his household and maintain hospitality, which in 1461 is known to have cost £180.[85] There were other expenses as well, including travelling, household fees and the regular drain of taxation; and the cost of maintaining the episcopal residences. It is clear that Bothe felt the need to economise. In 1448, with the permission of the archbishop of Canterbury and the chapters at Lichfield and Coventry, he rationalised the episcopal residences, receiving papal permission to do so in 1450.[86] The bull declared that the bishop's needs were well served by the palaces at Lichfield and Coventry, the manors of Haywood and Beaudesert, the castle and manor of Eccleshall, and the bishop's inn at Strand, London.[87] The bishop was empowered to demolish the surplus residences, which are not identified, and use their materials for repairing other residences. The abandoned residences are thought to have been Tachbrook (Warwickshire), Prees (Salop), and Sawley (Derbyshire).[88] Bothe adopted Haywood, about six miles east of Stafford, and twelve miles north-west of Lichfield, as his main residence in the diocese, although after 1450 Eccleshall castle, about 25 miles north-west of Lichfield, became his principal residence in the

---

[78] **277**.

[79] **232**.

[80] The Staffordshire Domesday refers to the lands held by the bishop after the Conquest as belonging to the bishop of Chester. The Rolls of Parliament also refer to the bishops of Coventry and Lichfield as bishops of Chester, a title still used well into the sixteenth century.

[81] *VCH Staffordshire* iii,

[82] *Valor ecclesiasticus* v, 128–9.

[83] *Ibid.*

[84] Staffordshire and Stoke-on-Trent Archive Service: Staffordshire County Record Office, D(W)1734/J1948.

[85] Staffordshire and Stoke-on-Trent Archive Service: Staffordshire County Record Office, D(W)1734/3/3/264.

[86] **276**.

[87] *CPL.* The bishop's inn at Strand is said to have stood at the south side next the river where Somerset House now stands. S. Pegge, *The History and Antiquities of Eccleshall Manor and Castle and of Lichfield House in London* (London, 1784), 10.

[88] *VCH Staffordshire*, iii. See also T. Harwood, *The History and Antiquities of the Church and City of Lichfield* (Gloucester, 1806).

diocese.[89] In 1452 he leased the inn at Strand, London, to William Cacemaker, at the same time confirming to him the lease of three tenements already held at an annual rent of 24s.[90]

As well as acting as chancellor to Queen Margaret, Bothe was engaged in other duties. In 1448 he was one of the seven men named to draw up statutes for the queen's foundation at Cambridge.[91] In 1449 he was commissioned a justice of the peace for Derbyshire, Shropshire, Staffordshire and Warwickshire.[92] He was again commissioned for Warwickshire in 1452.[93] He served on a commission to raise a loan in Staffordshire against sums granted in parliament to pursue the war in France.[94] He was present in the three parliaments called during his episcopate and was a trier of petitions for Gascony in the parliament of 1449–50.[95] He was at Westminster on 31 January 1450 when John Stafford resigned as chancellor,[96] and at the passing of the sentence of banishment on the duke of Suffolk on 17 March 1450. Acta for the summer of 1450 show that Bothe was at Leicester where parliament was meeting, and was, therefore, not attending the court in London during the suppression of Cade's rebellion.[97] His itinerary places him at Leicester on 7 June, the day after parliament had been dissolved;[98] at Eccleshall on 16 June;[99] and at Clayton, Lancashire, on 26 June.[100] There is no evidence to support Gascoigne's statement that Bothe was besieged in his palace by an angry mob.[101] Bothe's movements from Leicester direct to Eccleshall and then Clayton may be significant. Although he was far from the terror and bloodshed of Cade's rebellion, he must have been affected by the murders of Bishop Ayscough in his own diocese of Salisbury in 1450;[102] of Adam Moleyns;[103] and of his patron Suffolk.[104] Bothe remained in Lancashire throughout the summer of 1450 and into the early autumn, spending

---

[89] See itinerary in the appendix, which shows very clearly the way in which Bothe changed his residence after 1450.

[90] **273**.

[91] *CPR 1446–52*, 143–4. Nothing beyond the contents of the letters patent was known to W.G. Searle, *The History of the Queens' College of St Margaret and St Bernard in the University of Cambridge* (Cambridge Antiquarian Soc. Octavo Publications ix, xiii, 1867–71). Bothe's role is not mentioned by J.H. Gray, *The Queens' College of St Margaret and St Bernard in the University of Cambridge* (Cambridge, 1926).

[92] *CPR 1446–52*, 588, 594, 595, 596.

[93] *Ibid.*, 596.

[94] *Ibid.*, 299.

[95] *CPR 1446–52*, 412.

[96] *CPR 1446–52*, 194; *Proceedings and Ordinances of the Privy Council of England*, ed. Sir H. Nicolas (Record Commission, 7 vols, 1834–7), vi, 353.

[97] Gascoigne, *Loci*, 175.

[98] **202**.

[99] **203**.

[100] **254**.

[101] Gascoigne, *Loci*, 42, 175.

[102] R.L. Storey, *The End of the House of Lancaster* (London, 1966), 66.

[103] I.M.W. Harvey, *Cade's Rebellion*, 63.

[104] Harvey, *Cade's Rebellion*, 73, 75–6. The writer of the political poem on this event attributed Bothe's promotion to the influence of Suffolk: see 'Political Poems of the reigns of Henry VI and Edward IV', ed. F. Madden, *Archaeologia* 29 (1842), 320–1.

most of his time at the manor of his brother-in-law, Sir John Byron, at Clayton.[105] In July 1450 he was named to a commission to levy a subsidy in Warwickshire but could have taken little part in its work.[106] During that summer, safe with members of his family, Bothe busied himself with the work of diocesan administration, holding ordinations (which have about them a distinctly *ad hoc* flavour) in the chapel of the manor of Clayton.[107] He drew up the statutes for the chantry of St Katherine in the parish church of his native Eccles. The royal licence was dated 22 January 1450,[108] and the statutes for the chantry were completed on 28 July,[109] the first two chaplains being instituted on 1 August.[110] The apparent haste of the foundation may have been prompted by the events of 1450, of the summer in particular, and the fear that he might himself suffer the fate of Ayscough, Moleyns and Suffolk. While in the north-west Bothe visited Prescot, Lancashire, where he had once been rector, and no doubt visited his relatives in the area. He apparently began the journey south on 28 October 1450, when an act is dated at Clayton.[111] On 29 October he was at Bollin, Cheshire (part of the estates of his brother, Sir Robert Bothe),[112] and was at Lichfield on 1 and 2 November.[113] He was clearly on his way to London, where parliament opened on 6 November. In that parliament the pro-Yorkist commons introduced a bill urging the removal from the royal presence of some thirty persons. Bothe's name appeared fourth on the list, which also included his successor at Lichfield, Reginald Boulers, then abbot of Gloucester.[114] The king's reply to the petition was suitably non-commital. None of those named was banished from the royal presence, and in 1452 Bothe was translated to York while Boulers, now bishop of Hereford, moved to Lichfield.[115] Bothe remained at York until his death at Southwell on 12 September 1464. He was buried at Southwell in the chapel of St John on the north side. His brother Laurence was buried beside him in 1480; their graves were removed in the eighteenth century.[116] Bothe's will, proved on 24 November 1464, contained specific bequests of £1,506 13s 4d. He did not forget his two Lancashire churches at Leigh and Prescot, his chantries at Eccles, or the cathedral church of York.

On January 1450 Bothe received a papal indult allowing him to visit his diocese, and any other diocese he might receive in the future, by deputy for life.[117] At that

---

[105] Sir John Byron had married Bothe's sister Margery. He was a very powerful man in Lancashire and no doubt Bothe felt safer with him than with his own brother Sir Robert Bothe, whose estates lay only a few miles south of Manchester.

[106] *CPR 1446–52*, 412.

[107] **332**.

[108] *CPR 1446–52*, 322.

[109] **314**.

[110] **207, 208**.

[111] **143**.

[112] **48**.

[113] **103, 144, 260**.

[114] Anne Curry, ed., 'Henry VI: Parliament of November 1450, Text and Translation', in *The Parliament Rolls of Medieval England*, item 16.

[115] *Fasti* x, 2–3.

[116] For the wills of William and Laurence Bothe see *The Historians of the Church of York and its Archbishops*, ed. J. Raine (RS 1878–1894), iii, 334–5.

[117] *CPL* x, 59.

time he clearly expected to be regularly absent from his diocese, but this did not happen.

If attendance at the council is an indication of Bothe's importance, Bothe does not emerge as a significant political figure during his time at Lichfield.[118] Between 22 March 1450 and 29 August 1453 he attended only three out of a possible fifty councils. After his translation to York he attended a total of forty out of sixty-four councils, with a marked falling off towards the end of his life.[119] One of his last duties in Lichfield diocese in 1452 was to act as an arbitrator in a dispute between two Derbyshire men.[120] His political involvement continued until almost the end of his life; only in 1464 was he formally excused further attendance at the council due to old age and failing health.[121] If his assumed date of birth is correct he would then have been about seventy-four.

No churchman of his time has been more vilified than William Bothe. Thomas Gascoigne, who hated the family, is the contemporary commentator on whom later historians have drawn.[122] But he must be read with care, for (perhaps as a consequence of his own frustrated ambitions) he is not the most impartial of observers.[123] Following Gascoigne, Capes wrote that Bothe was perhaps 'the most unpopular prelate of his times'.[124] He was certainly the butt of contemporary scurrilous verses.[125] However, the evidence of the register suggests that Bothe was no worse, and perhaps somewhat better, than many of his contemporary bishops. He was present in his diocese more than he was absent from it, he instituted regularly to benefices in person, and showed a concern for the proper endowment of vicarages.[126] It is true that he showed little enthusiasm for holding ordinations, leaving that task to his suffragan even when he was in the diocese and could have conducted the ceremony in person.[127] He showed no greater enthusiasm for this duty after his translation.[128] But the evidence of the register does seem to show Bothe in a much less unfavourable light than usual, and must inevitably raise the question of the partiality of his critics. As Professor Storey has observed:

> ... our knowledge of the English church has been greatly extended by the study and publication of bishops' registers. It has been possible to modify conclusions once drawn only from the critical, and often adversely biassed accounts, of ecclesiastical practice and clerical

[118] The itinerary shows that Bothe spent very little time in London after 1450. See appendix below.
[119] R. Virgoe, 'The composition of the King's Council 1427–1461', *BIHR* 43 (1970), 134–60.
[120] *CCR 1447–54*, 358.
[121] CPR 1461–7, 341.
[122] Gascoigne, *Loci, passim*. On Bothe's promotion to York Gascoigne wrote 'quod memoria ejus erit in maledicione in saeculum': *ibid.*, 193–4.
[123] W. Pronger, 'Thomas Gascoigne', *EHR* 53 (1938), 54 (1939).
[124] W.W. Capes, *The English Church in the 14th and 15th Centuries* (London, 1900), 204.
[125] *Political Poems and Ballads*, ed. T. Wright (RS, 1859–61), ii, 225–9; 'Political Poems of the reigns of Henry VI and Edward IV', ed. F. Madden, *Archaeologia* 29 (1842), 320–1.
[126] **280, 283, 306**.
[127] **322, 323, 326, 343**.
[128] York, Borthwick Institute, Archbishop's Reg. 20. Bothe commissioned John, bishop *Insulensis*, as his suffragan on 21 October 1452 (*ibid.*, fo. 367).

behaviour provided by contemporary works of literature and political manifestoes.

THE REGISTER AND REGISTRAR

The register of William Bothe is numbered B/A/1/10 in the series of surviving pre-Reformation Lichfield episcopal registers, which runs unbroken from 1298 to the sixteenth century and is now kept in the Lichfield Joint Record Office.[130] It was rebound in 1975–6, but the binder produced a detailed report on its earlier condition and make-up.[131]

The register comprises 114 written folios, its condition being generally good. Some damp stains disfigure folios 72 to 74 but do not affect legibility badly. The pages have been numbered in arabic numerals in a consistent style, position and ink. These numbers were added prior to the excision of the now missing folio 75; but other excised leaves have not been included. The register now consists of nineteen quires varying from three to ten sheets (see following page).

The first quire contains the register of Mr Thomas Chestrefeld, B. Dec., keeper of the spiritualities, *sede vacante*. The quires were clearly not bound together until some years after Bothe's translation to York. Folio 88 in fact belongs to the register of Bothe's effective successor, Reginald Boulers.[132] The statutes for the chantry of St Katherine founded in Eccles parish church by Bothe and others in 1450 (folios 89 to 94), and for the chantry of Jesus and the Blessed Virgin Mary in the same church, founded by Bothe, then archbishop of York, and others in 1460 (folios 95 to 104) were clearly not part of the original register, even though the folios are numbered in the same style, position and ink, because the folios bear no scribal quire number. Instead they intrude into a sequence of numbered quires which otherwise continues from folios 86–8 (quire 16) to folios 105–12 (quire 17). Moreover, in the pre-1975 binding, folios 89–94 are included in a manner which suggests that they were a later addition.

This register had been produced with others from Lichfield, as evidence in Chancery proceedings in 1712.[133] An attempt had been made at keeping a somewhat rough and ready index of the more important matters in the register on the inside of the sheet of parchment in which the folios had been wrapped. This had been done in a contemporary hand, followed by some references to pensions in a later hand. Following this index is the entry relating to the production of the register in Chancery.

129 R.L. Storey, 'Ecclesiastical Causes in Chancery', in *The Study of Medieval Records: Essays in Honour of Kathleen Major*, ed. D.A. Bullough and R.L. Storey (Oxford, 1971), 237.
130 For the registers see D.M. Smith, *A Guide to Bishops' Registers in England and Wales, to the Abolition of Episcopacy in 1646* (London, 1981), esp. 53–66. For evidence of the survival of the register of Roger de Meuland (1258–1295) until the seventeenth century, see R.N. Swanson, 'The rolls of Roger de Meuland, bishop of Coventry and Lichfield (1258–1295)', *Journal of the Society of Archivists* 11, nos 1 and 2 (1990), 37–41.
131 This is now pasted on the inside of the back cover.
132 See **313**.
133 The note records that the register was shown in Chancery on 20 May 1712 in a case between John [Hough], Lord Bishop of Lichfield, and others, complainants, and Gilbert Walmsley, esq., and others, defendants.

Quire	Foliation	Leaves	Sheets
1	1–5	10	5
2	6–13	16	8
3	14–20	14	7
4	21–23	6	3
5	24–27	8	4
6	28–32	10	5
7	33–36	8	4
8	37–44	16	8
9	45–50	12	6
10	51–55	10	5
11	56–63	16	8
12	64–71	16	8
13	72–78	14	7
14	79–85	14	7
15	86–88	6	3
16	89–94	12	6
17	95–104	20	10
18	105–112	16	8
19	113–115	6	3

Bothe's register, with the *sede vacante* register of Mr Thomas Chestrefeld, is divided into three distinct sections:

(i) the archdeaconry section contains institutions and collations, exchanges and the confirmation of the heads of religious houses;

(ii) the general register containing commissions, compurgations of criminous clerks, dispensations for marriages within the prohibited degrees, appropriations, pensions, letters dimissory and many other matters;

(iii) the commission to the suffragan and a complete list of general and special orders celebrated in the diocese from 1447 to 1452.

No register of the vicar general, Mr George Radclyff, D. Dec., has survived; many, if not all, of his acta are in the bishop's register.

The register is not a diary of the bishop's acts but an important reference book, frequently consulted. It was made up from drafts which were entered onto the loose quires which were later bound up. The registrar kept a record of all acta as he travelled, entering them on the folios later when he had access to them. This delayed registration has resulted in occasional vagaries in chronology;[134] there are also some errors due to human failing.[135] The general register shows some attempt to classify material, grouping together pensions, appropriations, compurgation proceedings and other matters. The register was valuable not only to the bishop as a book of reference but to private individuals who had an interest in having certain

[134] **87** is dated 20 September 1448 and is followed by **88**, dated 28 May 1448.
[135] Edward Darleton appears twice as a deacon, in **329** and **330**. There are numerous errors of spelling of the names of ordinands and these are all indicated in the ordination lists and the person index. All deacons in **331** are subsequently 'lost'.

matters recorded in it for their own benefit. It is an often inadequate record of the bishop's acta; for instance the printed volumes of papal letters contain dispensations for marriages within the prohibited degrees that have not been included in the register. The decision as to what was entered in the register appears to have rested with the registrar. There is no means of knowing what was omitted, but doubtless much was.

Attempts to identify the scribal hands are not easy. A registrar commonly employed scribes to write up the folios that formed the register from the drafts that he himself had made, and it was quite rare for the registrar to do his own writing up. Richard Brancepeth, third registrar to Thomas Langley at Durham, did not employ a scribe to write for him.[136] Bothe's register records no creations of notaries, yet two notaries acted for the bishop. Their work appears in the register, and several others are named, some as having prepared instruments, others as witnesses. The first notary to appear in the register is William Gamull, acting in the diocese *sede vacante*, who drew up an instrument for Mr Thomas Chestrefeld, keeper of the spiritualities, during the vacancy,[137] and one for Bothe.[138] Gamull was a vicar in Lichfield cathedral,[139] but held no other benefice in the diocese. In 1452, before his translation to York, Bothe appointed Gamull as registrar and scribe in the consistory at Lichfield.[140]

The main hand in the register appears to belong to Mr William Brand or Brande. He was a notary who prepared several instruments for Bothe,[141] acted as a proctor for clerics on several occasions,[142] witnessed episcopal acta,[143] and is referred to as scribe in several places in the register and in papal letters.[144] Several times in the register Brand appears to have signed his name for different purposes in a hand that agrees closely with the main hand in the register.[145] The same hand appears in Bothe's archiepiscopal register at York.[146]

Little is known of Brand. He first appears in Bothe's register after the bishop's consecration, so it is quite probable that Bothe brought Brand with him from London. There is no record of his being appointed registrar. He was ordained acolyte by Bothe in the chapel of the manor of Clayton, Lancs., where Bothe spent the summer of 1450 following Cade's rebellion.[147] His orders were completed at successive ordinations in 1450–51, when the bishop was present in the diocese.[148]

---

[136] R.L. Storey, *Thomas Langley and the Bishopric of Durham 1406–1437* (London, 1961), 169.

[137] **5**.

[138] **281**.

[139] **312**.

[140] **274**. William Gamull, notary public, was appointed to the prebend of Berkswich and Withington on 1 July 1447 (Swanson, 'Lichfield Chapter Acts', no. 39).

[141] **278, 279, 280, 282, 283**.

[142] **32, 163, 198** as proctor for clerics at institution. **226, 231**, as witness to compurgations.

[143] **97, 167, 281**, as witness to acta.

[144] *CPL* xi, 49, 82; *ibid.* xii, 478.

[145] **88, 255, 279, 303**.

[146] York, Borthwick Institute, Archbishop's Reg. 20. I am grateful to Professor D.M. Smith for confirming this point for me.

[147] **332**.

[148] **334**: Subdeacon, 19 December 1450; **336**: Deacon, 20 March 1451; **337**: Priest, 10 April 1451. Had Brand taken his orders in the normal way he would have been ordained

Brand may have been a Lancashire man, possibly a native of Bothe's home town of Eccles. His title is given as the abbey of Whalley, Lancs., which frequently provided titles for ordinands from East Lancashire.[149] Brand received the prebend of Morehall in the collegiate church of Gnosall, Staffs., on 30 December 1450.[150] He received the rectory of Hodnet, Salop, from Bothe's successor, Reginald Boulers, in 1453.[151] He went with Bothe to York on his translation and prospered there, holding several prebends and ending his career as archdeacon of Cleveland.[152] He was also given the prebend of Oxton and Crophill, in the collegiate church of Southwell, once held by his master.[153] He was a witness to Bothe's will. Shortly after Bothe's death in 1464 Brand incepted in Canon Law at Cambridge.[154] He was dead by 1475.[155] Brand exemplifies the loyalty that Bothe appears to have reserved for his family and his trusted servants.

THE BISHOP'S OFFICERS

The administrative machinery that enabled the seventeen dioceses of England to function, even in the absence of their spiritual rulers, has been well described.[156] Lichfield was particularly well served by administrators, and Bothe, who was newly consecrated and therefore had no officials to bring with him to Lichfield, would have caused little upheaval in the administrative machinery of the diocese. He would appear to have continued with his predecessor's administration. During his tour of inspection of his diocese between 4 August and 12 October 1447 Bothe made the appointments that were to last the whole of his episcopate.

As his vicar general he appointed Mr George Radclyff, D. Dec., whose commission is dated 11 October, the day before Bothe started the journey back to London.[157] He renewed Radclyff's commission annually.[158] Radclyff was typical of that class of clergy, highly qualified in canon and/or civil law, who were attracted to diocesan administration with the rewards which were involved in such

subdeacon at general orders in Lichfield cathedral on 19 September 1450. He was still at that time with Bothe at Clayton.

[149] M.J. Bennett, 'The Lancashire and Cheshire clergy, 1379', *Trans. Lancs. & Ches. Antiq. Soc.* 124 (1972), 14–16.

[150] **106**.

[151] Lichfield Record Office, B/A/1/11 (Register of Masters John Wendesley and John Reedhill, D. C. and Can. L., keepers of the spiritualities, *sede vacante*), fo. 3v.

[152] *Fasti* vi, 21, 32, 57, 89. Prebendary of Holme, 1461–2; prebendary of Barnby, 1462; archdeacon of Cleveland, 1457–70; prebendary of Weighton, 1470–75. *CPL* xi, 163, 389. *ibid.* xii, 249–50, 251.

[153] *CPR 1452–61*, 278. Grant to William Brande, chaplain, of one of the prebends of Oxton and Crophill in the collegiate church of St Mary, Southwell, lately held by John Rider. It is interesting to note that Bothe exchanged this prebend with John Rider before 22 February 1422 for the rectory of Hackney. *CPR 1416–22*, 407.

[154] Emden i, 88.

[155] *Fasti* vi, 89.

[156] Thompson, *The English Clergy*, chapter 1.

[157] Storey, *Diocesan Administration*, 20–1, points out that diocesan ministers were well cushioned against displacement and at the worst they could live in their benefices.

[158] **11**.

work.[159] He was, like Bothe, a Lancashire man, and possibly related to him in some way. He was granted letters dimissory and was tonsured by Bishop Thomas Langley at Durham in 1408.[160] A graduate of Oxford University, he had obtained the degrees of Bachelor of Canon Law by 1414, Licentiate of Civil Law by 1424, and Doctor of Canon Law by 1432.[161] He had prospered under Langley, who had a preference for his fellow Lancastrians. Radclyff accumulated many benefices and dignities while in Langley's service, including the plum rectory of Winwick, Lancashire, acquired through Stanley influence.[162] He was also rector of the wealthy church at Wilmslow, Cheshire, in succession to Bothe.[163] While at Durham he frequently appeared as a witness to episcopal acta; but possibly Durham did not offer scope enough for a man of his abilities, and following a robbery at his Sedgefield rectory and a quarrel with a member of an important local family,[164] he returned to his native diocese through an exchange with Mr John Heyworth, treasurer of Lichfield cathedral and canon and prebendary of Sawley.[165] Heyworth received the rectory of Sedgefield and one other Durham rectory.[166] Radclyff continued to hold the treasurership until his appointment to the archdeaconry of Chester and the prebend of Bolton on 26 April 1449 following the death of Mr John Burdet.[167] Throughout his vicariate generalship Radclyff was resident at Lichfield, whence all his acta are dated.[168] The prebend of Bolton, valued at £65 in 1535, was the richest of the Lichfield prebends and its holder, the archdeacon of Chester, had a vote in the Lichfield chapter.[169] In 1452 Radclyff, then aged sixty-seven, obtained a papal indult permitting him to visit his archdeaconry by deputy for life.[170] Chester was still by far the most important town in the diocese, with the archdeacon, a virtual vicegerent in his archdeaconry, acquiring a house in Bacon Street, Lichfield, near the close, and leaving his archdeaconry in the charge of his officials.[171] In 1449 Bothe committed to George Radclyff his

159 **286, 290, 291, 294, 299**.
160 *Reg. Langley* i, nos 83, 61.
161 Emden iii, 1538–9.
162 Lichfield Record Office, B/A/1/9 (Register of William Heyworth), fo. 122. An undated letter from Humphrey, earl of Staffordshire, supporting his appointment to this rectory is extant in Thomas Baker's transcripts (R. Swanson, 'Lichfield Chapter Acts', no. 73).
163 *Reg. Catterick*, nos 166, 182: clearly there had been some dispute about the patronage of and presentation to the church at this date.
164 *Reg. Langley* iii, no. 883; TNA Palatinate of Durham, Chancery Enrolments no. 37 m. 5d.
165 Lichfield Record Office, B/A/1/9 (Register of William Heyworth), fo. 85v; Lichfield Chapter Acts I fo. 146.
166 *Reg. Langley* vi, 126.
167 **197**. *Fasti* x, 13.
168 **17, 18, 77, 78, 81, 82, 128, 170, 226**.
169 The prebend of Bolton had been attached to the archdeaconry of Chester since 1253. The church had been given to the bishop by Mattersey Priory, Notts., who retained the advowson (*Magnum Registrum Album*, 237–8).
170 *CPL* x, 228–9. The petition sets out that Radclyff was the son of a knight and then past his sixty-seventh year.
171 *Magnum Registrum Album*, nos 114, 121, 124–5, 561, 671–4, 737. Most of these law suits were heard before the official. It is clear that Radclyff had no accommodation in his

powers in the archdeaconry during pleasure by three separate agreements.[172] On 27 April 1449 he granted Radclyff all the usual powers of probate and wills including intestacy, the income of Peter's pence, sinodals, and mortuaries of deceased clerks, in return for an annual pension of £20 at Easter.[173] The same day he delegated to him power to hear and determine all causes whether instance, *ex officio* or *ex promoto*, and to exercise corrective jurisdiction in the archdeaconry, reserving to himself questions of heresy, simony, incest, and matrimony, and other causes which he might wish to reserve.[174] Competence in all divorce and matrimonial causes was conferred on Radclyff on 29 April 1449, with the proviso that he should inform the bishop of all the proceedings.[175] On 2 July 1449 Bothe appealed to the king for power to cite Cheshire offenders against the laws of the church to courts in other parts of the country, e.g. Lichfield, citing as his justification the protection afforded to offenders, adulterers, and fornicators in the city and county by maintenance and connexion.[176] The complaint appears to have been not without foundation.[177] John Burghill had tried to cite Cheshire clerks outside the palatinate, and had been forbidden to do so by the Prince of Wales.[178] Bothe secured a grant that was for his lifetime only, and Boulers ran into difficulty when he attempted to use it.[179]

Bothe appointed Master John Reedhill, B.Cn.L. and B.C.L., as his sequestrator general and commissary general on 20 September 1447.[180] The commission included probate jurisdiction as well as the sequestration of the goods of vacant benefices and of intestates, the correction of absentees, the punishment of illicit farming of benefices, and the examination of witnesses for the official of the consistory. Reedhill was prebendary successively of Ufton Cantoris and Pipa Minor or Prees in Lichfield cathedral,[181] and held a canonry and prebend in the collegiate church of St Chad, Salop, which he exchanged for a prebend in Salisbury

---

archdeaconry, though some of his predecessors had been dispensed to hold the church of Davenham in plurality so as to enable them to have a pied-à-terre in Cheshire.

[172], **238, 239**.

[173] For a full discussion of the exercise of the episcopal jurisdiction in Chester archdeaconry see P. Heath, 'The medieval archdeaconry and Tudor bishopric of Chester', *Journal of Ecclesiastical History* 19 (1969), 243–52.

[174] **238**.

[175] **239**.

[176] *Proceedings and Ordinances of the Privy Council*, ed. Sir H. Nicolas (Record Commission, 1834–37), vi, 75–6; *English Historical Documents 1327–1485*, ed. A.R. Myers (London and new York, 1969), 1228.

[177] G. Barraclough, 'The earldom and palatinate of Chester', *Tranasctions of the Historical Society of Lancashire and Cheshire* no. 103 (1951), 25–37. See also D. Jones, *The Church in Chester 1300–1540* (Chetham Society, 3rd series 7 (1957).

[178] Lichfield Record Office, B/A/1/7 (Register of John Burghill), fo. 89v. The prohibition did not apply to appeals and *querela*.

[179] Lichfield Record Office, B/A/1/11 (Register of Reginald Boulers), fos 68, 68v, 69. The documents are printed in Heath, 'The medieval archdeaconry and Tudor bishopric of Chester', 251–2.

[180] **240**.

[181] **66**. Reedhill was collated to Ufton Cantoris on 16 February 1452. There is no account of the negotiations for the exchange that appears to have taken place between Reedhill and Wendesley for Pipa Minor in 1459 (*Fasti* x, 49, 62).

cathedral in 1450.[182] A frequent witness to episcopal acta,[183] he presided over an inquest at Leek in 1450 to determine the true value of the vicarage there.[184] The register contains no other record of Reedhill and his work, nor of the appointment of any of the deputies he would have needed in so vast a diocese. Together with Mr John Wendesley he was keeper of the spiritualities in the vacancies following Bothe's translation to York and the death of Nicholas Cloos, Bothe's immediate nominal successor at Lichfield.[185]

Master John Wendesley, B.Cn.L. and B.C.L., continued to act as official principal throughout the episcopate and became, with Reedhill, a keeper of the spiritualities in the vacancies following Bothe's translation and the death of Cloos.[186] Wendesley was archdeacon of Stafford from 1442 to 1459,[187] prebendary of Prees from 1441 to 1459,[188] and then prebendary of Ufton Cantoris, apparently by exchange with John Reedhill. The only references to him in the register are of his acting as a commissary in the compurgation of a criminous clerk,[189] and of his being granted a clerical house in the close at Lichfield.[190] The one surviving record of his work is apparently a sentence in a dispute over the chapel at Alvanley, Cheshire.[191]

Among minor appointments in the register are those of an apparitor general,[192] a clerk of the bishop's courts in Staffordshire and Shropshire,[193] and in 1452 the appointment of William Gamull, notary and scribe, as such in the consistory.[194] Gamull, who had prepared instruments for Bothe during his episcopate, was apparently receiving the reward Bothe felt was due to a faithful servant for whom no place could be found at York.[195]

The archdeaconries of Coventry, Stafford, Derby, and Salop, unlike Chester, had no prebends attached to them, though their archdeacons did hold prebends. The archdeacons had only fees and perquisites for their support. Roger Wall served as archdeacon of Coventry from 1442 to 1488,[196] John Wendesley at Stafford from 1442 to 1459,[197] and Mr John Bride, B.C.L., held Derby from 1431 to 1473.[198] At Salop Bothe had to fill the vacancy caused by the resignation of Mr

---

[182] **176.**

[183] **97, 280, 303.**

[184] **306.**

[185] Lichfield Record Office, B/A/11/1.

[186] Lichfield Record Office, B/A/11/2–7.

[187] Lichfield Record Office, B/A/1/9 (Register of William Heyworth), fo. 70.

[188] *Ibid.*, fo. 105v.

[189] **226.**

[190] **287.**

[191] Cheshire and Chester Archives and Local Studies, CR 63/2/55. Details of a ruling by the official principal in a case concerning the chapel of Alvanley (1450).

[192] **292.**

[193] **293.**

[194] **274.**

[195] In the light of the uncertainty created when a bishop was translated and might bring with him his own officials this appointment might be seen as an insurance for Gamull, who, apart from being a vicar in Lichfield cathedral (**312**) does not appear to have held a benefice in the diocese.

[196] *Fasti* x, 15.

[197] *Ibid.*, 20. Wendesley succeeded Roger Wall, who was archdeacon briefly in 1442.

[198] *Ibid.*, 16.

Thomas Salisbury, archdeacon from 1437 to 1450, and collated the archdeaconry to Thomas Lye.[199] That Mr George Radclyff succeeded Mr John Burdet at Chester has already been noted. The register throws little light on the archdeacons, who were almost invariably mandated to induct within their archdeaconries.[200] No more light is thrown on the rural deans and their work, beyond the occasional reference in connexion with proclamations concerning criminous clerks.

As suffragan Bothe commissioned John, bishop *Insulensis*,[201] to replace the long-serving Robert Mulfield, bishop of Killaloe, who had been appointed in 1416.[202] Mulfield conducted his last orders in the diocese on 9 June 1447, *sede vacante*.[203]

There is some confusion over the identity of this suffragan bishop John and the see to which he was provided by Pope Nicholas V, which is named in the bull as *Insulensis*.[204] One identification of the see is Kilfernora, but it is almost certain that it was properly Scattery Island.[205] However, he certainly never set foot in Ireland, as is shown in his petition to Rome in 1458.[206] The religious who wished to gain episcopal status made free use of the smaller Irish sees to obtain their object, and thereafter a suffragan's commission in an English diocese. Although his provision restricted the exercise of his episcopal office to Ireland, John celebrated general and special ordinations in Lichfield diocese in September 1447 and regularly throughout Bothe's pontificate, conducting nineteen of the twenty general ordinations and four of the eight special ordinations held in the diocese between 1447 and 1452.[207]

The suffragan has been identified as John Grene, an Augustinian canon and former prior of Leighs, Essex.[208] He has also been confused with the bishop of Sodor and Man.[209] Bothe collated to him the vicarage of Dunchurch, Warwicks., vacant, by a strange coincidence, by the death of a John Grene, on 9 February 1449.[210] In October 1450 he was involved in an exchange for the rectory of

---

[199] *Ibid.*, 18. **173**.

[200] The calendar of the arhcdeaconry section includes a note of the person mandated to induct. There are few exceptions to the archdeacon or his official.

[201] **316**.

[202] Mulfield was a Cistercian of Meaux Abbey, Yorks. (*Registrum Sacrum Anglicanum*, 207; *CPL* vii, 7–8, 279).

[203] **9**.

[204] *CPL* x, 196 and note.

[205] The suffragan has in the past been wrongly included among the bishops of Sodor and Man (*Registrum Sacrum Anglicanum*, 212), but his Irish see was in fact Scattery Island in the province of Cashel.

[206] *CPL* xi, 181. The petition sets out that the suffragan had been unable to obtain possession of his church of Kilfernora, being prevented from entering his see by enemies of himself and King Henry VI. He asks to be allowed to receive, and to hold, *in commendam* for life, any benefice to be held with his vicarage of Godemanchester, Lincoln diocese, for his maintenance.

[207] *CPL* x, 296. 'He shall be able to exercise pontifical offices only in his said church and in a cathedral, even metropolitan, and other churches in Ireland.'

[208] Dugdale, *Monasticon* vi, 552. Grene is stated to have resigned his office as prior of Leighs priory on 16 November 1443.

[209] Thompson, *The English Clergy*, 42.

[210] **43**.

Blesworth, Northants, which evidently fell through.[211] In February 1451 he was again involved in an exchange, this time with the rector of Little Billing, Northants.[212] That both of the benefices he sought were in the same county suggests that he might have had some special reason for wishing to go there. Apart from his duties at ordinations there is no record of any other exercise of his jurisdiction, although he might be expected to have been involved in the re-consecration of polluted churchyards.

The date of the suffragan's provision raises the question of whether he was known to Bothe, chosen by him to be his suffragan, and provided to his Irish see in readiness to act as soon as Bothe himself had been consecrated. John went with Bothe to York, where he was again commissioned as suffragan and carried out ordinations.[213] He was also commissioned by Boulers at Lichfield,[214] and appears among the Canterbury suffragans.[215]

In 1452, following the death of John Stafford, there was a great change round in the dioceses of England. Kempe was translated from York to Canterbury, Bothe from Coventry and Lichfield to York, Nicholas Close from Carlisle to Coventry and Lichfield, while William Percy was appointed bishop of Carlisle, thereby increasing the Percy influence in the west march. Bothe's translation to York shows that he was still valued at a court that was still able to determine episcopal promotions, though it is doubtful whether he would have been promoted in 1454 or later. He took with him to York his suffragan, John, bishop *Insulensis*, Thomas Byrom, William Brande (his registrar and scribe), and his chaplain, Robert Bromezerde, canon of St John's, Chester, and rector of Hackney.[216]

EDITORIAL METHOD

This edition of the register of William Bothe gives in as concise a form as is consistent with clarity all the essential information from the register, including all personal and place names. The whole of the register has been produced, entries being calendared in the order in which they appear in the original, without omission or rearrangement and all numbered serially. Dates have been adjusted to show the year beginning on 1 January rather than following the year of grace but for the period 1 January to 24 March years are given in the form 1450/1. Latin transcripts of at least one entry of each type have been given, following a brief summary in English of their contents. Place names are given in modern form followed by the original spelling in parenthesis. Where surnames are not provided in the document but the individual can be identified surnames are given in square

---

[211] **48**.

[212] **55**.

[213] Borthwick Institute, Archbp Reg. 20, fo. 367. The commission is dated 21 October 1452. The suffragan conducted his first ordination ceremony in York diocese on 23 December 1452 (*ibid.*, fo. 412).

[214] Lichfield Record Office, B/A/1/11 (Register of Reginald Boulers), fo. 83v.

[215] *Handbook of British Chronology*, 329.

[216] Byrom and Brande were witnesses to Bothe's will. Bromezerde was dead before 23 December 1457 when his prebend at the collegiate church of St John Chester was filled (Lichfield Record Office, B/A/1/11 (Register of Reginald Boulers), fo. 42v).

brackets. Unidentified place names, of which there are only two, are italicised. In transcripts abbreviations and contractions have been expanded. The letters v/u have been standardised but i/j c/t are retained as in the original. Christian names have been modernised but surnames have been given in their original form.

The ordination lists are not reproduced in full. Only subdeacons are listed in full and all subsequent references to ordinands are restricted to surnames with a note of any discrepancy from the subdeacon entry and a reference to the number of that entry. This method, apart from saving space, has the merit of exposing errors which might not otherwise be detected.

Institutions to benefices in the register normally include a note that the appropriate archdeacon or his official has been mandated to induct and this is shown by Ind. Archdn. Institutions to vicarages and chantries invariably include a reference to the requirement of continued and permanent residence and this is omitted from the calendar.

1. [Fo. 1] REGISTRUM THOME CHESTREFELD, IN DECRETIS BACALLARII, CUSTODIS SPIRITUALITATIS EPISCOPATUS COVENTRENSIS ET LICHFELDENSIS SEDE IBIDEM VACANTE PER REVERENDISSIMUM IN CHRISTO PATREM ET DOMINUM DOMINUM JOHANNEM, DEI GRACIA CANTUARIENSIS ARCHI-EPISCOPUM, TOCIUS ANGLIE PRIMATEM, ET APOSTOLICE SEDIS LEGATUM, AD HOC SUFFICIENTER ET LEGITIME DEPUTATUM.

2. 28 March 1447. Commission of John [Stafford], archbishop of Canterbury,[1] to Mr Thomas Chestrefeld[2] as vicar general in spirituals, *sede vacante*.

COMMISSIO. Johannes, permissione divina Cantuariensis archiepiscopus, tocius Anglie primas, et apostolice sedis legatus, ad quem omnis et omnimoda jurisdictio spiritualis et ecclesiastica que ad episcopum Coventrensem et Lichfeldensem pertinet sede plena ipsa sede jam vacante dinoscitur notorie pertinere, dilecto nobis in Christo magistro Thome Chestrefeld in decretis bacallario, canonico residentiario ecclesie cathedralis Lichfeldensis, salutem, graciam, et bene-diccionem. Ad exercendum omnem et omnimodam jurisdiccionem spiritualem in civitatibus et diocesi Coventrensis et Lichfeldensis ad nos racione vacacionis eiusdem spectantem tibi committimus vices nostras, et plenam in domino potestatem; teque vicarium nostrum sive custodem spiritualitatis preficimus per presentes. Datum in manerio nostro de Otteford, vicesimo octavo die mensis Marcii, anno domini millesimo CCCC^mo quadragesimo septimo, et nostre translacionis anno quarto.

ARCHIDIACONATUS COVENTR'

3. Institution of John Kempe, priest, to the vicarage of Hillmorton (*Hulle morton*), vacant by the death of John Coton; presented by the dean and brethren of the collegiate church of the Blessed Virgin Mary, Astley (*Asteley*). Ind. Archdn. Coventry, 3 June 1447.

[Fo. 1v: BLANK]

ARCHIDIACONATUS DERB'

4. [Fo. 2] Institution of Roger Fysshewyk, chaplain, to the rectory of Walton-on-Trent (*Walton super Trent*), vacant by the resignation of John Thorneton: presented by Thomas de Ferrariis esq, lord of Walton. Ind. Archdn. Lichfield, 11 May 1447.[3]

5. [Fo. 2–v] Notarial instrument reciting a decree of the vicar general assigning a life pension of 8½ marks p.a., payable in four equal portions (at the Nativity of St

---

1 John Stafford, archbishop of Canterbury 1443 x 1452.
2 Thomas Chestrefeld, or Wursop, was canon of Tarvin in the diocese of Coventry and Lichfield 28 January 1425. Died by 23 August 1452 and archdeacon of Salop from 3 December 1425, resigning by 17 August 1433 (*Fasti* x, 18, 60; Swanson 'Lichfield Chapter Acts', no. 62).
3 For a pension paid by Roger Fysshewyk from this church see **5**.

John the Baptist, Michaelmas, Christmas, and the Annunciation) from the church of Walton-on-Trent at that church (following an inquiry into its value) by Roger Fysshewik [Fysshewyk, Fisshewik], now rector of Walton-on-Trent, to John Thorneton, formerly rector, who has resigned due to old age and infirmity (*propter senium et corporis debilitatem*), and on pain of sequestration, interdict, and excommunication if the pension is not paid within fifteen days of any of the set terms. Future rectors are to take an oath for their payment while Thorneton lives. Present: John Walton, chaplain, Ralph Maderer, literate, Coventry and Lichfield diocese. The keeper's house within the close at Lichfield, 14 April 1447.

Notarial attestation by William Gamull,[4] clerk, Coventry and Lichfield diocese, scribe of acts to the keeper of the spiritualities.

ARCHIDIACONATUS STAFFORD'

6. [Fo. 3] 16 May 1447. Ratification by the vicar general, following a visitation, of the appropriation of the parish church of Kinver (*Kynfare*), to the monastery of Bordesley.[5]

RATIFICATIO APPROPRIACIONIS ECCLESIE PAROCHIALIS DE KYNFARE MONASTERIO DE BORDESLEY. Universis sancte matris ecclesie filiis presentes litteras inspecturis, Thomas Chestrefeld,[6] in decretis bacallarius, canonicus residenciarius in ecclesia cathedrali Lichfeldensi, custos spiritualitatis episcopatus Coventrensis et Lichfeldensis sede ibidem vacante per reverendissimum in Christo patrem et dominum dominum Johannem dei gracia Cantuariensem archiepiscopum tocius Anglie primatem et apostolice sedis legatum ad hoc sufficienter et legitime deputatus, salutem in Christo Jesu omnium salvatore. Cum nuper coram nobis civitates et diocesim predictas auctoritate dicti reverendissimi patris actualiter visitantibus in nostra visitacione huiusmodi religiosos viros abbatem et conventum de Bordesley ordinis Cist' Wigorniensis diocesis ad proponendum, exhibendum, et ostendendum jus et titulum (si que haberent) super ecclesia parochiali de Kynfare dicte Coventrensis et Lichfeldensis diocesis cum suis juribus et pertinenciis universis, quam percibiebant et possidebant, percipiunt et possident, eciam in presenti, in diocesi Coventrensi et Lichfeldensi predicta, ipsis et eorum monasterio in proprios usus obtinentes, fecimus ex officii nostri debito ad certos diem et locum ad judicium legitime evocari; qui quidem religiosi viri dictis die et loco eisdem per nos auctoritate dicti reverendissimi patris assignatis secundum formam citacionis eiusdem legitime comparentes super assecucione et possessione canonicis de et super ecclesia parochiali de Kynfare predicta cum suis juribus et pertinenciis universis ipsis et eorum monasterio antedicto appropriata, unita, annexa, et incorporata ipsos et eorum monasterium per instrumenta publica, testes, litteras, et munimenta ac alias probaciones in ea parte legitimas et canonicas plenum jus et

---

[4] Granted the office of registrar and scribe in the consistory court of Lichfield 10 June 1452 (see **274**). A vicar of Lichfield cathedral (Eakwaker, *East Cheshire* i, 53).
[5] The original appropriation is in Lichfield Record Office, B/A/1/4 (the register of Robert Stretton), fo. 70a.
[6] See introduction, p. xxi.

titulum in dicta ecclesia habuisse et habere, necnon sufficienter fore munitos coram nobis docuerunt, ostenderunt, ac eciam probaverunt. Quibus in forma juris per nos admissis, visis, examinatis, rimatis, et plenius intellectis, invenimus eosdem religiosos viros de et super ecclesia predicta, ponderatis undique ponderandis, sufficienter fuisse et esse munitos; necnon eandem per tempora diuturna ac a tempore et per tempus cuius contrarii memoria hominum non existit pacifice possedisse et habuisse, possidere et habere, eciam in presenti. Unde nos, juris ordine qui in hac parte requiritur in omnibus observato, pro jure, titulo, et possessione ipsorum religiosorum virorum in et super ecclesia memorata eis et eorum monasterium antedictum rite et legitime appropriata, unita, incorporata, et annexa, ac dictos religiosos viros prefatam ecclesiam fuisse et esse canonice assecutos; necnon eandem percepisse, possedisse, et habuisse ab antiquo, et eiusdem fuisse et esse canonicos possessores in hiis scriptis pronunciamus et declaramus; ipsosque religiosos viros super eadem ecclesia a nostro et ipsius reverendissimi patris officio ac eiusdem officii examine sic sufficienter munitos absolvimus et tenore presencium dimittimus absolutos; necnon eandem ecclesiam cum suis juribus et pertinenciis universis eisdem religiosis viris et eorum monasterio antedicto auctoritate dicti reverendissimi patris ex certa nostra sciencia confirmamus. In cuius rei testimonium sigillum quo in hoc utimur officio presentibus apposuimus. Datum Lichfeld' sextodecimo die mensis Maii anno domini millesimo CCCC^{mo} xl^o septimo.

[Folio 3v: BLANK]

ARCHIDIACONATUS SALOP'

7. [Fo. 4] Institution of Mr Henry Bastard, M.A.,[7] priest, to the free chapel of St John the Baptist, Albrighton (*Adbrighton Husee*) and the college or perpetual chantry of St Mary Magdalene, Battlefield by Shrewsbury (*Batelfeld juxta Salop*) annexed thereto and vacant by the resignation of Roger Ive, formerly rector, and master or custodian of the new college or chantry aforesaid: presented by Richard Husee, esq., lord of the manor of Albrighton. Ind. Archdn. Lichfield, 14 April 1447.

8. Assignment of a life pension of £10 p.a., payable in four equal instalments (at the Nativity of St John the Baptist, Michaelmas, Christmas, and the Annunciation) in the college at Battlefield by Shrewsbury by Henry Bastard,[8] now master or custodian of the college to Roger Ive, formerly master or custodian (represented by John Prys, chaplain, as his proctor), '*Ad submovenda obprobria cleri que ex mendicitate inopinata sepius evenire noscuntur*'. Payment is to be made within 20 days of each of the assigned terms, on pain of excommunication, interdict, and sequestration. Succeeding rectors are to take an oath for payment whilst Ive lives. Lichfield, 14 April 1447.

[Fos 4v–5: BLANK]

---

7   Exhibited a caution in his own name for Little St Edmund Hall, 1445 and 1446 (Emden i, 127). For a pension paid to the former master by Henry Bastard see **8**.
8   See note 7.

9. [Fo. 5v] General orders in Coventry cathedral on 3 June 1447 by Robert [Mulfield], bishop of Killaloe,[9] by authority of the keeper of the spiritualities.

ORDINES GENERALES CELEBRATOS IN ECCLESIA COVENTRENSI DIE SABBATI QUATUOR TEMPORUM IN VIGILIA SANCTE TRINITATIS, VIDELICET TERCIO DIE MENSIS JUNII, ANNO DOMINI MILLESIMO CCCC^{mo} QUADRAGESIMO SEPTIMO, PER REVERENDUM IN CHRISTO PATREM ET DOMINUM DOMINUM ROBERTUM, DEI GRACIA LAONIENSEM EPISCOPUM, AUCTORITATE CUSTODIS PREDICTI SIBI ATTRIBUTA.

[col. a]

ACCOLITI SECULARES

Thomas Byllyngton
Ricardus Bury
Johannes Wylson
Willelmus Rydwalhurst
Willelmus Beke   Robertus Speke
Ricardus Pykeryn   Johannes Levys
Christoforus del Rowe   Willelmus Entwisill
Johannes Alkus   Robertus Dykson
Johannes Pertt

RELIGIOSI

Frater Ricardus Comyn ordinis Carmelitarum Coventr'

SUBDIACONI SECULARES

Willelmus Garard Lincoln' diocesis per litteras dimissorias ad titulum hospitalis sancti Johannis baptiste Coventr'
Johannes Jecok ad titulum domus de Osney ad omnes
Willelmus Wellis ad titulum domus sancte Anne ordinis Cartus' juxta Coventr' ad omnes
Ricardus Hawson ad titulum domus de Novo Loco in Shirewood
Johannes Herrymon ad titulum prioratus de Tuttebury ad omnes
Ricardus Deyne ad titulum domus de Dala ad omnes
Willelmus Orme ad titulum domus de Pollesworth ad omnes
Willelmus Lightwode ad titulum domus de Rowcester ad omnes
Johannes Marleston ad titulum domus de Combermer' ad omnes

DIACONI SECULARES

Henricus Watford ad titulum domus sancte Anne ordinis Cartus' juxta Coventr' ad omnes

---

9   Suffragan in Lichfield *c.* 1418–40. Provided to Killaloe 9 September 1409 but did not get possession.

Ricardus Sadeler ad titulum domus de Osney ad omnes
Johannes Boteler ad titulum domus de Chirbury ad omnes
Rogerus Wilkyn ad titulum domus de Bradewell ad omnes
Ricardus Cokke ad titulum domus de Haghmond ad omnes
Rogerus Whitlawe ad titulum Johannis Boteler militis et baronis de Weryngton ad
    omnes
Jacobus Wilson ad titulum domus de Landa ad omnes
Robertus Smalwode ad titulum domus de Osney ad omnes
Johannes Harewey ad titulum collegii de Tonge ad omnes
Robertus Walker ad titulum domus de Holond ad omnes
Thomas Prestbury ad titulum domus de Dieuleucres ad omnes
Johannes Balme ad titulum domus de Blida ad omnes
Thomas Legh ad titulum prioratus sancti Thome juxta Stafford ad omnes

[col. b]

RELIGIOSI

Frater Willelmus Colyns ordinis Carmelitarum Coventr'
Frater Thomas Brown ordinis Carmelitarum Coventr'

PRESBITERI SECULARES

Johannes Kempe ad titulum domus sancte Anne ordinis Cart' juxta Coventr', ad
    omnes
Nicholaus Tillesley ad titulum domus de Whalley ad omnes
Johannes Hodilston ad titulum domus de Osney ad omnes
Willelmus Benet ad titulum monasterii sancte Fredeswide in Oxon' ad omnes
Radulphus Kirkehalgh ad titulum domus de Whalley ad omnes
Ricardus Dey ad titulum domini Thome Stanley militis ad omnes
Ricardus Lee ad titulum prioratus sancti Thome martiris juxta Stafford ad omnes
Laurencius Bexwik ad titulum domus de Whalley ad omnes
Johannes Ferrour ad titulum domus de Whalley ad omnes
Johannes Mownford ad titulum domus de Myravalle ad omnes
Thomas Latener ad titulum prioratus sancti Thome juxta Stafford ad omnes

RELIGIOSI

Frater Willelmus Wirceter ordinis minorum Lich' ad omnes
Frater Thomas Moton ordinis fratrum hermitarum de Athirston
Frater Johannes Burton ordinis Cist' de Myravalle
Frater Thomas Glosur monachus de Stonley ad omnes

[Fo. 6]   **ARCHDEACONRY OF COVENTRY**

Annus Domini Millesimus CCCCxlvii^us[10]

10. REGISTRUM REVERENDI IN CHRISTO PATRIS ET DOMINI DOMINI
WILLELMI BOTHE, DEI GRACIA COVENTRENSIS ET LICHFELDENSIS EPISCOPI,
QUI CONSECRATUS FUIT IN EPISCOPUM IN ECCLESIA SANCTI PAULI, LONDON',
NONO DIE MENSIS JULII, IN FESTO VIDELICET RELIQUIARUM, LITTERA
DOMINICALIS ET ANNO DOMINI MILLESIMO QUADRINGENTESIMO QUAD-
RAGESIMO SEPTIMO. ET IDEM EPISCOPUS TRANSLATUS FUIT AD ECCLESIAM
EBORACENSEM VICESIMO PRIMO DIE MENSIS JULII, ANNO DOMINI MILLESIMO
QUADRINGENTESIMO QUINQUAGESIMO SECUNDO.

11. [Fo. 6–v] 11 October 1447. Commission to Mr George Radclyff, [11] D. Dec.,
treasurer and canon of Lichfield cathedral, to act as vicar general in spirituals
during pleasure.

COMMISSIO VICARII GENERALIS. Willelmus, permissione divina Coventrensis et
Lichfeldensis episcopus, universis et singulis Christi fidelibus (presertim civitatis et
diocesis nostrarum Coventrensis et Lichfeldensis) presentes litteras inspecturis,
salutem in auctore salutatis. Noveritis nos de circumspeccionis, industria, et
fidelitate, ac vite et morum honestate dilecti nobis in Christo venerabilis viri
Magistri Georgii Radclyff, decretorum doctoris, thesaurarii ecclesie nostre
cathedralis Lichfeldensis antedicte ac eiusdem ecclesie canonici et confratis nostri,
specialiter confidentes, eundem in nostra absencia in remotis agente in et per
totam nostram diocesim Coventrensem et Lichfeldensem ad causarum
spiritualium seu negociorum que ad forum pertinere consueverint ecclesiasticum
cognicionem, decisionem, et terminacionem ac sentenciarum execucionem;
criminumque et excessum spiritualium et ecclesiasticorum seu eorum que ad
forum consueverint pertinere ecclesiasticum inquisicionem, correccionem, et
punicionem, administracionem ammocionem, beneficiorum privacionem,
juramentorum canonice obedience ac fidelitatis recepcionem, censurarum –
eciam suspencionis excommunicacionis vel interdicti – fulminacionem, clerum ad
synodum convocandum, visitacionem ordinariam exercendum, eleccionesque
quascumque confirmandas seu infirmandas; necnon cuicumque episcopo
catholico potestatem et execucionem sui officii obtinenti ad celebrandum et
conferendum ordines majores et minores generales et speciales infra diocesim
nostram predictam, ac eciam benedicendum ecclesias, altaria, cimiteria, calices, et
alia ornamenta ecclesiastica quecumque consecranda, reconsilianda, et
benedicenda, ac quecumque alia que ad ordinem episcopalem spectantia facienda,
exercenda, et expedienda, nostris vice et nomine facultatem et licenciam danda et
concedenda; penitenciariosque unum seu plures, ut moris est, deputandos;
clericosque convictos quoscumque de judicibus secularibus quibuscumque
petendum et recipiendos, eosdemque a carceribus canonice liberandos;
jurisdiccionem omnimodam ecclesiasticam et spiritualem in dictis nostris civitatis

---

[10] This is in the top right-hand corner of the page, rather than written right across, as in
later instances.

et diocesis cum omnibus et singulis suis emergentibus, dependentibus, et connexis quibuscumque exercenda, expedienda, et gerenda, nostrum vicarium generalem et specialem – ita quod generalitas specialitati non deroget nec econtra – deputasse, preficisse, constituisse, et ordinasse quem sicut prefertur deputamus, preficimus, constituimus, et ordinamus ad beneplacitum nostrum duraturum, cum potestate unum vel plures (prout eidem melius videbitur expedire) ad predicta omnia et singula jurisdiccionalia (collacionibusque dignitatum et prebendarum ac aliorum beneficiorum ecclesiasticorum quorumcumque nostri patronatus aut eciam iure devoluto, necnon presentacionibus beneficiorum ecclesiasticorum nostri patronatus extra nostram diocesim existencium, et aliorum quorumcumque beneficiorum ecclesiasticorum cuiuscumque seu quorumcumque patronatus existant, et institucionibus eorundem, et confirmacionibus eleccionum abbathiarium et prioratuum quorumcumque infra nostram diocesim; necnon potestate de non residendo in beneficiis huiusmodi et aliis quibuscumque dumtaxat exceptis et nobis in hac parte specialiter reservatis) substituendi, delegandi, et committendi; ceteraque agendi et faciendi ac si nos in propria persona facere possumus si personaliter interessemus. In cuius rei testimonium sigillum nostrum presentibus apposuimus. Datum in palacio nostro Lichfeldensi, undecimo die mensis Octobris, anno domini millesimo quadringentesimo quadragesimo septimo, et nostre consecracionis anno primo.

12. [Fo. 6v] Institution of William Wodhouse, priest, to the vicarage of Coleshill (*Colleshull*), vacant by the resignation of John Wellefed; presented by the prioress and convent of Holy Trinity, Markyate (*Boscogh juxta Markyate*). Ind. Archdn. Coleshill, 4 August 1447.

13. Institution of William Erlle, priest, to the vacant vicarage of Bickenhill (*Chirchbykenhull*); presented by the prioress and convent of Holy Trinity, Markyate (*Boscogh iuxta Markyate*). Ind. Archdn. Haywood (*Heywode*), 6 August, 1447.

14. Institution of John Smalbroke, chaplain, to the chantry of John Peyto at the altar of St Mary in the parish church of Sheldon, vacant by the resignation of Thomas Blakeston; presented by Br. Richard Notyngham, prior of Coventry cathedral.[12] Ind. Archdn. Coventry (*Coventr'*), 18 August 1447.

15. Collation to John Austeley, priest, of the vacant rectory of Little Packington (*Pakynton parva*), in the bishop's patronage by lapse of time. Ind. Archdn. Coventry, 18 August 1447.

16. [Fos 6v–7] Exchange of the rectory of Claycoton, Lincoln diocese, and the vicarage of Wolston: (i) Commission of William [Alnwick], bishop of Lincoln, to William [Bothe], bishop of Coventry and Lichfield, to investigate and implement the exchange between Mr William Kilworth, rector of Claycoton (*Cleycot'*), Lincoln

---

[11] For other commissions to act as vicar general see **290**, **291**, **294**, **295**, **299**. He also established an altar in Lichfield cathedral (see **311**). For details of his career see introduction, pp. xxiv–xxvi.
[12] Elected prior 5 April 1437. Died before 7 March 1453 (*Fasti* x, 4).

diocese, and Mr Thomas Arkynden,[13] vicar of Wolverton (*Wolfricheston, Wolricheston*), Coventry and Lichfield diocese, instituting Arkynden on the presentation of the abbot and convent of St Mary de Pratis, Leicester, but reserving his induction and canonical obedience. Palace at Lincoln, 26 September 1447. (ii) Note of institution by Bothe of Kilworth to the vicarage of Wolston on the presentation of the prior and convent of St Anne by Coventry, O.Carth. Ind. Archdn. Lichfield, 3 October 1447. (iii) Note of institution by Bothe of Arkynden to the rectory of Claycoton at the presentation of the abbot and convent of St Mary de Pratis, Leicester. Lichfield, 3 October 1447. (iv) Note that a certificate was sent to the bishop of Lincoln. Lichfield, 3 October 1447.

17.   [Fo. 7] Institution by the vicar general of William Chapmon, priest, to the vicarage of Kenilworth (*Kenylleworth*), vacant by the resignation of John Smyth; presented by the prior and convent of Kenilworth. Ind. Archdn. Lichfield, 19 October 1447.

18.   Institution by the vicar general, by special mandate from the bishop, of Robert Bulmer, priest, to the rectory of Stretton on Fosse (*Stretton juxta Stratam*), vacant by the resignation of John Broke; presented by Thomas Twyforde esq. Ind. Archdn. The vacancy dates from the resignation made by John Broke in the house of John Swepeston of *Newam*, Lincoln diocese, 20 December 1447, witnessed by Stephen Jonson, vicar of Rotby, John Crownden, literate, and John Wynaway, Lincoln and Coventry and Lichfield dioceses, as shown in instrument by Mr John Paynyll, clerk, Coventry and Lichfield diocese, notary. Lichfield, 20 February 1447/8.

19.   [Fo. 7v] Institution of William Wore, priest, to the rectory of Grendon, vacant by the death of Simon Melburn; presented by Thomas Litelton and Joan his wife. Ind. Archdn. Hackney (*Hakeney*), 19 March 1447/8.

Annus domini millesimus CCCC^mus quadragesimus octavus

20.   Institution of Mr William Kele,[14] priest, in the person of Mr John Walbrond, clerk, his proctor, to a canonry and the prebend of Wolvey Astley in the collegiate church of the Blessed Virgin Mary, Astley, vacant by the resignation of John Druell; presented by Joan, lady of Astley, lately wife of Reginald Grey, lord of Hastings (*Hastyng*), Wexford (*Waifford*), and Ruthin (*Ruthyn*). Ind. Archdn. Strand, London (*le Strond iuxta London*), 6 May 1448.

21.   Institution of John Belebowch, priest, to the vicarage of Maxstoke, vacant by the death of Thomas Nassyngton; presented by the prior and convent of Maxstoke. Ind. Archdn. Haywood, 3 June 1448.

---

13 Bachelor of Canon Law by 1438. Vicar of St Giles' Oxford, and of Wolverton in Warwickshire, to which he was admitted 16 July 1438 (Emden i, 46).
14 Admitted as a fellow of All Souls College in 1438, elected warden 1445 a post he held until his death. Supplicated for his B.Th. 1453. Also held rectories in Sussex, Kent, Buckinghamshire and Lincolnshire. Died 22 October 1459 (Emden ii, 1028).

22. Collation to Ralph Wode, priest, of the vacant stall or vicarage of the canonry and prebend of Mylverton minor in the collegiate church of Astley, in the bishop's patronage by lapse of time. Mandate to the dean of the said church to induct. Haywood, 4 June 1448.

23. Institution of Geoffrey Clerk, priest, to the vicarage of Clifton on Dunsmore (*Clyffton*), vacant by the resignation of Ralph Bradeshagh; presented by the prior and convent of St Mary de Pratis, Leicester (*Leycestr'*). Ind. Archdn. Eccleshall (*Eccleshale*), 22 August 1448.

24. [Fos 7v–8] Institution of Thomas Coneway, priest, to the vicarage of Burton Dassett (*Chepyngdercet*), vacant by the resignation of Richard Leventhorp; presented by Ralph Boteller knight, lord of Sudeley (*Seudeley*), and the prior and convent of Arbury (*Erdebury*). Ind. Archdn. Coneway swore on the gospels in the presence of the bishop to pay a life pension of 12 marks p.a. to Richard Leventhorp. Hackney, 14 January 1448/9.

25. [Fo. 8] Institution of William Wore, chaplain, to the rectory of Grendon, in commend (*titulo commende*); presented by Thomas Litelton and Joan his wife. Ind. Archdn. Strand (*Stronde*), London, 5 February 1448/9.[15]

26. Institution of John Corryngham, priest, to the vacant vicarage of Alspath (*Allespath*); presented by the prior and convent of Coventry cathedral. Ind. Archdn. Hackney, 25 February 1448/9.

27. Collation to Henry Inse,[16] chaplain, of a canonry and the prebend of Wolvey in Lichfield cathedral, vacant by the resignation of Thomas Clerk.[17] Mandate to the dean and chapter to admit to the fraternity and to assign the customary stall in the choir and a place in the chapter and to induct. Strand, London, 18 March 1448/9.

28. Collation to Richard Bowier, priest, in the person of Mr Roger Draper, clerk, his proctor, of the rectory of Fenny Compton (*Fennycompton*), vacant by the resignation of Mr Thomas Lye. Ind. Archdn. Strand, London, 24 March 1448/9.[18]

Annus domini millesimus CCCC^{mus} quadragesimus nonus

29. Institution of Richard Donyngton, priest, to the rectory of Solihull, vacant by the death of Thomas Cullom; presented by James Fenys, lord Saye and Sele (*le Say de Sele*),[19] knight. Ind. Archdn. Strand, London, 28 March 1449.

---

[15] See also **19**.
[16] Archdeacon of Chester, collated 10 October 1467, died before 9 May 1474 (*Fasti* x, 14). Also rector of Yoxall, Staffs., and granted a house in the close at Lichfield (see **81**, **289**).
[17] Thomas Clark had been collated to the prebend of Wolvey 14 June 1427 (*Fasti* x, 70).
[18] 'ultimo die mensis et anni'. Given that the entry is immediately followed by the change of year, presumably 24 March rather than 31. Thomas Lye died by 1 June 1464 (*Fasti* x. 18).
[19] For James Fiennes, lord of Say and Sele, died 1450, see Joseph A. Nigota, 'Fiennes,

30.   [Fo. 8–v] Institution of John Kusener, chaplain, to the vicarage or stall of the prebend of Hillmorton (*Hulmorton*), in the collegiate church of Astley (*Asteley*), vacant by the resignation of Ralph Wode; presented by William Hull, canon and prebendary of the said prebend. Mandate to the dean to induct. Haywood, 10 April 1449.

31.   [Fo. 8v] Institution of Mr Richard Bulkyngton to a moiety of the chantry of Nicholas Percy and John Percy in the parish church of Holy Trinity, Coventry, vacant by the death of Robert Fawx; presented by Br. Richard Notyngham, prior of Coventry cathedral. Ind. Archdn. Haywood, 17 April 1449.

32.   Collation to William Worsley, clerk,[20] in the person of Mr William Brande, his proctor, of a canonry and the prebend of Tachbrook (*Tachebroke*) in Lichfield cathedral, vacant by the death of Walter Shiryngton. Mandate to the dean and chapter to induct etc. [as in 27]. Haywood, 29 April 1449.

33.   Institution of Richard Cokket, priest, to the vacant vicarage of Grendon; presented by Thomas Litelton and Joan his wife. Ind. Archdn. Haywood, 4 August 1449.[21]

34.   Institution of William Gregge, priest, to the vicarage of Bulkington (*Bulkyngton*), vacant by the resignation of Thomas Hill; presented by the abbot and convent of St Mary de Pratis, Leicester. Ind. Archdn. Haywood, 13 August 1449.

35.   Institution of Richard Grove, priest, to the vicarage of Aston by Birmingham *Aston juxta Bermyncham*), vacant by the resignation of John Drover; presented by the prior and convent of Tickford (*Tykforde juxta Neuport Paynell*), Ind. Archdn. Stone, 25 August 1449.

36.   [Fos. 8v–9v] 26 August 1449. Exchange of benefices, by authority of William [Alnwick], bishop of Lincoln, following letters dated 23 August 1449 at the manor of Lydington, between Mr Richard Dykelun, D. Dec., canon and prebendary of Bobenhull in Lichfield cathedral[22] and rector of Barnwell (*Bernwell*), diocese of Lincoln, and Augustine Whasch, rector of Deeping (*Depyng sancti Guthlaci*), diocese of Lincoln.

James, first Baron Saye and Sele (*c.*1390–1450)', *Oxford Dictionary of National Biography* (Oxford University Press, 2004); online edn, May 2005 [http://www.oxforddnb.com/view/article/9411].

[20] Dean of St Paul's from 1479, he was archdeacon of Nottingham from 1476. He took his first degree at Oxford, then transferring to Cambridge in 1459 to study canon and civil law (Michael J. Bennett, 'Worsley, William (*c.*1435–1499)', *Oxford Dictionary of National Biography* (Oxford University Press, 2004); [http://www.oxforddnb.com/view/article/29987, accessed 21 Sept. 2006]).

[21] Previous incumbent William Wore (see **19**).

[22] Also spelt Dekelan. Obtained the prebend by exchange November 1443 (*Fasti* x, 24).

PREBENDE DE BOBENHILL ET ECCLESIARUM PAROCHIALIUM DE BERNWELL ET DEPYNG, LINCOLNIENSIS DIOCESE, PERMUTACIO. Reverendo in Christo patri et domino domino Willelmo dei gracia Coventrensi et Lichfeldensi episcopo, Willelmus permissione divina Lincolniensis episcopus, salutem et fraternam in domino caritatem. Cum dilecti nobis in Christo magister Ricardus Dykelun, in decretis licenciatus, canonicus ecclesie vestre cathedralis Lichfeldensis et prebendarius prebende de Bobenhill in eadem ac rector ecclesie parochialis de Bernwell dicte nostre diocesis, et dominus Augustinus Whasch rector ecclesie parochialis de Depyng sancti Guthlaci eciam dicte nostre diocesis, intendant (ut asserunt) sua huiusmodi beneficia ex certis causis veris et legitimis ipsos ad hoc moventibus, dumtamen eorum quorum interest consensus et auctoritas interveniant in hac parte, adinvicem canonice permutare; nos huiusmodi permutacioni fiende quantum ad nos attinet nostrum prebentes consensum pariter et assensum, ad audiendum, examinandum, et plenarie discuciendum causas et negocium permutacionis predicte, ipsisque causis veris et legitimis inventis approbandum, easdem dictamque permutacionem auctorizandum, ac receptis per vos vice et auctoritate nostris resignacione dicti magistri Ricardi de ecclesia sua de Bernwell memorata prefatum dominum Augustinum ad eandem, ad quam per religiosos viros abbatem et conventum monasterii de Rameseye veros eiusdem ecclesie patronos nobis presentatus existit, necnon resignacione dicti domini Augustini rectoris ecclesie parochialis de Depyng sancti Guthlaci prefatum magistrum Ricardum ad eandem, ad quam per religiosos viros abbatem et conventum monasterii de Thorney veros dicte ecclesie patronos nobis eciam presentatus existit, admittendos, et ex causa permutacionis eiusdem eosdem instituendos canonice in eisdem. Ceteraque omnia alia et singula facienda, exercenda, et expedienda que in huiusmodi permutacionis negocio necessaria fuerint seu quomodolibet oportuna vobis tenore presencium committimus vices nostras; juribus nostris episcopalibus et ecclesie nostre Lincolniensis dignitate in omnibus semper salvis, ac obediencia canonica et induccione dictorum magistri Ricardi et Augustini nobis in hac parte debitis specialiter reservatis; attente rogantes quatinus onus commissionis huiusmodi si libeat amplectantes nos de toto processu vestro coram vobis in hac parte habendo, dicto negocio expedito, distincte et aperte certificare dignetur vestra fraternitas antedicta litteris vestris patentibus habentibus hunc tenorem. Datum sub sigillo nostro ad causas in manerio nostro de Lidyngton, vicesimo tercio die mensis Augusti anno domini millesimo quadringentesimo quadragesimo nono, nostrarumque consecracionis anno vicesimo quarto et translacionis terciodecimo.

PREBENDE DE BOBENHILL COLLACIO EX CAUSA PREDICTA. Et memorandum quod apud Heywode, xxvj^to die prefati mensis Augusti, anno domini proximo prescripto, per dominum Willelmum, Coventrensem et Lichfeldensem episcopum, expeditum fuit negocium permutacionis predicte, et idem reverendus pater prefatum canonicatum et prebendam de Bobenhill in ecclesia sua cathedrali Lichfeldensi predicta, per liberam resignacionem prefati magistri Ricardi Dykelun ex causa permutacionis fiende de eisdem ac ecclesia parochiali de Bernwell Lincolniensis diocesis, quos idem magister Ricardus ut canonicus et prebendarius ac rector prius obtinuit, cum ecclesia parochiali de Depyng sancti Guthlaci prefati Lincolniensis diocesis cuius rector dominus Augustinus Whasch prius extitit, in manibus prefati reverendi patris factam et per ipsum discussis primitus et approbatis, tam reverendi patris domini Willelmi dei gracia Lincolniensis episcopi sibi commissa quam sua auctoritate ordinaria causis et negocio dicte permutacionis legitime acceptatis vacantes et ad suam collacionem pleno jure spectantes, prefato domino Augustino dicte permutacionis obtentu contulit, ac ipsum per modum et ex causa predicta canonicum et prebendarium instituit canonice in eisdem cum suis juribus et pertinenciis universis. Et eodem die mandatum extitit decano et capitulo ecclesie cathedralis Lichfeldensis predicte de admittendo prefatum dominum Augustinum in canonicum et confratrem eiusdem, ac locum in capitulo et stallum in choro eisdem canonicatui et prebende ab antiquo debitos eidem domino Augustino assignandum. Necnon xxvj^{to} die predicto mandabatur archidiacono seu ejus officiali de inducendo eundem dominum Augustinum in corporalem dicte prebende possessionem, jurata primitus per eundem canonica obediencia.

ECCLESIE DE BERNWELL EX CAUSA PREDICTA INSTITUTIO. Eisdemque die et loco memoratis, dominus Augustinus admissus fuit ad ecclesiam parochialem de Bernwell predictam per liberam resignacionem dicti magistri Ricardi Dykelun ultimi rectoris eiusdem ex causa permutacionis fiende de eadem ac canonicatu et prebenda de Bobenhill predicta, ac dicta ecclesia parochiali de Depyng quam idem dominus Augustinus ut rector prius obtinuit, in manibus dicti domini Lincolniensi episcopi factam et per prefatum dominum Willelmum Coventrensem et Lichfeldensem episcopum discussis primitus (et cetera, ut supra) legitime admissam, vacantem, ad quam per religiosos viros abbatem et conventum monasterii de Rameseye, veros eiusdem ecclesie patronos, dicto domino Lincolniensi episcopo extitit presentatus, ac per eundem Coventrensem et Lichfeldensem episcopum vice et auctoritate dicti reverendi patris sibi (ut prefertur) ad hoc commissa, rector institutus canonice in eadem cum suis juribus et cetera, per modum et ex causa permutacionis predicte.

ECCLESIE DE DEPYNG EX CAUSA PREDICTA INSTITUTIO. Ceterum, die et loco memoratis prefatus magister Ricardus Dykelun admissus fuit ad dictam ecclesiam parochialem de Depyng sancti Guthlaci per liberam resignacionem dicti domini Augustini, ultimi rectoris eiusdem, ex causa permutacionis fiende de eadem cum canonicatu et prebenda de Bobenhill ac ecclesia parochiali de Bernwell predictis, quos idem magister Ricardus ut canonicus et prebendarius prius obtinuit, in manibus dicti reverendi patris domini Lincolniensis episcopi factam et per memoratum dominum Willelmum, Coventrensem et Lichfeldensem episcopum, discussis primitus et approbatis (et cetera, ut supra, et cetera), vacantem; rectorque vice et auctoritate quibus supra per prefatum Willelmum, Coventrensem et Lichfeldensem [?episcopum] institutus canonice in eadem cum suis juribus et cetera, ad presentacionem abbatis et conventus monasterii de Thorney verorum ipsius ecclesie de Depyng, ut asseritur, patronorum, memorato domino Lincolniensi episcopo factam. Et eodem xxvj^{to} die certificartum extitit dicto reverendo patri proximo predicto de expedicione permutacionis predicte.

37. [Fo. 9v] Institution of Richard Lynde, priest, to the chantry of John Peyto at the altar of St Mary in the parish church of Sheldon, vacant by the resignation of John Smalbroke; presented by Br. Richard Notyngham, prior of Coventry cathedral.[23] Ind. Archdn. Haywood, 1 October 1449.[24]

38. Institution of Thomas Shyngler, priest, to the chantry of St Mary in the parish church of Birmingham (*Birmyngham*), vacant by the death of William Pakewode; presented by Robert Ardern esq. Ind. Archdn. Haywood, 2 October 1449.

39. Institution of Mr William Eure, M.A., in the person of Laurence Sikylbrice, literate, his proctor, to the rectory of Wem (*Wemme*), vacant by the resignation of Mr William Lescrop; presented by Ralph (de Greystoke), lord of Greystock (*Graystok*) and Wem.[25] Ind. Archdn. Eccleshall, 15 October 1449.[26]

40. Collation of Mr Roger Wall,[27] priest, to the vacant vicarage of Maxstoke, in the bishop's patronage by lapse of time. Ind. Archdn. Strand, London, 9 December 1449.[28]

41. Institution of John Westourne, priest, to the vicarage of Farnborough (*Farneborgh*), vacant by the death of Richard Kele; presented by the abbot and convent of Lilleshall (*Lilleshull*). Ind. Archdn. Strand, London, 9 December 1449.

42. [Fos 9v–10] Institution of Mr Roger Wall, B. Dec., priest, to the rectory of Grendon, vacant by the resignation of Richard Cokett; presented by Thomas Litelton and Joan his wife. Ind. Archdn. London, 26 January 1449/50.[29]

43. [Fo. 10] Institution by the vicar general, by special mandate from the bishop, in commend (*titulo commende*), and in accordance with a papal dispensation, of John, bishop *Insulensis*,[30] to the vicarage of Dunchurch, vacant by the death of John Grene and in the bishop's collation. Ind. Archdn. Lichfield, 9 February 1449/50.

---

[23] See note 12 above.

[24] For institution of John Smalbroke see **14**.

[25] For Ralph (III) Greystoke, fifth baron Greystoke, see Keith Dockray, 'Greystoke family (*per.* 1321–1487)', *Oxford Dictionary of National Biography* (Oxford University Press, 2004); [http://www.oxforddnb.com/view/article/54524].

[26] Partially deleted, with 'vacat' written against it, and the note: 'vacat hic quia est in archidiaconatu Salop'. See **169**.

[27] Roger Wall obtained the prebend of Offley in 1440 by exchange, which he resigned by July 1449, and held the prebend of Eccleshall from March 1449. He went on to be archdeacon of Stafford and archdeacon of Coventry, collated to both in June 1442. He was also master of the hospital of Denwall as well as holding several benefices (*Fasti* x, 15, 20, 36, 47; see **93**, **95**, **198**, **312**).

[28] Precious incumbent, John Belebowch (see **21**).

[29] For institution of previous incumbent see **33**.

[30] Although identified as bishop of Kilfenora in the calendar of papal letters (*CPL* x, 296) John was almost certainly bishop of Scattery Island (*Handbook of British Chronology*, pp. 326–7). See introduction, p. xxviii.

44. Collation of the newly ordained vicarage of Mancetter (*Mancestre*), to John Moumforde, *alias* Barbour, priest. Ind. Archdn. London, 20 February 1449/50.[31]

Annus domini millesimus CCCC^{mus} quinquagesimus

45. Institution of Thomas Gamull, chaplain, in the person of Mr John Worsley, his proctor, to the chantry in the parish church of Hillmorton (*Hulmorton*), vacant by the resignation of John Russell; presented by John Astley esq. Ind. Archdn. Haywood, 15 April 1450.

46. Institution of John Smyth, priest, to the vicarage of Radway, vacant by the death of John Stevenes; presented by the abbot and convent of St Mary, Stoneleigh (*Stonley*). Ind. Archdn. Leicester (*Leycestr'*), 25 April 1450.

47. [Fo. 10–v] Institution of William Loveleis, chaplain, to the rectory of Allesley, vacant by the death of John Strangwais; presented by Edward Nevill, lord of Abergavenny (*Bergevenny*). Ind. Archdn. Clayton (*Claiton*), 29 August 1450.

48. [Fos 10v–11] Exchange of the vicarage of Dunchurch and the rectory of Blesworth, Lincoln diocese: (i) Commission from Marmaduke [Lumley], bishop of Lincoln, dated 24 October 1450 under the seal ad causas, to the bishop of Coventry and Lichfield to examine and implement the exchange between John, bishop *Insulensis*, vicar of Dunchurch (*Dunchirch, Dunchyrch*),[32] Coventry and Lichfield diocese, and Mr William Elmeshale, rector of Blesworth (*Blisworth, Blysworth*), Lincoln diocese, but reserving induction and canonical obedience. (ii) Note of the collation to Elmeshale of the vicarage of Dunchurch, in the person of William Barnard, literate, his proctor, following the resignation of John, bishop of *Insulensis*, offered by Robert Welford, literate, his proctor. Ind. Archdn. (iii) Note of the institution of John, bishop of *Insulensis*, to the rectory of Blesworth following the resignation of Elmeshale offered by Barnard as his proctor, at the presentation of Richard, duke of York, earl of *Ultoine*, and lord of Wigmore, Clare, Trym, and Connaght. (iv) Note that a certificate was sent to the bishop of Lincoln. Bollin (*Bolyn*), Cheshire, 29 October 1450.

49. [Fo. 11] Institution of John Stodeley, chaplain, in the person of Mr John Worsley, LL.B., his proctor, to the rectory of Hardborough Magna (*Herdburgh*), vacant by the death of Richard Wadilove; presented by Thomas de Ferrarus [*sic*] of Clunworth, Richard Byngham of Middleton (*Midleton*), and Robert Aston, esqs. Ind. Archdn. Strand, London, 20 November 1450.

50. Institution of Thomas Normanton, chaplain, in the person of Mr John Worsley, LL.B., his proctor, to the vicarage of Newbold, vacant by the death of Thomas Smyth; presented by the prior and convent of the house of the Visitation of the Blessed Virgin Mary in the isle of Axholme, Lincoln diocese, O.Carth. Ind. Archdn. Strand, London, 20 November 1450.

---

[31] The church of Mancetter was appropriated to Merevale Abbey in 1450 (see **280**).
[32] See **43** and note 30.

51. Institution of Thomas Cauke, priest, to the vicarage of Stoneleigh (*Stonley*), vacant by the resignation of William Loveles; presented by the abbot and convent of Kenilworth (*Kenilleworth*). Ind. Archdn. Eccleshall (*Eccleshale*), 22 January 1450/1.

52. Institution of Roger More, chaplain, to the vicarage of Cubbington (*Cobynton*), vacant by the resignation of John Hungeforde; presented by the abbot and convent of Kenilworth (*Kenylleworth*). Ind. Archdn. Eccleshall, 5 February 1450/1.

53. Institution of Henry Wele, chaplain, to the vicarage of Radford (*Radeford*), vacant by the resignation of Thomas Yonge; presented by the abbot and convent of Kenilworth. Ind. Archdn. Eccleshall, 5 February 1450/1.

54. [Fo. 11–v] Institution of William Haddon, chaplain, to the vicarage of Packington (*Pakynton*), vacant by the death of Richard Lache; presented by the abbot and convent of Kenilworth. Ind. Archdn. Eccleshall, 5 February 1450/1.

55. [Fo. 11v] Letters of Alexander Prowet,[33] inceptor in decrees, precentor and canon residentiary of Lincoln cathedral, Official of Lincoln, and keeper of the spiritualities of that see, *sede vacante*, dated at Lincoln 6 February 1450/1 acknowledging and reciting a commission of William [Bothe], bishop of Coventry and Lichfield, dated at the castle of Eccleshall 12 January 1450/1 to investigate and implement a proposed exchange of benefices between John, bishop *Insulensis*, vicar of Dunchurch, Coventry and Lichfield diocese,[34] and Mr Ralph Bradeshagh, rector of Little Billing (*Billynge parva*), Lincoln diocese. He has accepted the resignation of John, bishop of *Insulensis*, and has instituted Mr Ralph Bradeshagh to the vicarage (which is in the bishop's collation) in the person of Robert Welford, literate, his proctor, reserving his induction and canonical obedience.

Memorandum that the certificate was produced by Robert Welford, as proctor, who made obedience; and that a mandate was sent to the archdeacon or his official to induct. Eccleshall, 16 February 1450/1.

56. [Fo. 12] Institution of Richard Litilton, chaplain, to the vicarage of Fillongley, vacant by the resignation of William Estby; presented by the prior and convent of Maxstoke. Ind. Archdn. Eccleshall, 24 February 1450/1.

57. Institution of John Kusner, chaplain, in the person of Thomas Byrom, chaplain, his proctor, to the vicarage of Maxstoke (*Maxstok*), vacant by the resignation of Mr Roger Walle;[35] presented by the prior and convent of Maxstoke. Ind. Archdn. Eccleshall, 19 March 1450/1.[36]

---

33 Collated as precentor of Lincoln 4 April 1448, died by 23 February 1471 (*Fasti* i, 20).
34 See **43**, **48**.
35 See note 30.
36 For institution of previous incumbent see **40**.

Annus domini Millesimo CCCC^mus quinquagesimus primus

58. Institution of Br. William Turvey, priest, canon regular of Lavendon (*Lavenden*), O.Prem., in the person of Br. John Weston, his proctor, to the vicarage of Shotteswell (*Shoteswell*), vacant by the resignation of Br. Thomas Willyngham; presented by the abbot and convent of Lavendon. Ind. Archdn. Haywood, 31 July 1451.

59. Institution of Richard Barowe, chaplain, to the chantry of William [la Zouche], lord la Zouche and Seymour, knight, within his manor of Weston in Ardern, vacant by the resignation of James Pembreton in exchange for the parish church of Tattenhall; presented by William [la Zouche], lord la Zouche and Seymour. Ind. Archdn. Haywood, 31 July 1451.

60. Institution of Mr Henry Sharp, LL.D.,[37] priest, in the person of Robert Wodehowse, literate, his proctor, to a canonry and the moiety of the church of Olughton considered to be a prebend in Lichfield cathedral,[38] vacant by the death of Thomas Maclesfelde. Presented by the prior and chapter of Coventry cathedral. Mandate to the dean and chapter of Lichfield cathedral to induct and install. Eccleshall, 12 September 1451.

61. [Fo. 12v] Institution of Ralph Wode, chaplain, in the person of Thomas Byrom, chaplain, his proctor, to the vicarage of Morton (*Merton*), vacant by the resignation of Simon Billyngley; presented by the prioress and convent of Nuneaton (*Nuneton*). Ind. Archdn. Eccleshall, 29 October 1451.

62. Certificate of the official of the archdeacon of Coventry that he has executed the bishop's mandate (recited), dated at Leicester 18 May 1451 (recited), to examine and confirm the election of Br. Richard Evesham, canon of Maxstoke (*Maxstok*), O.S.A., as prior of Maxstoke, following the resignation of John Grene. The election had been examined and confirmed in Maxstoke parish church, 22 May 1451. Maxstoke parish church, 22 May 1451.
Memorandum that the certificate was brought to the bishop at Eccleshall on 31 October 1451.

63. Institution of Br. William Musselwike, O.E.S.A., *sacre pagine professor*, in the person of John Ferrers, literate, his proctor, to the vicarage of Aston, Birmingham (*Aston juxta Bermyngham*), vacant by the resignation of Richard Grove; presented by

---

[37] Principal of Little White Hall, Oxford, admitted 10 July 1439 and resigned 30 April 1444. Studied at Padua 1446 and 1447. Held many benefices and prebends in several cathedrals. Was archdeacon of Rochester in 1480 and also acted as a royal envoy during the 1460s. Member of the king's council under Edward IV. Died by April 1489 (Emden iii, 1680).

[38] Ufton Decani. Mr Henry Sharp resigned this prebend by 25 May 1461. He went on to hold prebends in the diocese of Lincoln: he was installed to the prebend of Milton Manor 17 December 1464 and resigned by 27 November 1493, was archdeacon of Bedford from 6 April 1471 and was collated to the prebend of Decem Librarum 22 December 1484, dying *c.* April 1489 (*Fasti* i, 17, 60, 93; x, 63).

the prior and convent of Tickford (*Tikford*). Ind. Archdn. Eccleshall, 2 December 1451.[39]

64. [Fo. 13] Collation to Robert Baguley, chaplain, in the person of Mr Thomas Lye, archdeacon of Salop,[40] his proctor, of the rectory of Fenny Compton (*Fennycompton*), vacant by the resignation of Richard Bowier. Ind. Archdn. Strand (*Stronde*), London, 1 February 1451/2.[41]

65. Institution of Henry Coventre, chaplain, to the rectory of Frankton (*Franketon*), vacant by the resignation of Richard Praty; presented by John Hereward and Katherine his wife, daughter and heiress of Thomas Palmer deceased. Ind. Archdn. Coventry, 15 February 1451/2.

66. Institution of Mr John Reedhill, LL.B., chaplain, to a canonry and the vacant moiety of the church of Ufton, considered to be a prebend in Lichfield cathedral;[42] presented by the prior and convent of Coventry cathedral. Mandate to the dean and chapter of Lichfield cathedral to install and induct. Lichfield, 16 February 1451/2.

67. Institution of John Parkyns, chaplain, to the vicarage of Grandborough (*Grenburgh*), vacant by the resignation of Henry Coventre; presented by the prior and convent of Ranton. Ind. Archdn. Haywood, 28 [?29] February 1451/2.

Annus Domini CCCC^mus Quinquagesimus secundus

68. Institution of John Lolleworth, chaplain, to the vicarage of Chilverscoton (*Chelverescoton, Chelverscoton*), vacant by the resignation of Br. William Wodecok; presented by the prior and convent of Arbury (*Erdebury*). Ind. Archdn. Haywood, 1 April 1452.

69. Collation to Br. John Welford, canon regular of Stone priory, O.S.A., of the vacant vicarage of Chesterton (*Chestreton*). Ind. Archdn. Haywood, 3 April 1452.

70. [Fo. 13v] Collation to Thomas Worsley, clerk,[43] in the person of Henry Wrightyngton, literate, his proctor, of a canonry and the prebend of Tachbrook (*Tachebroke*) in Lichfield cathedral, vacant by the resignation of William Worsley. Mandate to the dean and chapter to install and induct. Haywood, 28 June 1452.

71. Institution of William Parker, chaplain, in the person of John Menley, vicar

---

[39] For institution of the previous incumbent see **35**.
[40] See note 18.
[41] For previous institution see **28**.
[42] Ufton Cantoris. Reedhill apparently exchanged this prebend with Wendesley for the prebend of Pipa Minor in 1459, but no account of the exchange survives (*Fasti* x, 62). He was also a canon and prebendary of the collegiate church of St Chad in Salisbury, a prebend which he exchanged for one in Salisbury cathedral in 1450 (see **176**). For further details of his career see introduction, pp. xxvi–xxvii.
[43] Died before 1 May 1501 (*Fasti* x, 59).

of Holy Trinity, Coventry, his proctor, of the vicarage of Weston under Wetherley (*Weston subtus Wetheley*), vacant by the death of Richard Glowcestre; presented by the prior of Arbury. Ind. Archdn. Coventry, 26 August 1452.

[Fo. 14]   **ARCHDEACONRY OF STAFFORD**

72. Institution of Walter Flynton, priest, to the vacant rectory of Colton; presented by John Greseley, knight, Ind. Archdn. Haywood, 28 September 1447.

73. Institution of Mr Thomas Heywode,[44] priest, to the vacant rectory of Rolleston; presented by Queen Margaret, patron for this turn. Ind. Archdn. Lichfield, 12 October 1447.
Note that the vacancy dates from the resignation of John Catton, formerly rector of Rolleston, made in the south part of St Paul's cathedral, London, on 29 September 1447. Present: Mr Thomas Chopyn, notary public, Robert Hanneley, literate, Exeter and York dioceses. Shown in public instrument by Mr John Wardale, clerk, Lincoln diocese, notary.[45]

74. [Fo. 14–v] Certificate of Mr George Radclyff,[46] D. Dec., treasurer of Lichfield cathedral, vicar general, that he has executed the bishop's commission (recited, and dated at Kenilworth (*Kenylleworth*), 13 October 1447) receive the certificate of the archdeacon of Stafford on the proclamation citing opponents of the election of Br. Richard Collewich (*Collewych*) as prior of Stafford, St Thomas,[47] and to examine the election in Lichfield cathedral on 20 October, and if appropriate confirm and install the elect. The certificate of the proclamation (made by the archdeacon's Official) had been received, the election confirmed, and administration conferred. 21 October 1447.

75. [Fo. 14v] Institution by the vicar general, by special mandate of the bishop *in remotis*, of Richard Marchald, priest, to the chantry founded at the altar of St John the Baptist in the parish church of Walsall (*Walsale*), vacant by the death of Roger Spuryour; presented by Joan, widow of Henry Beaumount, knight, and Richard Whithill, *domicellus*. Ind. Archdn. Lichfield, 23 November 1447.

76. Institution of Richard Hancok, priest, to the rectory of Aldridge (*Alrewich*), vacant by the resignation of William Colyns; presented by William Ferrers, knight. Ind. Archdn. Hackney, 3 January 1447/8.

77. Institution by the vicar general, on special mandate of the bishop, of Geoffrey Powes, priest, to the vicarage of Sedgeley (*Seggesley*), vacant by the death of

---

[44] Thomas Heywood was prebendary of Gaia Minor, collated 7 May 1433, resigned by 24 August that year; of Hansacre in April 1439, and of Dasset Parva from 18 May 1434 which he exchanged with the prebend of Ryton. He was also dean of Lichfield from 21 April 1457 to his death on 25 October 1492 (*Fasti* x, 6, 30, 43–4, 52).
[45] See also **89**.
[46] See note 11.
[47] Richard Collewich was prior from 1447 to 1448. He had died by 11 December 1478 (*Heads of Religious Houses* iii, forthcoming).

John Walker; presented by the prior and convent of Dudley (*Duddeley*). Ind. Archdn. Lichfield, 24 January 1447/8.

78. [Fos 14v–15] Exchange of the rectory of Astley Abbots, Hereford diocese, and the vicarage of the prebendal church of Longdon. (i) Commission to William [Bothe], bishop of Coventry and Lichfield, from Thomas [Spofford], bishop of Hereford, to investigate and implement the proposed exchange of benefices between William Fernall, rector of Astley Abbotts (*Abbotley*), Hereford diocese, and Nicholas Colmon, vicar of Longdon, Coventry and Lichfield diocese, Colmon having been presented by Cicely, countess of Warwick. Manor of Whitburn, 7 November 1447. (ii) Institution by the vicar general, acting on special mandate from the bishop, of William Fernall to the vicarage of the prebendal church of Longdon, following the resignation of Colmon, at the presentation of Mr Robert Thwaytes, *sacre pagine professor*, proctor for Mr William Gray, canon and prebendary of Longdon in Lichfield cathedral,[48] *in remotis agente*. Mandate to the dean and chapter of Lichfield cathedral to induct. Lichfield, 6 March 1447/8. (iii) Institution by the vicar general of Nicholas Colmon to the rectory of Astley Abbotts, following Fernall's resignation, at the presentation of Cecily, duchess of Warwick. Lichfield, 6 March 1447/8. (iv) Note that a certificate was sent to the bishop of Hereford. 6 March 1447/8.

Sequitur Annus Domini Millesimus Quadringentiesimus Quadragesimus Octavus[49]

79. [Fo. 15] Institution of John Brounfeld, priest, to the rectory of Wednesbury, vacant; presented by King Henry. Ind. Archdn. Beaudesert, 18 May 1448.[50]

80. [Fo. 15a][51] Letters of John [Stafford], archbishop of Canterbury, concerning the dispute between John Bromefeld and William Smyth and the abbot and convent of Halesowen (Worcester diocese), rectors of the church of Walsall, concerning the possession of the chapel of Wednesbury.[52] Because the dispute is proceeding in the court of audience Bromefeld's induction into corporal possession of the said chapel is null and void; this fact is to be announced publicly and Bromefeld and Smyth are to be warned against any disturbance of the abbot and convent. Dated at the manor of Lambeth (*Lamehith*), 18 June 1448.

81. Institution by the vicar general of Henry Inse,[53] priest, to the rectory of Yoxhall (*Yoxhale*), vacant; presented by William Lovell knight, Lord of Lovell. Ind. Archdn. Lichfield, 25 March 1448.

---

[48] Collated 21 October 1442. Became bishop of Ely in 1454 (*Fasti* x, 46).
[49] At the top right-hand corner of the page is also written, 'Annus domini 1448'.
[50] See **80**.
[51] This is a separate piece of parchment, which has been sewn to the right-hand edge of the folio.
[52] See *VCH Worcestershire* ii, 163–6.
[53] See note 17.

82. [Fo. 15–v] Institution by the vicar general of John Leytwharte, alias Lovelady, priest, to the rectory of Handsworth, vacant; presented by John Stanley esq, patron this turn. Ind. Archdn. Lichfield, 28 October 1448.

83. [Fo. 15v] Institution of William Alkyn, priest, to the vacant rectory of Haughton (*Halughton*); presented by John Burghchier, knight. Ind. Archdn. Haywood (*Heywode*), 7 June 1448.

84. Institution of Nicholas Fyssher, priest, to the vicarage of the prebendal church of Alrewas (*Allerwas*), vacant by the resignation of John Careles; presented by Mr George Radclyff,[54] D. Dec., treasurer of Lichfield cathedral, and farmer of the canonry and prebend of Alrewas annexed to the chancellorship of Lichfield cathedral, patron for this turn by reason of the farm. Mandate to the dean and chapter of Lichfield cathedral to induct. Haywood (*Heywod*), 4 July 1448.

85. Institution of Humphrey Harryson, priest, to the vicarage of Alstonefield (*Alstonneffeld*), vacant by the resignation of Henry Sowter; presented by the abbot and convent of St Mary, Combermere, Ind. Archdn. Eccleshall, 20 August 1448.

86. Institution of William Wore, priest, to the rectory of Mucklestone (*Mocleston*), vacant by the death of John Wodelok; presented by William Morgan esq. Ind. Archdn. Eccleshall, 31 August 1448.

87. Collation to Thomas Daunesy, priest, of the chantry of St Nicholas in the parish church of Drayton Bassett, vacant and in the bishop's patronage by lapse of time. Ind. Archdn. Haywood, 20 September 1448.

88. Collation to Edward Croke, priest, *in commendam*, of the chantry called '*le Hilton chauntre*' in the prebendal church or chapel of St Michael, Lichfield, vacant and in the bishop's patronage by lapse of time. Mandate to the dean of Lichfield cathedral and James Langton,[55] canon of that church, *conjunctim vel divisim* to induct. Haywood, 28 May 1448.[56]

89. Institution of Mr Thomas Heywode,[57] priest, to the rectory of Rolleston, vacant by his own resignation; presented by Queen Margaret, patron for this turn. Ind. Archdn. Hackney, 23 January 1449.

90. [Fo. 16] (i) Letters of presentation from Thomas Stanley knight, reciting letters patent of King Henry VI (dated under the seal of the duchy of Lancaster, at Westminster, 21 January, 27 Henry VI [1448/9]),[58] granting to him, controller of

---

54 See note 11.

55 James Langton held the prebend of Stotfold from 5 July 1442 until his death, before 30 December 1450 (*Fasti* x, 56).

56 This is followed by a note: 'R. constat de rasura utriusque institucionis. W. Brand. R.' Each entry has a few words interlineated, but there is no immediate sign of any erasure.

57 See note 44.

58 This letter is not recorded in the Calendar of Patent rolls, although other grants to Thomas Stanley of a similar date do appear.

the household, the next presentation to the church of Stoke, and presenting Edward Stanley, priest, as rector following the death of Mr John Burdet. 24 January 1449. (ii) Institution of Edward Stanley, chaplain, in the person of Christopher Legh, priest, his proctor, to the rectory of Stoke, vacant by the death of Mr John Burdet, by virtue of the above presentation. Ind. Archdn. Hackney (*Hakeney*), 25 January 1448/9.

91. Institution of Roger Mersshe, priest, to a canonry and the prebend of Wigginton (Wygynton) in the collegiate church of Tamworth, vacant by the death of Mr Walter Sheryngton, presented by King Henry. Mandate to the archdeacon or his official to induct and install Mersshe or his proctor, John Boton, literate. Strand, London, 6 February 1448/9.

92. [Fo. 16–v] Collation to Thomas Walter, chaplain, of a canonry and the vacant prebend of Gaia minor (*Gaya minor*), in Lichfield cathedral. Mandate to the dean and chapter to induct and install. Strand, London, 18 February 1448/9.[59] Note that the vacancy dates from the resignation of Mr William Kynwolmersh, formerly canon and prebendary, made in the church of Kidlington (*Kydlyngton*), Lincoln diocese, on 20 January 1448/9. Present: Richard Harcourt, esq., and William Harcourt literate, Coventry and Lichfield diocese. Shown in instrument by Mr Stephen Braywell, clerk, York diocese, notary.[60]

93. [Fo. 16v] Collation to Mr Roger Wall (*Walle*),[61] chaplain, of a canonry and the prebend of Eccleshall (*Eccleshale alias Ionyston*), in Lichfield cathedral, vacant by the death of Mr Richard Leyot. Mandate to the dean and chapter to induct and install Wall or his proctor, Hugh Lache, priest. Strand, London, 7 March 1448/9.

Annus Domini Millesimus CCCC^{mus} Quadragesimus Nonus

94. Institution of Thomas Porter, priest, to the rectory of Leigh (*Legh*), vacant by the death of John Hichekyn; presented by James Ormonde, knight, patron for this turn. Ind. Archdn. Haywood, 16 April 1449.

95. Collation to Mr Laurence Bothe, Lic. Laws, priest, of a canonry and the prebend of Offley (*Offeley*), in Lichfield cathedral,[62] vacant by the resignation of Mr Roger Wall.[63] Mandate to the dean and chapter to induct and install Bothe or his proctor. Hackney, 17 July 1449.

96. Institution of John Kendale, priest, to the vicarage of Wombourn (*Womburn*),

---

59 Walter resigned this prebend by 27 November 1458 (*Fasti* x, 43).
60 Notary public by 1434. Died by December 1456 (Emden i, 256).
61 See note 27.
62 Bothe resigned this prebend the same year. He also held the Lichfield prebend of Gaia Major, by exchange of May 1444, which he resigned by 8 February 1445, and the prebend of Tervin, which he resigned in 1457 when bishop of Durham (*Fasti* x, 41, 48, 60). Le Neve stated that he exchanged the prebend of Offley for that of Tervin, but see **98**.
63 See note 27.

vacant by the resignation of Thomas Havkys; presented by the prior and convent of Dudley (*Duddeley*). Ind. Archdn. Haywood, 22 August 1449.

97. [Fo. 17] (i) Letters of John Stone and John Leder, canons regular of the priory of St Margaret, Calwich (*Calwych*), O.S.A., informing the bishop of the death on 25 October 1449 of Br. Robert Holynton, late prior of Calwich. Because of the notorious poverty of their house, and the intolerable expense involved in an election, for this occasion only they submit to the bishop the appointment of a new prior. Chapter house, Calwich, 29 October 1449. (ii) Decree of William [Bothe], bishop of Coventry and Lichfield, appointing Br. John Stone as prior of Calwich, in accordance with the powers conferred by the preceding letters, and conferring administration. Read in the main chapel of the manor of Haywood. Present; Masters Gregory Neuporte, B. Dec., and John Reedhill, LL.B., and William Brande, notary public. 1 November 1449. (iii) Note that John Stone took the oath of obedience, and a mandate was issued to the Archdeacon of Stafford or his Official to induct and install. 1 November 1449.

98. [Fo. 17v] Exchange of the canonry and prebend of Oxgate in St Paul's cathedral, London, and the canonry and prebend of Offley (*Offeley*) in Lichfield cathedral: (i) Commission from Thomas Lyseux [Liseux], dean and canon of St Paul's cathedral, London, Official and keeper of the spiritualities, *sede vacante*, to the bishop of Coventry and Lichfield, to investigate and implement a proposed exchange of benefices between between Thomas Pulter, canon and prebendary of Oxgate in St Paul's cathedral, London,[64] and Mr Laurence Both [Bothe], canon and prebendary of Offley in Lichfield cathedral,[65] the latter presented by Marmaduke [Lumley], bishop of Carlisle, by virtue of a grant to him by the king by letters patent.[66] Both's obedience, induction, and installation, are reserved. Hostel in London 12 November 1449. (ii) Memorandum of the institution of Mr Laurence Bothe to Oxgate, and of the collation of Offley to Thomas Pulter. The dean and chapter of Lichfield were mandated to induct and install Pulter or his proctor. Strand, London, 12 November 1449. (iii) Note that a certificate had been sent to Mr Thomas Lyseux. Strand, London, 12 November 1449.

99. [Fo. 18] Institution of Mr John Bate, dean of the collegiate church of Tamworth, to a canonry and the vacant prebend of Wylmecote in the said church; presented by King Henry. Mandate to the archdeacon or his official to induct and install. Strand, London, 22 November 1449.

100. Collation of Thomas Crowther, priest, to the rectory of Quatt [*Quatte*], vacant by the resignation of Richard Russheton. Ind. Archdn. London, 3 March 1449/50.
Memorandum that the same day, date, and place, Thomas Crowther swore on the gospels in the presence of the bishop that before he was able to receive or obtain the

---

64 Thomas Pulter had been installed in Oxgate prebend 13 March 1427. He resigned the prebend of Offley by 21 June 1452 (*Fasti* v, 48, 53). See **124**.
65 See note 62.
66 See *CPR 1446–52*, 260.

said rectory from the patrons, the prior and convent of Great Malvern (*Maioris Malverne*), Worcester diocese, O.S.B., he took an oath to pay to them an annual pension of 20s. It was for this reason that the bishop granted the church, having first absolved him from his oath.[67]

Annus Domini Millesimus CCCC^mus Quinquagesimus

101. Institution of Hugh Wetrenes, chaplain, to the vicarage of Caverswall (*Careswell*), vacant by the resignation of James Whitakres; presented by the prior and convent of Stafford, St Thomas. Ind. Archdn. Leicester (*Leycestre*), 22 April 1450.

102. Institution of Geoffrey Massy, chaplain, to the vicarage of Leek, vacant by the resignation of Hugh Wetrenes; presented by the abbot and convent of Dieuleucres (*Deuleucres*). Ind. Archdn. Clayton (*Claiton*), 30 July 1450.

103. Institution of William Alisaundre, chaplain, to the rectory of Leigh (*Legh*), vacant by the resignation of Thomas Porter by reason of his succession to the church of Cheselbourne (*Cheselborn*), Salisbury diocese; presented by Nicholas Mongomery, esq, patron for this turn. Ind. Archdn. Lichfield, 1 November 1450.

104. [Fo. 18v] Collation to Mr Thomas Edmond, M.D., of a canonry and the prebend of Bishopshull (*Bisshophill*), in Lichfield cathedral,[68] vacant by the death of Mr William Berford.[69] Mandate to the dean and chapter to induct and install. Strand, London, 14 December 1450.

105. Collation to Thomas Byrom, chaplain, of a canonry and the prebend of Stotfold in Lichfield cathedral,[70] vacant by the death of James de Langton. Mandate to the dean and chapter to induct and install. Eccleshall, 30 December 1450.

106. Collation to William Brande, clerk, of a canonry and the prebend of Morehall [*Morehalle*] in the collegiate church of Gnosall (*Gnowsale*), vacant by the death of James de Langton. Mandate to Robert Grene, chaplain, vicar choral of the said church, to induct and install. Eccleshall, 30 December 1450.

---

67 The memorandum is at the foot of the page, after **103**. The first part of **100** ends with the added words, 'Et memorandum' and a mark which is reproduced at the start of the continuation.

68 Winchester College scholar 1427, admitted to New College Oxford 1433 and a fellow 1435, vacated 1451. As well as this prebend he held the benefice of Amersham, Bucks., and was vicar of St Michael's Coventry (following papal dispensation) 1457 until his death. Deceased by 23 October 1481 (Emden i, 626; *Fasti* x, 22).

69 For Master William Berford's will, see Swanson, 'Lichfield Chapter Acts', no. 72.

70 Byrom's successor in this prebend was collated 9 October 1451 (see **112**, *Fasti* x, 56). Byrom also held the prebend of Longdon from 24 October 1458 to his resignation before 18 May 1466 and the prebend of Curborough where his next known successor was collated 28 October 1458 (*Fasti* x, 28, 46; **113**).

Annus Domini Millesimus CCCC^{mus} Quinquagesimus Primus

107. Institution of Hugh Adwley, chaplain, to the rectory of Kingsley (*Kyngesley*), vacant by the death of Mr Richard Faltherst; presented by Thomasine, widow of Hugh Yerdeswike, esq. Ind. Archdn. Eccleshall, 8 July 1451.

108. Collation to John Eton, chaplain, of the chantry of St Mary in the parish church of Drayton Bassett (*Drayton Basset*), vacant and in the bishop's patronage by lapse of time. Ind. Archdn. Haywood (*Haywode*), 21 July 1451.

109. Institution of Thomas Billyngham, chaplain, to the rectory of Gratwich (*Grotewich*), vacant by the death of Roger Banister; presented by Thomas Litelton. Ind. Archdn. Haywood, 31 July 1451.

110. [Fo. 19] Institution of John Chircheyerde, chaplain, to the rectory of Norbury, vacant by the death of William Freman; presented by Phillip Botiller, esq. Ind. Archdn. Haywood, 3 August 1451.

111. Institution of Br. Robert Twysse, canon of St Mary, Rocester (*Roucester*), chaplain, to the vicarage of Rocester, vacant by the resignation of Br. William Welforde; presented by the abbot and convent of Rocester. Ind. Archdn. Haywood, 21 August 1451.

112. Collation to Mr John Thurston, B. Dec., priest, of a canonry and the prebend of Stotfold in Lichfield cathedral,[71] vacant by the resignation of Thomas Byrome. Mandate to the dean and chapter to induct and install. Eccleshall, 9 October 1451.[72]

113. Collation to Thomas Byrom, chaplain, of a canonry and the prebend of Curburgh in Lichfield cathedral,[73] vacant by the death of Mr Gregory Broun. Mandate to the dean and chapter to induct and install. Eccleshall, 10 October 1451.

114. Collation to Thomas Aron, priest, of the vicarage of Brewood (*Brewode*), vacant and in the bishop's patronage by lapse of time. Mandate to the dean and chapter of Lichfield cathedral to induct. Eccleshall, 3 November 1451.

115. Institution of John Nobull to the vicarage of Biddulph (*Bedulf*), vacant by the resignation of John Beryngham; presented by the abbot and convent of Hulton (*Hilton*). Ind. Archdn. Eccleshall, 18 November 1451.

116. [Fo. 19v] Institution of William Beke, chaplain, to the rectory of Cheadle (*Chedull*), vacant by the resignation of Mr William Hudale; presented by Ralph Basset, esq., patron for this turn. Ind. Archdn. Eccleshall, 3 December 1451.

[71] Thurstan had died by 28 July 1457 (*Fasti* x, 56).
[72] See note 69.
[73] See note 70.

117. Institution of Br. Thomas Wolscote, canon of St Mary, Rocester (*Roucestre*), to the vacant rectory of Colton; presented by John Greseley, esq. Ind. Archdn. Eccleshall, 22 December 1451.[74]

118. Letters of Mr George Radclyff,[75] D. Dec., archdeacon of Chester, acknowledging and reciting the bishop's commission dated 24 January 1451/2, to institute a suitable person to the rectory of Standon (*Staundon*), vacant by the death of Hugh Priamour, on the presentation of the patrons. On 1 February 1451/2 he instituted Richard de Wode, clerk, in the person of John Wode, literate, his proctor, at the presentation of John Roger, esq, and Elizabeth *consortis sue*. Ind. Archdn. Lichfield, 1 February 1451/2.

Annus Domini Millesimus CCCC^{mus} Quinquagesimus Primus

119. Institution of Richard Worthyngton, chaplain, to the rectory of Mavesyn Ridware (*Mawesyn Ridware*), vacant by the death of Richard Tilly; presented by John Cawardyne, Edmund Vernon, and Hugh Davenporte, esqs., patrons this turn. Mandate to the chancellor of Lichfield cathedral or his commissary to induct. Haywood, 18 April 1452.

120. [Fo. 20] Institution of John Brigham, chaplain, to the vicarage of Weston on Trent (*Weston super Trent*), vacant by the resignation of John Nobull;[76] presented by the prior and convent of Stafford, St Thomas. Ind. Archdn. Heywood, 20 April 1452.

121. Collation to Elizabeth Botery, nun of the priory of the black nuns of Brewood (*Brewode*), O.S.B., of the priorate of the house, vacant by the resignation of Margaret Chilterne, and in the bishop's patronage by lapse of time.[77] Memorandum that Henry Inse,[78] chaplain, was mandated to install and induct. Haywood, 24 April 1452.

122. Institution of Hugh Witterens, chaplain, to the vicarage of Dilhorne (*Dulverne*), vacant by the resignation of John Colton; presented by John Verney, dean,[79] and the chapter of Lichfield cathedral. Ind. Archdn. Haywood, 28 April 1452.

123. Institution of John Witterens, chaplain, to the vicarage of Caverswall (*Careswall*), vacant by the resignation of Hugh Witterens; presented by the prior and convent of Stafford, St Thomas. Ind. Archdn. Haywood, 28 April 1452.[80]

---

[74] Previous incumbent William Parker (see **72**).
[75] See note 11.
[76] See **115**.
[77] Elizabeth Botery was prioress from 1452 to 1485. She had died by 5 August 1485 (*Heads of Religious Houses* iii, forthcoming).
[78] See note 16.
[79] Dean from 1 October 1432 to his death before 19 June 1457. Previously held the prebend of Hansacre by exchange from April 1439 until appointed dean (*Fasti* x, 6, 44).
[80] For the institution of his predecessor see **101**.

124. [Fo. 20–v] Collation to Mr Laurence Bothe,[81] Lic. Leg., of a canonry and the prebend of Offley (*Offeley*), in Lichfield cathedral, vacant by the resignation of Thomas Pulter. Mandate to the dean and chapter to induct and install. Strand, London, 21 June 1452.[82]

125. [Fo. 20v] Institution of William Ferrour, priest, to the vacant vicarage of Bushbury (*Busshebury*); presented by the prior and convent of Stafford, St Thomas. Ind. Archdn. Haywood, 18 July 1452.

126. Institution of Robert Davy, chaplain, to the vicarage of Madeley, vacant by the death of Richard Hawkyn; presented by the prior and convent of Stone. Ind. Archdn. Haywood, 19 August 1452.

[Fo. 27]   **ARCHDEACONRY OF DERBY**
          Anno Domini Millesimo CCCC^mo xlvij^o[83]

127. [Fo. 21] Institution of John Whithals, priest, to the second chaplaincy of the chantry at the altar of St Mary in the chapel of Chaddesden (*Chadesden*), vacant by the resignation of Gilbert Boterworth; presented by the abbot and convent of St Mary, Darley (*Derley*). Ind. Archdn. Strand, London, 19 January 1447/8.

128. Institution by the vicar general, by special mandate of the bishop, of Richard Langton, priest, to the chantry of St Katherine the virgin in the church of St Michael the archangel, Melbourne (*Melburn*), vacant; presented by Robert Wyllen and Cecilia his wife. Ind. Archdn. Lichfield, 25 January 1447/8.

129. Judicial writ of King Henry VI, notifying the bishop that Robert Wilne [Wylne] and Cecilia his wife have recovered the right of presentation to the chantry at the altar of St Katherine the virgin in the nave of the parish church of St Michael, Melbourne, by writ *de quare impedit*, against the claim of Robert Newton, and ordering the bishop to admit a suitable person presented by them. Tested by R. Neuton, Westminster, 10 April, 26 Henry VI.[84]

130. Institution of Thomas Monyasshe, priest, to the vicarage of St Werburge, Derby, vacant by the resignation of John Whithals; presented by the prioress and convent of the nuns of Derby. Ind. Archdn. Strand, London, 8 February 1447/8.

Annus Domini Millesimus CCCC^mus Quadragesimus Octavus

131.[85] Institution of John Watson, priest, to the vicarage of Ault Hucknall (*Hawte Hukenall*), vacant by the death of John Wyntworth; presented by the prior and convent of Newstead (*Novo Loco in Shirewode*). Ind. Archdn. Haywood, 15 July 1448.

---

81 See note 52.
82 See **98**.
83 The date actually appears on the same line as the heading for the archdeaconry.
84 See **128**.
85 This entry is marked with several 'B's, and also 'infra'. Their purpose is to indicate that this should be the second entry for this year, the first being **134**, which also has markings to indicate its misplacement (see below).

132. [Fo. 21v] Institution of Thomas Sayntur, priest, to the vicarage of Scarcliffe (*Charclyff, Skarclyff*), vacant by John Stubbar's acceptance of the church of Lynby (*Lymby*), York diocese; presented by the abbot and convent of Darley. Ind. Archdn. Haywood, 20 July 1448.

133. Institution of Robert Parker, priest, to the rectory of Kirk Ireton (*Kirke Ireton, Kirke Irton*), vacant by the resignation of Henry Scortred; presented by Mr John Macworth, D. Dec., dean of Lincoln cathedral. Ind Archdn. Haywood, 21 September 1448.

134.[86] Collation to John Crecy *alias* Smyth of the rectory of Stoney Stanton (*Stonnystaunton, Stonystaunton*), vacant and in the bishop's patronage by lapse of time. Ind. Archdn. Beaudesert, 17 May 1448.

Annus Domini Millesimus CCCC^mus Quadragesimus Nonus

135. Collation to Mr William Radclyff, LL.B., priest, in the person of Seth Worsley, literate, his proctor, of the vacant treasurership of Lichfield cathedral,[87] and a canonry and the prebend of Sawley (*Sallow*) annexed thereto. Mandate to the dean (or his *locum tenens*) and chapter of Lichfield to induct and install. Haywood, 29 April 1449.

136. Institution of Richard Bellerby, priest, to the rectory of Sutton in the Dale (*Sutton in le Dall*), vacant by the resignation of John Bithekyrk; presented by Alice Leeke, lady of Landeford. Ind. Archdn. Haywood, 16 October 1449.

137. Institution of John Porter, priest, to the rectory of Clowne (*Cloune*), vacant by the death of John Marshall; presented by the prior and convent of Worksop (*Wirkesopp*). Ind. Archdn. Haywood, 29 October 1449.

138. [Fos 21v–22] Institution of Thomas Sharpe, priest, to the vicarage of Mickleover (*Magna Overa*), vacant by the resignation of Richard Rotour; presented by the abbot and convent of Burton upon Trent (*Burton super Trentt*). Ind. Archdn. London, the bishop's hostel near St Paul's cathedral, 23 January 1449/50.

139. [Fo. 22] Collation to John Freman, chaplain, of the vicarage of Hope, vacant and in the bishop's patronage by lapse of time. Mandate to the dean and chapter of Lichfield cathedral to induct. Strand, London, 4 February 1449/50.

Annus Domini Millesimus CCCC^mus Quinquagesimus

140. Institution of Br. James Doram, canon regular of the priory of Newstead, O.S.A., York diocese, to the vicarage of Ault Hucknall (*Hawte Hukenall*), vacant by

[86] This entry is marked with a letter 'A' and 'supra', to indicate that it is misplaced and should appear first among this year's entries (see previous note).
[87] Radclyffe died before 24 October 1458 (*Fasti* x, 12).

the resignation of William Watson;[88] presented by the prior and convent of Newstead. Ind. Archdn. Sawley (*Sallowe*), 18 April 1450.

141. Institution of John Balme, chaplain, to the chantry of St Michael in the church of All Saints, Chesterfield (*Chestrefeld, Chestrefelde*), vacant by the death of William Worsley; presented by Nicholas Durant, *domicellus*, of Chesterfield. Leicester, 6 May 1450.

142. Collation to William Boydon,[89] chaplain, of a canonry and the prebend of Sandiacre in Lichfield cathedral, vacant by the resignation of John Werkeworth. Mandate to the dean (or his *locum tenens*) and chapter of Lichfield to induct and install. Prescot (*Prestcote*), 18 July 1450.

143. [Fo. 22–v] Institution of John Tonge, chaplain, to the rectory of Stoney Stanton (*Sonystaunton, Stonystaunton*), vacant by the resignation of John Crecy *alias* Smyth, who has secured the parish church of Mottram in Longdendale (*Mottrom*), incompatible with Stoney Stanton; presented by John Fraunces of Tiknale. Ind. Archdn. Clayton (*Claiton*), 28 October 1450.[90]

144. [Fo. 22v] Institution of Henry Russell, deacon, to the vicarage of Doveridge (*Dovebrugg, Dovebrugge*), vacant by the resignation of John Yeveley; presented by the prior and convent of Tutbury (*Tuttebury*). Ind. Archdn. Lichfield, 1 November 1450.

145. Institution of Mr Robert Colynson, D. Dec., to the rectory of Bradley vacant by the death of Br. Thomas Richard; presented by Mr John Macworth, D. Dec., dean of Lincoln cathedral.[91] Ind. Archdn. Eccleshall, 21 January 1450/1.

146. Institution of William Tailleour, chaplain, to the vicarage of Castleton (*Castelton in pecco*), vacant by the resignation of Thomas Tailleour; presented by the abbot and convent of Vale Royal (*Valle regali*). Ind. Archdn. Eccleshall, 24 January 1450/1.

147. Collation to Peter Berdesley, deacon, of the rectory of Trusley (*Trusseley*), vacant and in the bishop's patronage by lapse of time. Ind. Archdn. Eccleshall, 21 March 1450/1.

Annus Domini Millesimus CCCC^mus Quinquagesimus

148. Institution of Richard Smyth, chaplain, to the rectory of Carsington (*Kersyngton*), vacant by the resignation of Thomas Porter; presented by Mr John Macworth, D. Dec.,[92] dean of Lincoln cathedral. Ind. Archdn. Eccleshall, 27 March 1451.

---

88 Called John at his institution, see **131**.
89 Boyden resigned this prebend before 23 September 1489 (*Fasti* x, 54).
90 For the institution of his predecessor see **134**.
91 Elected dean by 26 May 1412. Died by 12 January 1452 (*Fasti* i, 4).
92 See note 91.

149. Institution of Richard Hawson, chaplain, in the person of Robert Dawbriggecowrte, literate, his proctor, to the chantry of St Mary Magdalene in the parish church of All Saints, Chesterfield (*Chestrefeld*), vacant by the death of Robert Isabell; presented by Nicholas Durant, *domicellus*. Ind. Archdn. Eccleshall, 19 April 1451.

150. [Fos 22v–23] Institution of Robert Hesull, chaplain, to the rectory of Brailsford (*Brailesforth, Braillesforth*), vacant by the death of Robert Keyngham; presented by Thomas Blounte, knight, Edward Langforth, Walter Blount and Thomas Blount, esqs. Ind. Archdn. Haywood, 2 August 1451.

151. [Fo. 23] Institution of John Fyton, chaplain, to the rectory of Barton Blount, vacant by the resignation of Robert Hesull by reason of his securing the parish church of Brailsford (*Brailesforth*), incompatible with Barton Blount: presented by Thomas Blount, knight. Ind. Archdn. Haywood, 9 August 1451.

152. Institution of James Hyton, chaplain, to the rectory of Morton, vacant by the death of William Snowe: presented by Nicholas Longforde, knight. Ind. Archdn. Haywood, 17 August 1451.

153. Institution of John Fesande, chaplain, to the vicarage of Crich (*Criche*), vacant by the resignation of James Hyton by reason of his securing the parish church of Morton, incompatible with Crich: presented by the abbot and convent of Darley. Ind. Archdn. Eccleshall, 9 September 1451.

154. Institution of John Salt, chaplain, to the vicarage of Church Broughton (*Kirkbroghton*), vacant by the death of John Tirpyn: presented by the prior and convent of Tutbury (*Tuttebury*). Ind. Archdn. Eccleshall, 9 October 1451.

155. Institution of Br. John Basset, canon regular of the priory of Repton (*Repingdon*), O.S.A., chaplain, to the vacant vicarage of Croxall [*Croxhale*]; presented by the prior and convent of Repton. Ind. Archdn. Eccleshall, 24 October 1451.

156. Institution of William Felowe, chaplain, to the rectory of Shirland (*Shurland, Shurlande*), vacant by the death of Hugh Penyale: presented by Thomas, lord of Richmond, and Margaret his wife, lately wife of Richard Grey, lord of Wilton. Ind. Archdn. Eccleshall, 29 October 1451.

157. Institution of Thomas Knangresse to the rectory of Langwith (*Langewath*), vacant by the death of Richard Malkey: presented by the prior and convent of Thurgarton. Ind. Archdn. Eccleshall, 20 December 1451.

Annus Domini Millesimus CCCC^{mus} Quinquagesimus

158. [Fo. 23v] Institution of Thomas Smyth, chaplain, to the rectory of Bradley (*Bradeley*), vacant by the resignation of Mr Robert Colynson, D. Dec.: presented by Mr Robert Flemmynge,[93] dean of Lincoln cathedral.[94] Ind. Archdn. Haywood, 17 April 1452.[95]

159. Institution of William Wattson, chaplain, to the rectory of Thorpe (*Thorp*), vacant by the resignation of Richard Gararde: presented by Mr Robert Flemmyng, dean of Lincoln cathedral.[96] Ind. Archdn. Strand, London, 12 May 1452.

[Fo. 24] **ARCHDEACONRY OF SALOP**

160. Institution of William Jowkys, priest, to the vicarage of Shifnal (*Ideshale*), vacant by the resignation of John Smyth; presented by the master or warden of the new college or chantry of St Mary Magdalene, Battlefield by Shrewsbury (*Batelfeld iuxta Salop'*). Ind. Archdn. Strand, London, 13 January 1447/8.

161. Institution of William Estby, priest, to the vicarage of Baschurch (*Bassechurch*), vacant by the resignation of Mr Thomas Condor offered by Thomas Longe, clerk, his proctor; presented by the abbot and convent of St Peter, Shrewsbury. Ind. Archdn. Hackney, 14 February 1447/8.

Annus Dominus Millesimus Quadringentesimus Quadragesimus Octavus

162. Institution of Hugh Newton, priest, to the rectory of Norton in Hales, vacant by the acceptance by William Wore of the parish church of Grendon; presented by William Boerley esq. Ind. Archdn. Strand, London, 12 April 1448.[97]

163. [Fo. 24–v] Exchange of the vicarage of Notholt [*Northall*], London diocese, and the rectory of Stockton (*Stokton*), Coventry and Lichfield diocese. (i) Commission from Walter Shiryngton [Sheryngton, Shyryngton], canon residentiary of St Paul's cathedral, London,[98] official and keeper of the spiritualities, *sede vacante*, to William [Bothe], bishop of Coventry and Lichfield, to investigate and implement a proposed exchange of benefices between Hugh Grene, vicar of Northolt, London

---

93 Dean of Lincoln from 12 January 1452, deceased by 18 August 1483 (*Fasti* i, 4).
94 This entry includes a note: 'Et memorandum quod dictus magister Robertus scripsit in presentacione obedienciam episcopo ut tenetur, ut patet in eadem'. This presumably alludes to some dispute concerning the bishop's jurisdiction over the enclaves in Derbyshire, which were in the patronage of the dean of Lincoln.
95 For the institution of his predecessor see **145**.
96 See note 93.
97 See **19, 25**.
98 Walter Shiryngton was prebendary of Sidlesham by exchange with Thomas Morton for the prebend of Barnby in Howden collegiate church, from December 1433, probably until his death by 14 February 1449 (*Fasti* v, 42).

diocese (in the keeper's collation for this turn), and John Rowlow, rector of Stockton, Coventry and Lichfield diocese, reserving Rowlow's induction and canonical obedience. London 10 August 1448. (ii) Memorandum of the institution of Hugh Grene, to the rectory of Stockton, following Rowlow's resignation offered in the person of Mr William Brande, clerk, his proctor, at the presentation of Richard Archer of Stotfold (*Stodfolde*), esq. Ind. Archdn. Haywood, 13 September 1338. (iii) Note of the institution of John Rowlow, in the person of Mr William Brande, clerk, his proctor, to the vicarage of Northolt, following Grene's resignation, and reserving his canonical obedience and induction. Haywood, 13 September 1448. (iv) Note that a certificate had been sent to the keeper of the spiritualities. Haywood, 13 September 1448.

164. [Fo. 24v] Institution of Roger Phelips, priest, to the vicarage of Baschurch, vacant by the resignation of William Estby; presented by the abbot and convent of St Peter, Shrewsbury. Ind. Archdn. Haywood (*Heywode*), 26 September 1448.[99]

165. Institution of John Launcell, chaplain, to the deanery of the collegiate church of St Mary, Shrewsbury, vacant by the death of Mr John Burdet; presented by King Henry VI. Mandate for induction to the archdeacon or his official, and Mr John [Chircheyerde], *conjunctim vel divisim*. Hackney, 1 February 1448/9.

166. Institution of Richard Bell, priest, in the person of Mr Thomas Lye,[100] his proctor, to the vicarage of Attingham (*Attyngham*), vacant by the death of Richard [Glover]; presented by the abbot and convent of Lilleshall (*Lilleshull*). Ind. Archdn. Hackney, 1 February 1448/9.

167. [Fos 24v–25] Exchange of the rectories of Broughton (*Byryghton*) and Adderley (*Aderley*), both within the diocese of Coventry and Lichfield. (i) Institution of John Cook to the rectory of Broughton, vacant by the resignation of Robert Catrik (Catryk) in exchange for the rectory of Adderley, at the presentation of the abbot and convent of St Peter, Shrewsbury. Ind. Archdn. Cook swore on the gospels that he would pay the pension anciently due from his church to the sacristan of Lichfield cathedral. Present; Mr William Brand, clerk,[101] William Coton, *domicellus*, Bernard Fyssher, literate, and others. Strand, London, 18 March 1448/9, (ii) Institution of Robert Catrik, in the person of Mr Robert Kent, clerk, his proctor, to the rectory of Adderley, for the above exchange, at the presentation of Thomas, lord of Roos and Hamlake (*Hamelak*). Ind. Archdn. Strand, London, 18 March, 1449.

Annus Domini Millesimus CCCC^mus^ Quadragesimus Nonus

168. [Fo. 25] Institution of William Shery, priest, to the rectory of Norton in Hales, vacant by the resignation or dimission of Hugh de Newton by reason of his

---

99   For the institution of his predecessor see **161**.
100 See note 18.
101 William Brand, public notary and proctor, his is probably the main hand of the register. This hand also occurs in Archbishop William Bothe's register at York.

securing the parish church of Clungunford (*Clongonvas*), Hereford diocese, incompatible with Norton in Hales; presented by William Boerley, esq. Ind. Archdn. Haywood, 31 July 1449.[102]

169. Institution of Mr William Eure, M.A., priest, in the person of Laurence Sikilbrice, literate, his proctor, to the rectory of Wem (*Wemme*), vacant by the resignation of Mr William Lescrop;[103] presented by Ralph [de Greystoke], lord of Greystock (*Graistok*) and Wem.[104] Ind. Archdn.
Memorandum that this vacancy dates from the resignation of Mr William Lescrop in the house of William Pierson, Newcastle on Tyne (*Novo castro super Tynam*), Durham diocese, on 16 June 1449. Present; Mr Alexander Cok, clerk, Thomas Chartres, chaplain, Durham diocese; as shown in instrument by Mr Christopher Roche, clerk, Durham diocese, notary. Eccleshall, 15 July 1449.

170. Institution by the vicar general, by special mandate of the bishop, of John Hoope, priest, to the rectory of Pitchford (*Picheford, Pycheforde*), vacant by the death of John Adyse; presented by James [Butler], earl of Wiltshire.[105] Ind. Archdn. Lichfield, 22 December 1449.[106]

171. [Fo. 25v] Institution of Br. Richard Trussell, canon of Haughmond (*Haghmond*), O.S.A., in the person of Mr Thomas Lye,[107] priest, his proctor, to the vicarage of Stanton on Hine Heath (*Stanton super Hyneheth*), vacant by the resignation of John Donne; presented by the abbot and convent of Haughmond. Ind. Archdn. Strand, London, 3 March 1449/50.

172. Institution of Thomas Milis, priest, in the person of Mr Thomas Lye, notary public, his proctor, to the rectory of Stockton (*Stokton*), vacant by the resignation of Hugh Grene; presented by Richard Archer of Lapley (*Lappeley*), esq. Ind. Archdn. Strand, London, 4 March 1449/50.

Annus Domini Millesimus CCCC^mus Quinquagesimus

173. Collation to Mr Thomas Lye, priest, of the archdeaconry of Salop,[108] vacant by the resignation of Mr Thomas Salesbury. Mandate to John Churcheyorde and Walter Brown, priests, *conjunctim vel divisim*, to induct Lye or William Disceleden or [*blank*] Lutte, priests, his proctors, into the archdeaconry by

102 For the institution of his predecessor see **162**.
103 Son of Stephen, second lord Scrope of Masham, held many ecclesiastical honours and benefices, including a prebend at Ripon and the mastership of Greatham Hospital, Durham, 1451 until his death and of St Leonard's Hospital, Yorkshire, 1431–48. Died 12 May 1463. Buried in York Minster (Emden iii, 1361).
104 See note 25.
105 For James Butler see John Watts, 'Butler, James, first earl of Wiltshire and fifth earl of Ormond (1420–1461)', *Oxford Dictionary of National Biography* (Oxford University Press, Sept. 2004); online edn, May 2006.
106 This entry refers to the certificate returned by the vicar general to the bishop.
107 See note 18.
108 See note 18.

handing over the ring of the door of a church within the archdeaconry which is subject to episcopal jurisdiction, and delivery of the archidiaconal procurations of that church.[109] Leicester, 22 May 1450.

174. Collation to Thomas Marshall, priest, of a canonry and prebend in the collegiate church of St Chad, Shrewsbury, formerly occupied by Mr Thomas Lye and vacant by his resignation.[110] Mandate to the dean of the collegiate church, his *locum tenens*, or the president, to induct and install. Leicester, 23 May 1450.

175. [Fos 25v–26] Institution of Richard Lopynton to the vicarage of Montford (*Monford*), vacant by the resignation of William Leche; presented by the prioress and convent of the white nuns of Brewood (*Brewode*). Ind. Archdn. Clayton (*Claiton*), 23 October 1450.

176. [Fo. 26] Exchange of the prebend of Grantham in Salisbury cathedral, and a prebend in the collegiate church of St Chad, Shrewsbury. (i) Certificate of John Paslew, LL.B., keeper of the spiritualities, Salisbury diocese, *sede vacante*, recording his receipt on 1 September 1450 of a commission from William [Bothe], bishop of Coventry and Lichfield (recited, and dated 23 August 1450) to investigate and implement the proposed exchange of benefices between Mr Edmund Dutton, LL.B., canon of Salisbury cathedral and prebendary of Grantham in the same,[111] and Mr John Reedhill, LL.B., canon and prebendary of the collegiate church of St Chad, Shrewsbury. He has accepted Reedhill's resignation and has collated the canonry and prebend in the collegiate church of St Chad, Shrewsbury, to Edmund Dutton, in the person of his proctor, John Dutton, literate, reserving his induction and canonical obedience. Salisbury 1 September 1450. (ii) Memorandum that the certificate was delivered by John Dutton, literate, proctor for Mr Edmund Dutton who made obedience. The sacristan of the collegiate church was mandated to induct and install. Eccleshall, 23 February 1450/1.

[Fo. 26v] **Annus Domini Millesimus CCCC^mus Quinquagesimus Primus**

177. Institution of Richard Asshe to the rectory of Donnington (*Donynton*), vacant by the death of Thomas Clous; presented by the abbot and convent of St Peter, Shrewsbury. Ind. Archdn. Eccleshall, 11 September 1451.

178. Institution of Matthew Cloit to the parish church or chapel of Hordley (*Hordeley*), vacant by the death of Thomas Rotour; presented by the abbot and convent of St Peter, Shrewsbury. Ind. Archdn. Eccleshall, 23 September 1451.

179. Collation to Robert Baguley, chaplain, of a canonry and prebend in the collegiate church of St Chad, Shrewsbury, formerly held by John Neuton, and

109 This would reflect the formal termination of episcopal exercise of archidiaconal jurisdiction during the vacancy of the archdeaconry.
110 See **173**.
111 Edmund Dutton. Collated 26 April 1416. Exchanged this prebend 11 August 1450 with John Reedhill for a prebend in St Chad's collegiate church, Shrewsbury (*Fasti* iii, 56).

vacant by his death. Mandate to the sacristan to induct and install. Eccleshall, 9 October 1451.

180. Institution of Richard Astley, chaplain, to the vicarage of Shawbury, vacant by the resignation of William Aleyne; presented by the abbot and convent of St John the Evangelist, Haughmond. Ind. Archdn. Eccleshall, 6 November 1451.

181. Collation to Richard Bowier, chaplain, of a canonry and prebend in the collegiate church of St Chad, Shrewsbury, formerly held by Robert Baguley and vacant by his resignation. Mandate to the sacristan to induct and install Bowier or his proctor, John Whitefelde. Strand, London, 1 February 1451/2.

182. Institution of William Lech, chaplain, to the rectory of Myddle (*Mudele*), vacant by the death of John Newton; presented by the abbot and convent of St Peter, Shrewsbury. Ind. Archdn. Haywood, 26 February 1451/2.

[Fo. 27]   **Annus Domini Millesimus CCCC^mus Quinquagesimus Secundus**

183. Institution of William Bikeley of Ruyton, chaplain, to the newly ordained vicarage of Great Ness (*Nesse Straunge*), vacant; presented by the abbot and convent of St Peter, Shrewsbury. Ind. Archdn. Haywood, 3 April 1452.[112]

184. Institution of Hugh Webbe, chaplain, to the vicarage of Leighton under the Wrekin (*Leghton*), vacant by the resignation of Hugh Carier *alias* Bispan; presented by the abbot and convent of Buildwas (*Bildewas*). Ind. Archdn. Haywood, 21 April 1452.

185. Institution of Richard Porter, chaplain, as warden of the college or collegiate church of St Mary, Newport (*Neuport*), newly erected and ordained, vacant; presented by the abbot and convent of St Peter, Shrewsbury.[113] Ind. Archdn. Haywood, 25 April 1452.[114]

186. Collation to Mr Wystan Brown, M.A.,[115] in the person of William Brown, literate, his proctor, of a canonry and prebend in the collegiate church of St Chad, Shrewsbury, formerly held by Mr Edmund Dutton and vacant by his resignation. Mandate to the sacristan to induct and install. Haywood, 19 July 1452.[116]

[112] For the appropriation of Great Ness see **279**.
[113] The marginal title refers to this as 'prima institucio'.
[114] For the appropriation of this church at the request of Thomas Draper to found a college and for its statutes see **278**, **284**. The college was connected with the gild of St Mary's (*Medieval Religious Houses in England and Wales*, 433).
[115] Exhibited a caution in his name for Little University Hall, Oxford, in 1446. Junior proctor of the University 1450–51. Ordained subdeacon, deacon and priest in 1448 and 1449 held benefices in Oxfordshire, Northamptonshire and London. Died by March 1480 (Emden i, 287).
[116] The remainder of the page has been cut away, but there is no indication that it had contained any entries.

[Fo. 27v: BLANK]

[Fo. 28]   **ARCHDEACONRY OF CHESTER**

187.   Institution of Br. William Catton, prior of Arbury (*Erdebury*), O.S.A., by papal dispensation, to the rectory of Leigh (*Leght*), vacant by the consecration (*per munus consecracionis*) of William Bothe as bishop of Coventry and Lichfield: presented by Ralph Buttiller knight, lord of Sudeley, patron for this turn. Ind. Archdn. London, 13 July 1447.

188.   Institution of Adam Irelond to the moiety of the rectory of Malpas, vacant by the death of Mr Richard Wodewarte: presented by John [de Sutton], lord of Dudley (*Duddeley*).[117] Ind. Archdn. London, 28 July 1447.

189.   Institution of Thomas Weston, priest, to the rectory of Rostherne (*Routhestorn*), vacant by the death of Mr Richard Dutton: presented by Hugh Venables of *Kynderton*, esq. Ind. Archdn. Wilmslow (*Wilmeslow*), 20 September 1447.

190.   Institution of William Smyth, priest, to the rectory of Thurstaston, vacant by the resignation of William Gylowe: presented by the abbot and convent of St Werbergh, Chester. Ind. Archdn. Strand, London, 11 November 1447.

Annus Domini Millesimus CCCC^{mus} Quadragesimus Octavus

191.   Institution of Mr Reginald Neuton, priest, to the moiety of the rectory of Malpas, vacant by the death of Adam Irelond: presented by John [de Sutton], lord of Dudley (*Duddeley*), knight. Ind. Archdn. Beaudesert, 25 May 1448.[118]

192.   Collation to Peter Bothe, clerk, of the rectory of Northenden (*Northerden*), vacant and in the bishop's patronage by lapse of time. Ind. Archdn. Eccleshall, 5 September 1448.[119]

193.   [Fo. 28–v] Institution of Mr Ralph Dukworth, *sacre pagine professore*, priest, to the newly-ordained vicarage of Prescot (*Prestcote*): presented by the provost and scholars of the royal college of St Mary and St Nicholas [King's College], Cambridge, Ely diocese. Ind. Archdn. Haywood, 5 October 1448.

194.   [Fo. 28v] Institution of Nicholas Bridde, priest, to the vicarage of

---

[117] For John de Sutton see Hugh Collins, 'Sutton, John (VI), first Baron Dudley (1400–1487)', *Oxford Dictionary of National Biography* (Oxford University Press, Sept. 2004); online edn, May 2006.
[118] For the institution of his predecessor see **188**.
[119] On 8 June 1444 Peter Bothe had received papal dispensation to hold any benefice with cure of souls after he had attained his twenty-second year. The dispensation described him as a scholar who had completed his tenth year and whose uncle and father were both knights (*CPL* x, 26). He was dead by 5 April 1453 when he was succeeded by another of the Bothe family (Lichfield Record Office, B/A/1/11(Register of Reginald Boulers), fo. 3v).

Prestbury, vacant by the resignation of John Duncalff: presented by the abbot and convent of St Werbergh, Chester. Ind. Archdn.

Memorandum that Bridde swore on the gospels to pay a life pension of 100s p.a. to John Duncalff which the abbot and convent were accustomed to pay him '*nomine augmentacionis*'. Strand, London, 22 November 1448.

195. Institution of Laurence Huet, priest, to the rectory of Pulford (*Pulforde*), vacant by the death of William Feysande; presented by Robert le Grosvenour, esq. Mandate to Mr Oliver Legh, the bishop's official within the archdeaconry of Chester, to induct. Hackney, 17 January 1448/9.

196. Institution of Thomas Tarleton, priest, to the vicarage of Croston, vacant by the death of Richard Dalton: presented by the abbess and convent of the Holy Saviour and the Blessed Virgin Mary and St Bridget of Syon, O.S.A., London diocese, the appropriators. Mandate for induction to the rector of Eccleston and the vicar of Leyland (*Leylond*) and the parish priest of Croston *conjunctim vel divisim*, the archdeaconry of Chester being vacant due to the death of Mr John Burdet. Strand, London, 7 March 1448/9.

Annus Domini Millesimus CCCC^mus Quadragesimus Nonus

197. [Fos 28v–29] Collation to Mr George Radclyff, D. Dec.,[120] priest, of the archdeaconry of Chester and a canonry and the prebend of Bolton in Lichfield cathedral annexed thereto, vacant by the death of Mr John Burdet. Mandates (i) to the dean and chapter of Lichfield cathedral to admit and install; (ii) to the vicar of the prebendal church of Bolton to induct to the prebend; (iii) Masters Roger Asser, dean of the collegiate church of St John,[121] Chester, and William Asser, clerk, *conjunctim vel divisim*, to induct into the archdeaconry by handing over the ring of the door of a church within the archdeaconry which is subject to episcopal jurisdiction, and delivery of the archidiaconal procurations of that church.[122] Haywood, 26 April 1449.

198. [Fo. 29] Collation to John Bothe, clerk, of the hospital of Denwall and the parish church of Burton in Wirral (*Burton in Wirall*) annexed thereto, in the person of Mr William Brande, clerk, his proctor, vacant by the resignation of Mr Roger Wall.[123] Mandate to Mr Roger Asser, John Holme, and Henry Medwall, to induct, *conjunctim vel divisim*. Haywood, 28 April 1449.[124]

199. Election of a prioress for the Benedictine nuns of Chester: (i) Beatrice le Heyre, sub-prioress of the house of the nuns of Chester, O.S.B., has been elected as

---

[120] See note 11.

[121] Bachelor of Canon and Civil Law 1438, held several benefices, in the diocese of Coventry and Lichfield and in London, and was dean of St John's College, Chester, from 8 February 1444 until his death, by July 1471 (Emden i, 63).

[122] See also **173**.

[123] See note 27.

[124] In 1452 John Bothe received papal dispensation to hold the hospital and the church together following his petition (*CPL* x, 128–9).

prioress of the house, following the resignation of Alice Leyot.[125] The bishop quashes the election due to procedural defects (*ex variis ipsius forme defectibus non ex vicio persone electe*). (ii) Episcopal provision of Beatrice le Heyre as prioress. (iii) Ind. Archdn. Haywood, 16 August 1449.

200. [Fo. 29v] Institution of Henry Bancrofte, priest, to the rectory of Cheadle (*Chedle*), vacant by the death of Thomas Bysby: presented by Richard de Bulkeley of Cheadle, esq. Ind. Archdn. Strand, London, 22 November 1449.[126]

201. Institution of Br. Hugh Goldburn, priest, canon regular of the monastery of St Mary, Norton, O.S.A., to the vicarage of Runcorn (*Roncorn, Roncorne*), vacant by the death of Robert Brekerake; presented by the prior and convent of Norton. Ind. Archdn. Strand, London, 23 December 1449.

Annus Domini Millesimus CCCC^{mus} Quinquagesimus

202. Institution of Thomas Bonell, chaplain, in the person of Nicholas Hogge, his proctor, to the rectory of Holy Trinity, Chester, vacant by the death of John Mynys; presented by Thomas Stanley, knight, Ind. Archdn. Leicester, 7 June 1450.

203. Institution of Gilbert Hesketh, priest, to the vicarage of Backford (*Bacforde*), vacant by the death of Thomas Calffe; presented by the prior and convent of Birkenhead (*Birkehed*). Ind. Archdn. Eccleshall, 16 June 1450.

204. Institution of [*no name given*] Whitstones, chaplain, to the vicarage of Childwall (*Childewall*), vacant by the succession of Thomas Bonell to the church of Holy Trinity, Chester; presented by the prior and convent of Upholland (*Holand*). Ind. Archdn. Prescot (*Prestcote*), 17 July 1450.

205. Institution of Thomas Byrom,[127] chaplain, to the rectory of Grappenhall (*Gropenhale*), vacant by the resignation of William del Heth; presented by the abbot and convent of Norton. Ind. Archdn. Clayton (*Claiton*), 26 July 1450.

206. Institution of John Crecy, *alias* Smyth, chaplain, to the rectory of Mottram in Longdendale (*Mottrom in Longedendale*), vacant by the death of John Yoxale; presented by Peter de Legh esq, patron this turn by virtue of the grant to him of the next presentation by William, lord of Lovell. Ind. Archdn. Clayton, 5 September 1450.

207. [Fo. 30] Collation to Robert Baguley, chaplain, of the first chaplaincy in the newly-founded chantry for two chaplains of St Katherine in the parish church

---

[125] Beatrice le Heye last occurs as prioress September 1458 and her successor Ellen Blundell first occurs April 1459 (*Heads of Religious Houses* iii, forthcoming).
[126] For a previous institution of William Beke to this church see **116**.
[127] See note 60.

of the Blessed Virgin Mary, Eccles. Mandate to the vicar of Eccles to induct. Clayton, 1 August 1450.[128]

208. Collation to Peter Berdesley, chaplain, of the second chaplaincy in the newly-founded chantry for two chaplains of St Katherine in the parish church of the Blessed Virgin Mary, Eccles. Mandate to the vicar of Eccles to induct. Clayton, 1 August 1450.[129]

209. [Fo. 30–v] Certificate of John Verney, dean of Lichfield cathedral,[130] and Mr Thomas Chestrefeld (*Chestrefelde*), B. Dec., canon residentiary of Lichfield cathedral,[131] that they have executed the bishop's mandate dated at Eccleshall castle, 2 January 1450/1 (recited), and have examined Oliver de Langton, clerk, who has been presented to the bishop by Henry de Langton, esq., as a suitable person to be admitted to the rectory of Wigan, vacant by the death of James de Langton.[132] They had found him suitable; had instituted him to the rectory; issued the mandate for his induction; issued letters patent of the institution, reserving a pension of £20 payable to the dean and chapter of Lichfield; and received his canonical obedience on behalf of the bishop. They recite their mandate for induction (addressed to the Archdeacon of Chester or his Official, dated at Lichfield, 3 January 1450/1, and sealed with the seal of the Official of the episcopal consistory of Lichfield), setting out that they had received the episcopal mandate on 3rd January, and had implemented it. Following his institution, Oliver de Langton swore on the gospels in their presence in the chapter house of Lichfield cathedral that he would pay the annual pension of £20 due from Wigan to the dean and chapter of Lichfield, in equal instalments within the fifteen days after Easter and within the fifteen days following Michaelmas, and entered into a bond in £200 to secure the pension. Attestation of sealing by the Official of the episcopal consistory at Lichfield. Dated at Lichfield, '*quo ad sigillacionem*', 30 January 1450/1.

210. [Fo. 30v] Institution of John Bothe, clerk, in the person of Mr Gregory Neuport, canon of Lichfield cathedral,[133] his proctor, to the rectory of Thornton in the Moors (*Thornton super le more*), vacant by the death of Thomas Radclyff;

---

[128] For the foundation of the chantry see **314**. For the collation of the second of the two chaplains here see **208**.

[129] For the collation of the first of the chaplains here see **207**.

[130] See note 79.

[131] See note 2.

[132] James Langton was probably rector of Wigan from *c.* 1428, until his death, in 1450. He ceratinly appears as rector by 1432 (G.T.O. Bridgeman, *The History of the Church and Manor of Wigan in the County of Lancaster* (Cheetham Society, n.s. 15, 1888), p. 64). He also held the prebend of Stotfold (*Fasti* x, 56). The proving of his will in December 1450, with a transcript, appeared in the lost Lichfield Chapter Act Book, and can be found in Baker's transcript. This will includes a bequest to James' brother, Oliver. (Swanson, 'Lichfield Chapter Acts', no. 69).

[133] Prebendary of Flixton 26 May 1443 to his death by 6 December 1459 and prebendary of Dasset Parva 13 August 1426 until his appointment as archdeacon of Salop, to which he was collated 17 August 1433 until he exchanged his archdeaconry and a prebend in St Chad's College Shrewsbury with John Weborn for the church of Hanbury (*Fasti* x, 18, 30, 36).

presented by Robert Bothe, knight. Mandate to the archdeacon or his official to induct John Bothe or his proctor, James Hall, priest. Eccleshall, 15 February 1450/1.

211. Institution of Edmund Redich, chaplain, to the rectory of Taxal (*Taksale*), vacant by the resignation of Robert Wightmon; presented by Reginald de Downes, esq. Ind. Archdn. Eccleshall, 19 February 1450/1.

212. Collation to James Hall, priest, of the vacant newly ordained and endowed vicarage of Leigh (*Leght*). Ind. Archdn. Eccleshall, 20 March 1450/1.[134]

Annus Domini Millesimus CCCC^mus Quinquagesimus Primus

213. [Fo. 31] Institution of Ralph Dutton, chaplain, in the person of John Kyngeley, literate, his proctor, to the rectory of Christleton (*Cristelton*), vacant by the death of John ap Gruff' ap Guyth; presented by the abbot and convent of St Werbergh, Chester. Ind. Archdn. Eccleshall, 18 May 1451.

214. Institution of Richard Thyknes, chaplain, to the rectory of Woodchurch (*Wodchurch*), vacant by the death of Thomas Coppenall; presented by Robert Fouleshurst, esq. Ind. Archdn. Eccleshall, 7 June 1451.

215. Institution of James Pembreton, chaplain, to the rectory of Tattenhall (*Tatenhall*), vacant by the resignation of Richard Barowe, with whom he has exchanged the chantry in the manor of Weston in Ardern, Coventry and Lichfield diocese; presented by the abbot and convent of St Werbergh, Chester. Ind Archdn. Haywood, 31 July 1451.

216. Institution of Richard Barowe, chaplain, in the person of Richard Brodehede, his proctor, to the rectory of Christleton (*Cristelton, Crystelton*), vacant by the death of Ralph Dutton; presented by the abbot and convent of St Werbergh, Chester. Ind. Archdn. Haywood, 18 August 1451.[135]

217. [Fo. 31–v] Certificate of Mr Gregory Neuport, B. Dec., canon of Lichfield cathedral, that he has executed the bishop's mandate dated at Eccleshall castle, 2 November 1451 (recited), to receive the certificate of the official of the archdeacon of Chester of his proclamation of the summons of opponents of the election of Br. Robert Leftwich, canon regular of Norton abbey, O.S.A., as abbot of Norton, and to examine and if appropriate confirm the election and grant administration of the house, in the parish church of Wybunbury (*Wibbenbury, Wibbynbury*), on 4 November 1451, but reserving the canonical obedience of Br. Thomas Westbury, lately abbot of Norton. The commission had been fulfilled, the archdeacon or his Official being mandated to induct and install. Sealed with the seal of John, bishop *Insulensis*,[136] because the seal of Mr Gregory Brown [*sic*] is unfamiliar. Attestation of John, bishop of *Insulensis*. 6 November 1451.

---

[134] For the appropriation of Leigh to Arbury priory see **283**.
[135] For the institution of his predecessor see **213**.
[136] See note 30.

218. [Fo. 31v] Institution of Thomas Blakeburn to the vicarage of Walton, vacant by the resignation of John Iremonger; presented by Ralph Stanley, rector of Walton. Ind. Archdn. Eccleshall, 8 November 1451.

219. Collation to Mr Edward Whitforde, B. Dec.,[137] of a canonry and the third prebend of the cross in the collegiate church of St John, Chester, on the north side, vacant by the resignation of John Seton, chaplain. Mandate to the dean and chapter of St John to induct and install. Eccleshall, 15 November 1451.

220. [Fos 31v–32] Collation to Mr Robert Bromeyerde, chaplain, of a canonry and the fourth prebend of the cross in the collegiate church of St John, Chester, on the north side, vacant by the death of Mr Thomas Flygh. Mandate to the dean and chapter to induct and install. Eccleshall, 26 November 1451.

Annus Domini Millesimus CCCCmus Quinquagesimus Secundus

221. [Fo. 32] Collation to Mr Robert Thornton (*Thorneton*), B. Dec., in the person of Mr John Sutton, his proctor, of a canonry and the second prebend of the cross in the collegiate church of St John, Chester, on the south side, vacant by the resignation of Mr John Southewell. Mandate to the dean and chapter to induct and install. Strand, London, 21 May 1452.

222. Institution of Thomas de Coghull, priest, in the person of Richard Osbaldeston, literate, his proctor, to the vicarage of Backford (*Bacforde*), vacant by the death of Gilbert Hesketh; presented by the prior and convent of Birkenhead (*Birkeheud*). Ind. Archdn. Haywood, 3 July 1452.[138]

223. Institution of Edmund Bothe, clerk, in the person of Mr Thomas Lye, archdeacon of Salop,[139] his proctor, to the rectory of Thornton in the Moors (*Thorneton super le Morez*), vacant by the resignation of John Bothe; presented by Robert Bothe, knight, and Dulcie his wife. Mandate to the archdeacon or his official to induct the said Edmund or his proctor. Haywood, 8 July 1452.[140]

224. [Fo. 32–v] Institution of Richard Wodwarde, chaplain, in the person of Richard Barow, chaplain, his proctor, to the mastership or wardenship of the collegiate church of St Boniface, Bunbury, vacant by the resignation of William Arden; on the election and nomination of his confreres as chaplains of the church, and on the presentation of Hugh de Chaveley, esq., founder and patron of the church. Ind. Archdn. Haywood, 9 August 1452.

225. [Fo. 32v] Collation to Ralph Byrom, clerk, of a canonry and the prebend of Tervin (*Tervyn*), in Lichfield cathedral, vacant by the death of Mr Thomas

---

137 Tendered a caution for Nightingale Hall 9 September 1444. Held churches in Oxfordshire, Wales, Hertfordshire, Lincolnshire and Northamptonshire (Emden iii, 2038).
138 For the institution of his predecessor see **203**.
139 See note 18.
140 For the institution of his predecessor see **209**.

Chestrefeld.[141] Mandate to the dean and chapter to induct and install. Haywood, 24 August 1452.[142]

[GENERAL LETTERS]

226. [Fos 33–4] Documents relating to the canonical compurgation of Edward Lech (*Leche*), labourer, of Goostrey, Cheshire, who was convicted for theft at Chester and granted benefit of clergy. The documents include (i) the certificate of Oliver de Legh, B. Dec., official in the archdeaconry of Chester, citing the vicar general's commission and certifying that proclamation had been made; (ii) the commission of Mr George Radclyff, D. Dec.,[143] vicar general, to Mr John Wendesley, LL.B.,[144] to receive the canonical compurgation; and (iii) the note that this has been done.[145]

CERTIFICATORIUM SUPER PROCLAMACIONE EDWARDI LECHE CLERICI INCARCERATI, ETC. Reverendo ac discreto viro magistro Georgio Radclyff, decretorum doctori, thesaurario ecclesiae cathedralis Lichfeldensis, reverendi in Christo patris et domini domini Willelmi, dei gracia Coventrensis et Lichfeldensis episcopi, in remotis agente vicario in spiritualibus generali, vester humilis et devotus Oliverus de Legh, in decretis bacallarius, reverendi patris supradicti saltem infra archidiaconatu Cestrie officialis, obedienciam et reverenciam debitam cum honore. Litteras vestras reverendas sexto die instantis mensis Decembris ea cum qua decet reverentia recepi sub ea que sequitur verborum serie: Georgius Radclyff, decretorum doctor, thesaurarius ecclesie cathedralis Lichfeldensis, reverendi in Christo patris et domini domini Willelmi, dei gracia Coventrensis et Lichfeldensis episcopi, in remotis agente vicarius in spiritualibus generalis, dilecto nobis in Christo magistro Olivero de Legh, in decretis bacallario, in archidiaconatu Cestrie prefati reverendi patris officiali, salutem in auctore salutis. Cum Edwardus Lech, nuper de Gostre in comitatu Cestrie, labourer, coram Willelmo de la Pole comite Suffolciensi, justiciario domini regis in dicto comitatu Cestrie, felonice indictatus existat (prout in tenore dicti indictamenti ut sequitur plenius liquet), comitatu Cestrie tento apud Cestriam die martis proximo post festum sancte Marie Magdalene anno regni regis Henrici sexti vicesimo: coram Willelmo de la Pole, comite Suffolciensi, iusticiario domini regis hic ad comitato tento die Martis proximo post festum sancte Trinitatis, anno regni eiusdem regis nunc nunc Anglie vicesimo

[141] See note 2.

[142] Byrom also held the prebend of Ottley, which he resigned before 7 December 1452 (*Fasti* x, 48).

[143] See note 11.

[144] Natural son of Sir Thomas Wendesley, knight, received papal dispensation to be promoted to all orders despite his illegitimacy 1427, as well as holding prebends in Lichfield and becoming archdeacon of Stafford 29 June 1442, held the church of All Saints Pavement in York and was official principal of Coventry and Lichfield 1440 (Emden iii, 2014). One of the keepers of spiritualities in the vacancy after Bothe's translation to York and in the vacancy following the death of Nicholas Cloos (Lichfield Record Office, B/A/11/1). See also introduction, pp. xxvii–xxviii.

[145] See also **263–5** for Edward Leche's 1451 compurgation for burglary and theft, 1448 and 1449.

presentatus fuit, quod Edwardus Lech, nuper de Gostre in comitatu Cestrie, labourer, die lune proximo post festum sancti Hillarii, anno regni regis Henrici sexti vicesimo, castrum Cestrie apud Cestriam fregit, et deinde unam cistam cum una zona phalaratura cum argento et aliis diversis bonis et catallis Elianore Holes ad valenciam xl^a solidorum furatus fuit, per quod preceptus fuit vicomiti quod non omittur et cetera, quoniam caperet eum et cetera. Et modo ad istum eundem comitatum et coram prefato justiciario hic venit predictus Edwardus in propria persona sua, per Thomam Stanley, militem, constabularium castri domini regis Cestrie, ductus, et cetera. Et vicomiti indictamento predicto per justiciarum instanter allecutus est qualiter ipse de felonia predicta superius ei imposita velit se acquietare, dicit quod ipse in nullo est inde culpabilis et de hoc de bono et malo ponit se super patriam et cetera. Venit inde jurata hic hac instanter die, etc. Iurati venerunt, qui ad hoc electi et jurati dicunt super sacramentum suum quod predictus Edwardus culpabilis est de felonia predicta superius ei imposita et quod nulla habuit bona neque catalla terras necque tenementa die felonie predicte facte nec umquam postea in comitatu predicta. Iam consideratum est quod ipse per collum suspe[n]datur et cetera. Et super hoc idem Edwardus dixit se fore clericum et petit beneficium ecclesiasticum, et cetera. Et super hoc venit Jacobus de Huyton, commissarius et procurator Johannis Burdet, archidiaconi Cestrie, ordinarii hic et tradidit prefato Edwardo librum, et legit, et cetera. Et super hoc predictus commissarius nomine dicti ordinarii petit hic in curia prefatum Edwardum tanquam clericum sibi deliberari, et cetera. Et ei liberatur salvo et securo sub suo periculo custodiendum, et cetera. Super premissis falso (ut asserit) diffamatus extitisset, et propter hoc per potestatem laicalem captus et incarceratus, ac bone memorie Willelmo, nuper Coventrensis et Lichfeldensis episcopo, per justiciarium domini nostri regis predicti tanquam clericus liberatus existat in foro ecclesiastioo secundum canonicas sancciones omnino iudicandum. Super quibus omnibus et singulis prefatus Edwardus post diutinam ipsius in carcere detencionem obtulit se suam innocenciam coram nobis canonice purgature; et super hoc nobis humiliter supplicavit et devote. Nos vero suis supplicacionibus in hac parte misericordia ducti inclinantes, vobis firmiter injungendo mandamus, quatinus diebus dominicis et festivis in singulis civitatis Cestrie ecclesiis parochialibus intra missarum solempnia dum major affuerit populi multitudo in eisdem, ac in mercatis publicis civitatis predicte, et aliis quibus visum fuerit expediens, proclametis palam et publice, proclamaciones faciatis, seu per alios sic fieri faciatis, quod siquis sit qui velit aut valeat prefatum Edwardum clericum super premissis accusare vel aliter in forma juris prosequi aut contra ipsius purgacionem obicere, compareat coram nobis seu nostro in hac parte commissario in ecclesia prebendali de Eccleshale dicti patris diocesis die Jovis (videlicet quarto die mensis Januarii) proximo futuro, quem diem pro termino peremptorio precise eisdem assignamus quicquid sibi de jure competat contra memoratum Edwardum clericum in forma juris proposite, prosequiture, et probature cum effectu, ulteriusque facture et recepture in hac parte quod canonice dictaverunt sancciones. De diebus recepcionis presencium et proclamacionum ac locis in quibus feceritis easdem et qualiter premissa fuerit executi nos aut dictum commissarium nostrum dictis die et loco distincte et aperte certificare curetis per litteras vestras patentes harum seriem continentes sigillo auctentico signatas. Datum Lichfeld', sub sigillo quo in hoc utimur officio, tercio die mensis Decembris anno domini millesimo CCCC^{mo} quadragesimo septimo. Auctoritate quarum litterarum reverendarum diebus dominicis et festivis in singulis ecclesiis civitatis Cestrie intra missarum solempnia in eisdem dum major affuerit populo multitudo, ac merketis civitatis predicte et aliis convicinis quibus visum fuerat expediens, palam et publice proclamari feci quod siquis sit qui velit seu valeat Edwardum Leche, nuper de Goostre, clericum, de comitatu Cestrie, olim coram Willelmo de la Pole, comite Suffolciensi, justiciario domini regis in dicto comitatu Cestrie felonice indictatum super premissis accusare vel aliter in forma juris prosequi, aut contra ipsius purgacionem obicere, quod compareant coram vobis aut alio commissario vestro in ecclesia prebendali de Eccleshale dicti patris diocesis die Jovis (videlicet, quarto die mensis Januarii) proximo futuro quem terminum pro termino peremptorio precise eis assignavi quicquid sibi de jure competat contra memoratum Edwardum, clericum, in forma juris propositure, prosequiture, et probature cum effectu, ulteriusque facture et recepture in ea parte quod canonice dictaverint sancciones. Et sic presens mandatum vestrum reverendum humiliter sum executus, que omnia et singula vestre reverencie significo per presentes, sigillo officii mei in premissorum testimonium sigillatas. Datum Cestrie, quantum ad sigillacionem presentis certificatorii, xiij° die mensis instantis Decembris, anno domini millesimo CCCC^mo quadragesimo septimo predicto.

COMMISSIO IN EODEM NEGOCIO. Georgius Radclyff, decretorum doctor, thesaurarius ecclesie cathedralis Lichfeldensis, reverendi in Christo patris et domini domini Willelmi, dei gracia Coventrensis et Lichfeldensis episcopo, in remotis agente vicarius in spiritualibus generalis, dilecto nobis in Christo magistro Johanni Wendesley, in utroque jure bacallario, salutem in auctore salutis. Cum Edwardus Leche, nuper de Gostre in comitatu Cestrie, laborer, felonice indictatus fuerit et ad carceros prefati reverendi patris condempnatus, prout in cedula pergameni presentibus annexa de toto processu ejus indictamenti plenius continetur, ipse tamen Edwardus post diutinam in carcere dicti reverendi patris detencionem nobis cum instancia supplicavit, ut purgacionem suam canonicam de et super indictamento predicto misericorditer reciperemus; nolentes ei in sua justicia deesse sicuti nec debemus, ad recipiendum igitur certificatorium super proclamacione de et super premissis in ea parte (si pro eo fecerit), necnon purgacionem ejus de et super criminibus huiusmodi in numero sufficienti compurgatorum; receptaque purgacione canonica eiusdem prefatum Edwardum Leche sue bone famam quantum cum deo poteritis restituendum; necnon eundem[146] a carcere dicti reverendi patris finaliter liberandum, vobis, auctoritate dicti reverendi patris et ejus mandato nobis specialiter transmisso, de cuius circumspeccionis industria plene in domino confidimus, vices nostras committimus per presentes, sigillo quo in hoc utimur officio sigillatas. Datum xij° die mensis Decembris, anno domini millesimo CCCC^mo quadragesimo septimo predicto.

DELIBERACIO A CARCERE EPISCOPI EDWARDI LECHE CLERICI PER LAICALEM POTESTATEM CONVICTI, ETC. Quo quidem die Jovis, videlicet quarto die mensis Januarii, adveniente coram prefato magistro Johanno Wendesley, commissario antedicto, in ecclesia prebendali predicta judicialiter sedente, productus fuit

---

[146] MS reads eosdem.

prefatus Edwardus Leche; publicaque proclamacione habita pro obicientibus (ut moris est) in ea parte siqui sint, et cetera. Et quia nullus oppositor aut contradictor comparuit, eidem Edwardo indicebatur sua purgacio canonica. Propositumque fuit ejus indictamenta, prout supranotatur, que quidem omnia et singula in prefato indictamento contenta, tactis per ipsum Edwardum sacrosanctis dei evangeliis, denegavit; et conpurgatores suos, tam clericos et literatos, in numero sufficienti et legitime secum adduxit, qui crediderunt ipsum verum jurasse. Et sic fame sue pristine restitutus, auctoritate predicta, et a carceribus dicti domini episcopi dismissus est, et liberatus quocumque ire voluerit ad placitum. Presentibus tunc ibidem magistro Willelmo Gamull, publico auctoritate appostolice notario, scriba in hac parte assumpta, ac Willelmo Coton et Rogero Swyneshed, et aliis, etc.

227. Letters testimonial assigning a life pension of 100s p.a., to be paid by Nicholas Bridde, now vicar of Prestbury (instituted on the presentation of the abbot and convent of St Werburgh, Chester), to John Duncalff, formerly vicar of Prestbury, who has resigned on account of age and bodily weakness (*propter senium et sui corporis debilitatem*), and for other reasons. The pension had originally been paid by the abbot and convent, but is now to be paid by Bridde out of the vicarial receipts. Strand, 22 November 1448.[147]

228. [Fo. 34–v] Commission of the bishop to Thomas Byrome, canon of the royal free chapel of St Michael, Penkridge [*Penkrich*], to receive the canonical compurgation of Richard Banyster of Chester, *alias* Richard Banyster late of Hesketh, Lancashire, gentleman, and Thomas Walton, late of Westminster (*Westmynster*), Middlesex, yeoman, imprisoned convicted clerks. Manor of Haywood, 10 July 1448.[148]

229. [Fos 34v–35] Certificate of Oliver de Legh, B. Dec., official of the archdeacon of Chester, reciting the bishop's mandate (dated at Haywood, 12 June 1448) to make proclamation on Sundays and feast days in the collegiate church of St John, Chester, the churches of St Peter and St Oswald, Chester, the chapel of Daresbury, and in market of the city and neighbouring places citing opposers of the proposed compurgation of Richard Banyster of Chester, alias Richard Banyster of Hesketh, Lancashire, gentleman, convicted for stealing a missal value 10 marks, and a silver gilt chalice value 40s the property of John Pykeryn and Thomas de Hatton, then churchwardens (*prepositi ecclesie*), from Daresbury (*Deresbury*) church, Cheshire, on the Tuesday after Easter, 19 Henry VI [1440], and imprisoned in the bishop's prison as convicted clerks during the episcopate of William [Heyworth], to appear at Eccleshall prebendal church on 11 July 1448. Proclamation had been made in the named churches on the Sunday after receipt, and on the eve of the Nativity of St John the Baptist during the markert or fair of the city, and elsewhere at times and places as seemed appropriate. Chester, 26 June 1448.

230. [Fo. 35–v] Certificate of the official of the archdeacon of Coventry, setting out that on 14th June he had received the bishop's mandate (recited) dated at

---

[147] See also **194**.
[148] See **229–31**.

Haywood 12 June 1448, and addressed to the official of the archdeacon of Coventry, the dean of Christianity of Coventry, and the parish priests of Holy Trinity and St Michael, Coventry, *coniunctim et divisim*, to make proclamation in churches and markets on Sundays and feast days of the proposed compurgation of Thomas Walton of Westminster (*Westmynster*), Middlesex, yeoman, and to cite opponents to appear in Eccleshall prebendal church on 11 July 1448. The accusations against Walton were that (i) at Coventry on 24 April, 24 Henry VI [1445], together with others by night, and *vi et armis*, he had broken into the building called *Seyntmary Hall*, set fire to it, and stole therein one silver gilt standing cup, two silver dishes with two covers of silver gilt, one silver gilt chalice cup, two silver spice dishes, one small silver gilt table, two bosses, one silver trumpet, one silver dish with a cover called a boll cup, two silver dishes, four silver gilt spoons, one silver standing cup, six silver dishes with two silver covers, one cup called a *gilde* cup, one silver standing cup, one silver dish, one silver salt cellar with a cover, and twenty-four silver spoons, to the total value of 200 marks, the property of the master of the gild of the Holy Trinity, St Mary, St John the Baptist and St Katherine the virgin; (ii) at Coventry on 27 October, 25 Henry VI [1446], together with others *vi et armis* (that is, with sword, bows and arrows, and divers instruments), he broke into the house of John Hosteler of Coventry, and stole therein 14s 1d in money, the property of the said John Hosteler. He had been convicted and handed over to Mr Thomas Chestrefelde, B. Dec.,[149] keeper of the spiritualities on behalf of John [Stafford], archbishop of Canterbury, during the vacancy of the see of Lichfield. Proclamation has been made in every church in Coventry and in market places and other convenient places, on 16th and 30th June. Coventry, 5 July 1448.

231. [Fo. 35v] Note that the bishop had appointed Thomas Byrom, canon of the royal free chapel of St Michael, Penkridge (*Penkrych*); and that on 11 July 1448, in the prebendal church of Eccleshall, Richard [Banyster] and Thomas [Walton] were admitted to canonical compurgation, no opposers appearing, in the presence of compurgators and clerks in sufficient number, and of Mr William Brand, notary and scribe, Roger Swyneshed and William Coton, *doimicelli* and literates of the diocese of Coventry and Lichfield, and others.

232. [Fos 35v–36] 7 October 1448. Certificate of John Verney, dean,[150] and the chapter of Lichfield cathedral, that they have executed the bishop's monition dated 15 July 1448 at the manor of Haywood (recited), and have brought to the notice of those concerned the ruinous state of the houses in the close at Lichfield.[151]

CERTIFICATORIUM DECANI LICHFELDENSIS DE MONICIONIBUS EPISCOPI SIBI FACTIS ET CAPITULO PRO REPARACIONEM DOMORUM INFRA CLAUSUM LICHFELDENSIS. Reverendo in Christo patri et domino, domino Willelmo [etc.], vestri humiles et devoti filii Johannes Verney, decanus ecclesie cathedralis Lichfeldensis obediencias, et eiusdem loci capitulum reverencias tanto patri debitas, cum

---

149 See note 2.
150 See note 79.
151 A similar mandate was issued by Bishop Boulers (Lichfield Record Office, B/A/1/11 (Register of Reginald Boulers), fo. 83).

honore. Mandatum vestrum reverendum nobis in hac parte directum nuper recipimus in hec verba: Willelmus [etc.], dilectis in Christo filiis decano ecclesie nostre cathedralis Lichfeldensis, seu ejus locum tenenti sive presidenti, et capitulo salutem, graciam et benediccionem. Ad nostrum fama publica referente, ymmo (quod deterius est) ipsa rei notarietas manifestat, quod vos, decanus et canonici prefati ecclesie nostre cathedralis Lichfeldensis, domos et alia edificia infra clausum vestrum Lichfeldense existencia et alibi (videlicet, in singulis quasi prebendis vestris et suis) sine correccione aliquo dimittitis et dimittunt penitus irreparata in tantum quod adeo sunt ruinosa et lapsui vicina; quod nisi cicius repararentur et emendentur finalem ruinam pati verisimiliter formidatur ex incuria et necligencia vestris manifestis, cum huiusmodi defectuum reparacio, correcio et punicio vobis (ut asseritur) notorie dinoscitur pertinere, in animarum vestrarum et prebendariorum dicte ecclesie grave periculum, domorumque et edificorum huiusmodi destruccionem et ruinam, et aliorum subditorum nostrorum exemplum per maxime perniciosum. Unde nos, prout ex officii nostri debito obligamur et tenemur, verum eciam ad querelosam populi supplicacionem premissis remedium apponere volentes, vobis in virtute obediencie et sub pena contemptus firmiter injungendo mandamus, quatinus circa congruam reparacionem domorum infra clausum vestrum Lichfeldense predictum existencium (videlicet decani et prebendarum de Olughton alias Ulfton tantum; necnon et aliorum domorum ac edificiorum prebendarum dicte ecclesie nostre adextra, jurisdiccioni vestre notorie subditarum) juxta formam constituccionis legatine que sic incipit: 'Improbam quorundam avariciam, et cetera' cum omni celeritate omnino procedatis. Monendo, videlicet, ac defectus huiusmodi debite reparari faciendo in omnibus prout decet. Et quid feceritis in premissis nos infra mensem proximam post recepcionem presencium distincte et aperte certificare curetis per litteras vestras patentes harum seriem ac discripcionem locorum et defectuum eorundem plenius in se continentes autentico sub sigillo. Datum sub sigillo nostro in manerio nostro de Heywode, quintodecimo die mensis Julii, anno domini millesimo CCCC^{mo} quadragesimo octavo et nostre consecracionis anno secundo. Cuius auctoritate mandati vestri reverendi circa ruinam mansorum non reparatorum, tam infra clausum vestrum predictum quam eciam extra (infra tamen civitatem), diligenter inspeximus. Et mansa decanatus et prebendarum de Oulghton alias Ulfton sunt competenter reparata, preter mansum domini Thome Maxfeld quod caret coquina; ad infra, videlicet mansa magistri Willelmi Kynwelmersh et magistri Johannis Wendesley maxime sunt defectiva, videlicet in coopertura, muris, et meremio; ad extra vero (infra tamen civitatem), videlicet mansa archidiaconatus Cestrie et prebende de Gaia majori ac prebende de Wyford finalem paciuntur ruinam. Item mansa prebendarum de Wollvey et Curburgh sunt defectiva in coopertura dawbatura muris et meremio. Quantum vero ad monicionem dictis prebendariis faciendum pro reparacione predicta dominacioni vestre humiliter supplicamus quatinus nos finaliter habeat dominacio prelibata excusatos, pro eo quod extra jurisdiccionem nostram omnino commorantur. Que omnia et singula dominacioni vestre notificamus per presentes. Datum in domo nostra capitulari, sub sigillo nostro communi ad causas, septimo die mensis Octobris, anno domini suprascripto.

233. [Fo. 36–v] 21 December 1448. Commission to the prior and subprior of Coventry cathedral to visit certain chantries in Coventry.

COMMISSIO AD VISITANDUM CANTARIAS IN ECCLESIA CATHEDRALI COVENTRENSI.
Willelmus [etc.], dilectis nobis in Christo priori ecclesie nostre cathedralis
Coventrensis et eiusdem ecclesie suppriori, salutem, graciam et benediccionem.
Quia nos ex causis nonnullis legitimis et probabilibus per nos pensatis certas
cantarias civitatis nostre Coventrensis predicte (videlicet cantariam domini
Henrici Prioris in ecclesia cathedrali predicta; ac cantariam Willelmi de Copston
in quadam capella dicte ecclesie nostre cathedrali annexa; necnon cantarias
Willelmi Celett, domini Johannis Percy, Nicholai Percy, Willelmi de Allesley, et
Rogeri de Lodyngton in ecclesia sancte Trinitatis civitatis nostre predicte; et
cantarias Laurencii Shepey, Jordani Shepei, Henrici del Hay, Hugonis de
Meryngton, et Johannis Preston in ecclesia parochiali sancti Michaelis dicte
civitatis pro peccatorum remedio et animarum quiete saluberime fundatas pariter
et ordinatas) earumque cantariarum capellanos altissimo propositum nostrum
adimplenter decrevimus actualiter visitare, debitumque visitacionis nostre
officium pro criminibus, excessibus et delictis dictorum capellanorum corrigendis
et puniendis, ipsorumque moribus (quatenus ad nos attinet) reformandis, exercere
in eisdem variis negociis arduis sumus prepediti, quominus eidem visitacioni
personaliter intendere valeamus. Ad visitandum igitur omnes et singulas cantarias
predictas, ac de et super criminibus, excessibus et delictis capellanorum earundem
cantariarum qualitercumque delinquencium in eisdem; necnon et super defectibus
reparacionis edificiorum et aliorum huiusmodi ad easdem cantarias pertinencium
que propter incuriam et necligenciam dictorum capellanorum deformantur ruine
et non mediocriter (ut dicitur) dilabuntur; ac super ipsarum cantariarum
ornamentorum, jocalium, utensilium, fructuum, reddituum et proventuum
substraccione, abduccione et dilapidacione inquirendum; criminaque et excessus
huiusmodi, eciam majora, in visitacione huiusmodi comperta, ac aliis coram vobis
(auctoritate nostra canonice procedentibus) detecta seu inposterum detegenda
nomine et auctoritate nostris (quatenus ad nos attinere dinoscitur) corrigendum,
puniendum et reformandum; defectus reparacionis [edificorum] seu aliorum
huiusmodi ad dictas cantarias pertinencium fideliter juxta iuris exigenciam taxari,
et taxatas reparari faciendum pariter et compellendum; ceteraque omnia et singula
statuendum, decernendum, exercendum et expediendum que as nos seu officium
visitacionis huiusmodi de jure vel consuetudine ac dictarum cantariarum
fundacione sive ordinacione pertinent seu quomodolibet requiruntur, eciam si ad
amocionem aliquorum capellanorum predictorum a cantariis vel officiis suis seu
ad fructuum, reddituum sive proventuum sequestracionem vel alia huiusmodi
majora (forsan fuerit) procedendo vobis, de quorum fidelitate, prudencia ac zelo
quem ad salutem animarum procurandum haberi dicimini plenam in domino
fiduciam gerimus conjunctim et divisim tenore presencium committimus vices
nostras donec eas ad nos duxerimus revocandas, cum cuiuslibet cohercionis et
execucionis canonice eorumque in hac parte decreveritis potestate. Datum sub
sigillo nostro, in hospicio nostro apud le Stronde, London', xxj° die mensis
Decembris, anno domini millesimo CCCC^{mo} quadragesimo octavo et nostre
consecracionis anno secundo.

234. [Fos 36v–37] 16 January 1449. Assignment of a life pension of 12 marks
p.a. in four equal portions to be paid by Thomas Coneway, now vicar of Burton
Dassett [*Chepyngdercet*], to Richard Leventhorp, formerly vicar of Burton Dassett.

ASSIGNACIO PENSIONIS VICARIE DE CHEPYNGDERCET. Universis sancte matris
ecclesie filiis presentes litteras inspecturis, Willelmus [etc.], presertim domino
Ricardo Leventhorp nuper vicario perpetuo ecclesie parochialis de
Chepyngdercet, nostre diocesis, et domino Thome Coneway nunc vicario dicte
ecclesie de Chepyngdercet, salutem in eo qui est omnium vera salus. Ad
submovenda obprobria que ex mendicitate inopinata sepius evenire noscuntur,
noverit universitas vestra quod personaliter constituti coram nobis, die loco et
anno domini infrascriptis, dicti domini Ricardus et Thomas nostris ordinacioni,
laudo, decreto et arbitro in alto et in basso cuiuscumque annue pensionis de
fructibus et proventibus prefate vicarie de Chepyngdercet predicto domino
Ricardo Leventhorp durante vita sua pro vite sue neccessariis per nos assignande
pure, sponte et absolute submiserunt et eorum uterque submisi;, promittentes se
ratum et gratum firmiter habituri quicquid nos in dicte pensionis annue
assignacione seu limitacione ordinaremus seu statueremus in hac parte, juramento
corporali ad sancta dei evangelia super hoc per eosdem dominos Ricardum et
Thomam prestito. Unde nos, Willelmus, episcopus antedictus, attentes per nos
facultatibus atque proventibus prefate vicarie de Chepyngderset, diligenter pariter
et pensatis, statuimus, ordinamus et decernimus auctoritate nostra ordinaria, cum
consensu et assensu omnium quorum interest in hac parte, quod prefatus dominus
Thomas Coneway, nunc dicte vicarie vicarius, et successores sui ipsius vicarie de
Chepyngdercet vicarii qui pro tempore fuerint, fideliter solvat et solvant singulis
annis prefato domino Leventhorp pro victu et vestitu suis quoad vixerit ut
premittitur neccessariis, annuam pensionem duodecim marcarum ad quatuor
anni terminos, videlicet ad festa annunciacionis beate Marie Virginis, nativitatis
sancti Johannis baptiste, ac sancti Michaelis archangeli et natalis domini, vel
saltem infra viginti dies post lapsum cuiuslibet festi festorum predictorum, equis
porcionibus, in ecclesia de Chepingdercet predicta de fructibus et proventibus
vicarie memorate. Insuper monemus prefatum dominum Thomam Coneway,
nunc vicarium supradictum, et successores suos dicte vicarie vicarios futuros,
primo, secundo et tercio ac peremptorie, et sub pena excommunicacionis majoris
in ipsius domini Thome Coneway et ipsorum vicariorum futurorum personas, ac
interdicti in vicariam predictam, sequestracionisque fructuum et proventuum
eiusdem, quatinus predictam annuam pensionem duodecim marcarum eidem
domino Ricardo Leventhorp sub modo et forma predictis ad festa predicta (seu
saltem infra viginti dies ut prefertur post lapsum cuiuslibet festi festorum
predictorum) in loco predicto persolvat et persolvant realiter et cum effectum;
alioquin prefatum dominum Thomam Coneway et successores suos ipsius vicarie
vicarios qui pro tempore fuerint in solucione huiusmodi deficientes, mora, culpa et
dolo suis precedentibus id merito exigentibus, ac huiusmodi canonica monicione
premissa, excommunicacioni ac vicariam predictam interdicto decernimus
subjacere. In cuius rei testimonium sigillum nostrum fecimus hiis apponi. Datum
in hospicio nostro apud Hakeney, xvjº die mensis Januarii, anno domini millesimo
CCCCmo quadragesimo octavo et nostre consecracionis anno secundo.

235. [Fos 37] Indenture between the bishop and Thomas Tarleton, vicar of
Croston, in which the bishop grants to Tarleton the tithe of sheaves of Croston for
one year, in accordance with the custom of the archdeaconry of Chester because
the vicarage was vacated before the preceding feast of St Chad by the death of
Richard Dalton, and had remained vacant without a presentation being made

until the 7 March then next following, being the feast of St Chad, in return for a sum of money to be agreed. 8 March, 27 Henry VI [1448/9].

236. [Fo. 37–v] Assignment of a life pension of 5 marks p.a. in four equal portions to be paid in St Paul's cathedral, London, by Henry Inse, now canon and prebendary of Wolvey in Lichfield cathedral,[152] to Thomas Clerk, formerly canon and prebendary of Wolvey.[153] Strand, London, 18 March 1449.

237. [Fos 37v–38] 27 April 1449. Composition between the bishop and Mr George Radclyff, archdeacon of Chester,[154] by which the archdeacon is granted powers of probate and administration of wills, including intestacy, the income of Peter's pence, synodals, and mortuaries of deceased clerks, in return for an annual payment of £20 to the bishop at Easter.

COMPOSICIO INTER COVENTRENSEM ET LICHFELDENSEM EPISCOPUM ET ARCHIDIACONUM CESTRIE DE JURISDICCIONE EPISCOPALI SIBI COMMISSA INFRA ARCHIDIACONATUM CESTRIE. Universis Christi fidelibus presentes litteras indentatas visuris vel audituris, innotescat et notum sit tenore earumdum quod reverendus in Christo pater dominus Willelmus [etc.], ac venerabilis vir magister Georgius Radclyff, archidiaconus Cestrie in ecclesia cathedrali Lichfeldensi, composuerunt et convenerunt in hunc modum, videlicet, quod dictus magister Georgius Radclyff, archidiaconus, vice et auctoritate dicti reverendi patris, ad beneplacitum predicti reverendi patris episcopi, exercebit et habebit auctoritatem et plenam potestatem insinuandi, probandi et approbandi testamenta et ultimas voluntates defunctorum quorumcumque subditorum eiusdem archidiaconatus; ac administracionem bonorum huiusmodi defunctorum et aliorum infra eundem archidiaconatum ab intestato decedencium committendi; et compotum sive calculum administracionis bonorum huiusmodi petendi, recipiendi, et audiendi; ac administratores huiusmodi acquietendi et liberandi. Et dictus magister Georgius, archidiaconus predictus, vice et auctoritate dicti reverendi patris habeat eciam potestatem petendi, exigendi, et recipiendi (ad beneplacitum prefati reverendi patris domini episcopi) omnes denarios vocatos denarios sancti Petri, vacaciones ecclesiarum, et synodalia infra ambitum archidiaconatus predicti, ac mortuaria curatorum decedencium infra ambitum dicti archidiaconatus, salva subditis archidiaconatus predicti potestate querelandi ad dictum reverendum patrem quociens eis placuerit, et appelandi ad prefatum reverendum patrem quociens et quando eos contigerit a dicto archidiacono vel suis officiariis aut ministriis quibuscumque in aliquo ledi seu gravari. Ac dictus magister Georgius, archidiaconus sepedictus, pro indempnitate prefati reverendi patris occasione premissorum concessorum solvet annuatim prefato reverendo in Christo patri episcopo predicto viginti libras sterlingorum in festo Pasche realiter et cum effectum. Et si contingat dictum magistrum Georgium, archidiaconum predictum, aretro fore in solucione predictarum viginti librarum in parte vel in toto in aliquo

---

152 See note 16.
153 Collated to the prebend of Wolvey 24 June 1427. Resigned by 18 March 1449 (*Fasti* x, 70).
154 See note 11.

festo quo solvi debeat per quinquaginta dies, quod extunc bene liceat prefato reverendo patri episcopo omnia et singula premissa dicto magistro Georgio per sepedictum reverendum patrem episcopum concessa reassumare, ac eadem omnia pro libito sue voluntatis exercere et rehabere presenti composicione indentata in aliquo non obstante; et tunc predictus magister Georgius, archidiaconus sepedictus, de premissis omnibus et singulis se in aliquo non intromittet. In quorum omnium et singulorum premissorum testimonium atque fidem sigilla nostra alternatim presentibus apposuimus. Datum apud Heywode vicesimo septimo die mensis Aprilis anno domini millesimo CCCC^{mo} quadragesimo nono.

238. [Fo. 38] 27 April 1449. Further composition between the bishop and the archdeacon whereby the bishop concedes to the archdeacon power to hear and determine all causes, whether ex officio or instance, and to exercise corrective jurisdiction in the archdeaconry, reserving cases of heresy, simony, incest, and matrimony are to the bishop, with appeals.

ALIA COMPOSICIO INTER EOSDEM DE EXERCICIO JURISDICCIONIS PER ARCHIDIACONUM CESTRIE. Universis Christi fidelibus presentes litteras indentatas visuris vel audituris innotescat et notum sit tenore earundum quod reverendus in Christo pater dominus Willelmus [etc.] ac venerabilis vir magister Georgius Radclyff, archidiaconus Cestrie in ecclesia cathedrali Lichfeldensi, de et super exercicio jurisdiccionis ecclesiastice infra archidiaconatum predictum ac modo et forma utendi eadem composuerunt et convenerunt in hunc modum; videlicet quod dictus magister Georgius Radclyff, archidiaconus predictus, vice et auctoritate dicti reverendi patris domini episcopi exercebit et habebit ad bene placitum predicti reverendi patris domini episcopi auctoritatem et plenam potestatem cognoscendi et procedendi in omnibus et singulis causis ex officio mero, mixto, seu promoto, vel ad alicuius partis instanciam, infra ambitum archidiaconatus predicti, et subditos eiusdem qualitercumque movendis; ac eas et ea fine debito canonice terminandi; ad corrigendum insuper et debite puniendum crimina et excessus subditorum quorumcumque archidiaconatus predicti, et pro criminibus et excessibus predictis penas et penetencias canonicas infligendum et injungendum (exceptis causis majoribus, ut puta heresie, symonie, incestus, matrimonii, et divorcii, ac aliis quibuscumque ad beneplacitum dicti reverendi patris eidem specialiter reservatis), salva eciam subditis archidiaconatus predicti potestate querelandi ad dictum reverendum patrem quociens eis placuerit, et appellandi ad dictum reverendum patrem quociens et quando eos contigerit a dicto archidiacono vel suis officiariis aut ministris quibuscumque in aliquo ledi seu gravari, superius ordinatis in aliquo non obstantibus. In quorum, etc., ut supra. Datum ut supra.

239. 29 April 1449. Commission to the archdeacon to proceed in all matrimonial and divorce causes provided that he informs the bishop of all cases.

COMMISSIO ARCHIDIACONO CESTRIE PRO CAUSIS MATRIMONIALIBUS ET DIVORCII. Willelmus [etc.] dilecto nobis in Christo archidiacono nostro Cestrie salutem, graciam, et benediccionem. Ad cognoscendum et procedendum in quibuscumque causis matrimonialibus et divorcii inter subditos archidiaconatus Cestrie predicti qualitercumque movendis; ipsasque causas cum suis emergentibus, incidentibus, dependentibus pariter et annexis fine debito terminandum; ceteraque omnia et singula faciendum, exercendum, et expediendum que in premissis et circa ea necessaria fuerint seu quomodolibet oportuna vobis, de cuius circumspeccionis industria et fidelitate fiduciam in domino gerimus specialem, committimus vices nostras, et plenam in domino potestatem cum cuiuslibet cohercionis canoniceque exequendi que decreveritis in hac parte potestate, ad nostrum beneplacitum duraturum. Et quid feceritis in premissis nos pro re loco et tempore oportunis distincte et aperte certificare curetis per vestras litteras patentes harum seriem continentes, ac tocius processus vestri formam sigillo autentico consignatam. Datum sub sigillo nostro in manerio nostro de Heywode, xxix° die mensis Aprilis, anno domini M°CCCC^mo^xlix°, et nostre conseoracionis anno ii°.

240. [Fo. 38v] 20 September 1447. Commission to Mr John Reedhill, LL.B., as sequestrator and commissary general for the diocese during pleasure.

COMMISSIO PRO OFFICIO SEQUESTRATORIS. Willelmus [etc.], dilecto nobis in Christo magistro Johanni Redehill, in utroque jure bacallario, salutem, graciam, et benediccionem. Ad corrigendum et puniendum crimina et excessus ac errores quorumcumque subditorum nostrorum; moresque eorum reformandum; testamentaque eorundem subditorum nostrorum admittendum, probandum, approbandum, et insinuandum, et pro ipsis pronunciandum et decernendum; calculum sive raciocinium administracionum ipsa testamenta concernencium committendum, petendum, audiendum, et examinandum; ac eciam quietancias inde faciendum, fructusquoque redditus et proventus quorumcumque beneficiorum ecclesiasticorum nostre diocesis vacancium seu inofficiatorum legitime sequestrandums sequestrarique faciendum; bona eciam quecumque subditorum nostrorum predictorum ab intestato decedencium committendum, sequestrandum, et disponendum, ac sequestrari et disponi faciendum; ac insuper contra quoscumque beneficiatos dicte nostre diocesis in beneficiis suis minime residentes qui de jure seu consuetudine in eisdem residere tenentur procedendum, ac eosdem seu alios beneficia sua ad firmam tradentes licencia nostra minime petita aut obtenta ac beneficia sua huiusmodi collabi permittentes canonice puniendum, et huiusmodi non residentes ad residendum in eisdem beneficiis suis, necnon beneficia sua ruere permittentes ad reparacionem eorundem per penas sequestracionis fructuum et proventuum dictorum beneficiorum suorum huiusmodi ac alias censuras ecclesiasticas debite compellendum et faciendum; eciam testes quoscumque in concistorio nostro Lichfeldensi in quibuscumque causis productos, ac per dicti concistorii officialem nostrum in forma juris admissi et juratos rite et legitime examinandum, ac eorum testimonia eidem officiali prout moris est debite transmittendum; ceteraque omnia et singula faciendum, exercendum, et expediendum que in premissis et circa ea necessaria fuerint, seu quomodolibet oportuna et que ad officium sequestratoris et commissarii de jure seu consuetudine juxta morem preteriti temporis pertinere noscuntur vobis vices nostras committimus, cum cuiuslibet cohercionis canonice potestate, per presentes, ad nostrum beneplacitum duraturum. Datum sub sigillo nostro, xx^mo^ die mensis Septembris, anno domini millesimo CCCC^mo^ quadragesimo septimo, et nostre consecracionis anno primo.

241. Assignment of a life pension of 5 marks p.a. in four equal portions to be paid in Wombourn (*Womburn*) church by the patrons, the prior and convent of Dudley, out of the fruits and income of the rectory, to Thomas Hawkys, formerly vicar of Wombourn, who has resigned broken with age and weak in body (*senecutem et corporis debilitatem quam alias mundi tribulaciones*). The present vicar of Wombourn, John Kendale and his successors, shall reimburse the patrons the five marks. Haywood, 22 August 1449.

Ratification of the above by the prior and convent of Dudley under their common seal dated in the chapter house at Dudley 22 August 1449.

Ratification of the above by John Kendale, vicar of Wombourn, under his seal dated 22 August 1449.

242. [Fo. 40] Assignment of a life pension of 7 marks p.a. in four equal portions to be paid in Aston church by Richard Grove, now vicar of Aston, to John Drover, formerly vicar (*ad submovenda opbrobria* etc.). Haywood, 25 August 1449.

243. [Fo. 40v] 14 October 1449. Dispensation for the marriage of John Barette and Joan Barette who have been living together and have begotten children, though related in the third and third degrees of consanguinity, in accordance with letters of Nicholas V dated at Rome, 16 kalends December [15 November] 1448.

DISPENSACIO MATRIMONII INTER JOHANNEM BARETTE ET JOHANNAM BARETTE.
Willelmus [etc.], dilectis in Christo filiis Johanni Bareite, laico, et Johanne Bareite, mulieri, nostre diocesis, salutem, graciam, et benediccionem. Litteras apostolicas sanctissimi in Christo patris et domini domini nostri domini Nicholai divina providencia pape quinti cum cordula canapis more romane curie bullatas sanas et integras, omni prorsus suspicione carentes, pro parte vestra nobis presentatas nuper recipimus, tenorem qui sequitur in se continentes: Nicholaus, episcopus, servus servorum dei, venerabili fratri Lichfeldensi et Coventrensi episcopo, salutem et apostolicam benediccionem. Oblate nobis pro parte dilecti filii Johannis Bareite, laici, et dilecte in Christo filie Johanne Bareite, mulieris, tue diocesis, peticionis series continebat quod ipsi, qui se actu fornicario pluries cognoverunt, prole exinde suscitata, illius favore necnon pro sedandis que alias inter eorum parentes et amicos verisimiliter erumperent scandalis et discordiis ac confovendis inter eosdem parentes et amicos pacis et concordie, nexibus insimul desiderant matrimonialiter copulari. Sed quia Johannes et Johanna predicti tercio et tercio consanguinitatis gradibus invicem conjuncti sunt, huiusmodi eorum desiderium adimplere nequeunt, dispensacione super hoc apostolica non obtenta; quare pro parte dictorum Johannis et Johanne nobis fuit humiliter supplicatum, ut super hiis ipsius de oportune dispensacionis gracia providere de benignitate apostolica dignaremur. Nos, igitur, qui inter fideles quoslibet pacem et tranquillitatem confoventes scandalorumque materias adimere studiis querimus indefessis, ex premissis et certis aliis nobis expositis causis huiusmodi supplicacionibus inclinati, fraternitati tue (de qua in hiis et aliis specialem in domino fiduciam obtinemus) per apostolica scripta committimus et mandamus quatinus si est ita, dictaque Johanna propter hoc rapta non fuerit, cum eisdem Johanne et Johanna ut, impedimentis non obstantibus supradictis, matrimonium inter se libere contrahere, et in illo postquam contractum fuerit remanere licite valeant, apostolice auctoritate dispenses, premissam et ex ipso contrahendo matrimonio suscipiendam prolem

legitimam decernendo. Datum Rome, apud sanctam Potencianam, anno incarnacionis dominice millesimo quadringentesimo quadragesimo octavo, sextodecimo kalendis Decembris, pontificatus nostri anno secundo. Nos, vero, Willelmus, episcopus antedictus, super suggestis in litteris apostolicis prenotatis diligenter inquirentes, et ipsa deposicione veridica virorum auctoritate nostra in forma juris examinatorum noticiam pleniorem suggestorum huiusmodi verisimiliter obtinencium, invenientes veritate fulciri, necnon vos, Johannem et Johannam, tercio et tercio consanguinitatis gradibus adinvicem attigisse, teque Johannam in hac parte propter hoc ab aliquo raptam non fuisse sed ex causis racionabilibus et honestis desideratis adinvicem matrimonialiter copulari; ut, igitur, dicto consanguinitatis impedimento minime obstante matrimonium inter vos libere contrahere et in illo postquam contractum fuerit remanere licete valeatis, vobiscum juxta exigenciam litterarum apostolicarum predictarum et auctoritate earundem tenore presencium misericorditer in domino dispensamus, prolem susceptam et exinde suscipiendam legitimam decernendo. In quorum omnium et singulorum testimonium atque fidem sigillum nostrum fecimus hiis apponi. Datum in castro nostro de Eccleshale, quartodecimo die mensis Octobris, anno domini millesimo CCCC^{mo} quadragesimo nono, et consecracionis nostre anno tercio.

244. Commission of the bishop to Thomas Byrome, canon of the royal free chapel of St Michael, Penkridge, to receive the canonical compurgation of imprisoned clerk Hugh Bostoke, late of Poynton, Cheshire, yeoman, in the prebendal church of Eccleshall on 23 October 1449. Haywood, 22 October 1449.

245. [Fo. 41] Certificate of Nicholas Bridde, dean of Macclesfield, Cheshire, reciting the bishop's mandate dated at Haywood, 20 September 1449 to make proclamation of the compurgation of Hugh Bostoke, late of Poynton, Cheshire, in Eccleshall prebendal church on 23 October 1449. He certifies that proclamation has been made concerning this matter and that details of Hugh Bostoke, convicted for stealing a white horse value 20s at Poynton, Cheshire, *vi et armis contra pacem*, the property of William Assheton of Poynton, on the Monday after the feast of St Michael 1443 (22 Henry VI), have been given in the churches of Stockport, Prestbury, and Gawsworth, and in all market places and other churches in the deanery of Macclesfield and opposers cited to appear at Eccleshall prebendal church on the appointed day, that is, 23 October 1449. Macclesfield, 21 October 1449.[155]

246. Certificate of Thomas Byrom, canon of the royal free chapel of St Michael, Penkridge, that on 23 October 1449 in the prebendal church of Eccleshall Hugh Bostoke was admitted to canonical compurgation, no opposers appearing, in the presence of the following as compurgators; John Halyngbury, vicar of Eccleshall, Thomas Worly, John Harwar', priests, William Coton, Ralph Henshagh, John Shirley, John Russheton, William Hewster, Roger Russheton, Robert Careswell, Robert Underwode, and Thomas Cronage, literates. Eccleshall, 23 October 1449.

[155] See **246**.

247. [Fo. 41v] 20 December 1449. Licence to Robert Catryke, rector of Adderley, and John Hoton, chaplain of the chapel of Wrenbury, to marry John Starky and Agnes Nedham in the chapel or oratory of John Nedham, *domicellus*, providing banns are called and there is no canonical objection.

LICENCIA AD CELEBRANDUM MATRIMONIUM INTER JOHANNEM STARKY ET AGNETEM NEDHAM IN ORATORIO. Willelmus [etc.], dilectis in Christo filiis domino Roberto Catryke, rectori ecclesie parochiali de Aderley, et domino Johanni Hoton, capellano divina celebranti in capella de Wrenbury, nostre diocesis, salutem, etc. Ad solempnizandum matrimonium inter Johannem Starky et Agnetem Nedham in capella sive oratorio mansionis Johannis Nedham, domicelli dicte nostre diocesis, dummodo banna matrimonialia inter eosdem Johannem and Agnetem (prout moris est) fuerint et sint debite edita et proclamata, nullumque impedimentum canonicum obstitat in hac parte, vobis conjunctim et divisim tenore presencium concedimus facultatem et licenciam specialem. In cuius rei testimonium sigillum nostrum fecimus hiis apponi. Datum in hospicio nostro apud le Stronde, London', vicesimo die mensis Decembris, anno domini millesimo CCCC^mo quadragesimo nono, et nostre consecracionis anno tercio.

248. [Fos 41v–42v] 5 December 1449. Certificate of the bishop to the treasurer and barons of the treasury naming the collectors of the various clerical subsidies granted in convocation, and the names of those exempted from them.

CERTIFICATORIUM COLLECTORUM INTEGRE DECIME ET QUARTE PARTIS DECIME DE PERSONIS A COLLECCIONE EXEMPTIS. Venerabilibus et discretis viris dominis thesaurario et baronibus de scaccario domini nostri regis, Willelmus [etc.], salutem in Christo Jesu omnium salvatore. Breve regum nobis directum nuper reverenter recipimus in hec verba: Henricus, dei gracia, etc., cuius datum est apud Westmonasterium, xviij° die Octobris, anno Henrici sexti nunc xxviij°, cuius brevis auctoritate in archidiaconatu Coventrensi Johannem abbatem et conventum monasterii de Miravall, ac in archidiaconatu Derbie Rogerum abbatem et conventum monasterii de Derley, et in archidiaconatu Staffordie Ricardum abbatem et conventum monasterii de Hulton, in archidiaconatu vero Salopie Johannem abbatem et conventum monasterii de Lilleshull, ac eciam in archidiaconatu Cestrie (tam in comitatu eiusdem quam in comitatu Lancastrie in eodem archidiaconatu Cestrie) Johannem abbatem et conventum monasterii sancte Wereburge Cestrie nostre diocesis, ad levandum et colligendum primam medietatem dicte integre decime eidem domino regi (ut prefertur) concesse de quibuscumque bonis, beneficiis, et possessionibus ecclesiasticis prefate nostre diocesis taxatis et non taxatis, ac quartam partem decime de personis huiusmodi per litteras regias (ut premittitur) a collecione decimarum exemptis juxta formam dicte concessionis collectores deputavimus; pariter et assignavimus, eisque et eorum singulis firmiter dedimus in mandatis, quatinus tam de dicta prima medietate decime quam de quarta parte decime de personis huiusmodi (ut predicitur) a collecione decimarum exemptis, in festo annunciacionis beate Marie Virginis quod erit anno domini millesimo CCCC^mo quinquagesimo prefato domino nostro regi in scaccario suo plenarie satisfiat per eosdem. Necnon in archidiaconatu Coventrensi predictos Johannem abbatem et conventum monasterii de Miravall, et in archidiaconatu Derbie abbatem et conventum[156] monasterii de Dala nostre diocesis, ac insuper in archidiaconatu Staffordie Johannem abbatem et conventum de Dyeuleucrece, et eciam in archidiaconatu Salopie Ricardum abbatem et conventum monasterii de Haghmond, et in archidiaconatu Cestrie (tam in comitatu eiusdem quam in comitatu Lancastrie eiusdem archidiaconatu Cestrie) priorem[157] et conventum prioratus de Birkeheved prefate nostre diocesis, ad levandum eciam et colligendum alteram sive secundam medietatem dicte integre decime dicto nostro regi (ut prefertur) concessam de quibuscumque bonis, beneficiis, et possessionibus ecclesiasticis prefate nostre diocesis (ut prefertur) taxatis et non taxatis juxta formam concessionum predictarum collectores deputavimus; et assignavimus, ac eisdem et eorum singulis firmiter dedimus in mandatis, quod dicta altera sive secunda medietas dicte integre decime in festo annunciacionis beate Marie quod erit anno domini millesimo CCCC[mo] quinquagesimo primo prefato domino regi in scaccario suo fideliter persolvatur per eosdem. Exceptis a concessione et solucione dicte integre decime bonis, beneficiis, et possessionibus ecclesiasticis pauperum monalium de Pollesworth, Nuneton, Brewod, Derbie, Cestrie, hospitalis sancti Johannis Cestrie, ac hospitalis de Denwall et ecclesie parochialis de Burton in Wyrall eidem hospitali annexe, per ruinam et alios casus fortuitos depauperatorum, monasteriorumque de Crokesden, Roucestre, Hulton, de bello capite, de Bildewas (per inundaciones aquarum), et de Dala (per incendium) ac prioratus de Stone cum ecclesiis parochialibus de Stone, Melwych et Madeley eidem prioratui appropriatis, ac prioratuum de Trentham, Erdebury, Tuttebury, Repyngdon, sancti Thome martiris juxta Staffordie, Ronton, Burschogh, et de Braydeshale Parke, dicte nostre diocesis, per diversos casus fortuitos nimium destructis ac depauperatis[158] et diminutis; exceptis eciam a concessione et solucione dicte decime beneficiis ecclesiasticis (videlicet ecclesia de Tachebroke in archidiaconatu Coventrensi, et ecclesia de Sallowe in archidiaconatu Derbie) que per incendium ruinam et alios fortuitos casus depauperatis et nimium diminutis existunt; ac beneficiis ecclesiasticis de Bedworth, Stretton, Herdeburgh, Bathekynton, Stokton, Arley, Dercet parva, Lalleford, Boroughton, Competon Mordoke et Sheldon in archidiaconatu Coventrensi, et beneficiis de Longley, Cloune, Morton, Shirland, Normanton, Whytyngton, Sutton in Dall, Barleburgh, Irton, Bentley, Bradeley, Rodeburn, Morley, Trusseley, Hertishorn, Bondeshale, Ravenston, Swerkeston, ac vicariis de Chestrefeld, Dovebrugge, Wirkesworth et de Mershton in archidiaconatu Derbie; ac insuper beneficiis de Draycote, Kyngeley, Rydeware, Alrewich, Haroughton, Norbury, Blymmehull, Weston subtus Luzeyerd, Eyton et Quate in archidiaconatu Staffordie; exceptis eciam beneficiis ecclesiasticis de Picheforde, Biryghton, Stokton, Chetwynde et Aderley in archidiaconatu Salopie; necnon beneficiis sancte Trinitatis Cestrie, Cristelton, Codyngton, Norworthyn, Dodelaston et Brereton in archidiaconatu Cestrie nimium depauperatis et diminutis ac taxatis et ad decimam solvere consuetis, quorum verus valor annuus modernis temporibus ad summam xij marcarum se extendit et non ultra, quorum

---

[156] The next three words are written over an erasure, which continues for a line and more with the vacated space being filled with squiggles until 'nostre diocesis'.

[157] priorem written over erasure.

[158] MS reads depauperatorum.

rectores et vicarii personalem fecerunt et faciunt residenciam in eisdem. Exceptis eciam a concessione et solucione decime predicte bonis, beneficiis, et possessionibus ecclesiasticis nostris quibuscumque infra nostram diocesim predictam, ac aliis beneficiis in prefati brevi regio preexceptis. Beneficia vero non taxata nostre diocesis nec ad decimam solvere consueta, verusque valoravimus juxta estimacionem eorundem, secuntur in hunc modum; videlicet archidiaconatus Coventrensis (xx marcas); archidiaconatus Derbie (xx marcas); archidiaconatus Staffordie (x libras); archidiaconatus Salopie (xiiij marcas); archidiaconatus Cestrie (xx marcas); et in archidiaconatu Coventrensi vicaria sancte Trinitatis ibidem (xiiij marcas), vicaria de Kirkby (xiij marcas), vicaria de Newbolde (xiij marcas), vicaria de Dercet magna (xij marcas et dimidia), vicaria de Aston (xiij marcas), vicaria de Hampton (xij marcas et dimidia), et cantaria de Copeston Coventrensis (xij marcas et dimidia); et in archidiaconatu Derbie vicaria de Glossop (xij marcas et dimidia), vicaria de Hertyngton (xiij marcas) et vicaria de Duffeld (xiiij marcas); et in archidiaconatu Staffordie vicaria de Bromley Abbatis (xiij marcas), vicaria de Leke (xiij marcas), vicaria de Astonesfeld (xiij marcas), et vicaria de Walsale (xiij marcas); et in archidiaconatu Salopie vicaria de Wellyngton (xiij marcas) et vicaria sancti Alkmundi Salop' (xiij marcas; et in archidiaconatu Cestrie vicaria de Bowdon (x libras), vicaria de Sondebache (x libras), vicaria de Prestbury (xiij marcas), vicaria de Croston (xx marcas), vicaria de Leylonde (x libras), et vicaria de Whalley (xiij marcas). Ac insuper, ad colligendum et levandum dictum subsidium sex solidorum et octo denariorum infra diocesim nostram de singulis presbyteris secularibus et aliis juxta formam dicti brevis regii prefato domino regi concessum (videlicet in archidiaconatu Coventrensi magistrum Rogerum Wall, archidiaconum eiusdem archidiaconatus, et in archidiaconatu Derbie magistrum Johannem Bridde, archidiaconum eiusdem, ac eciam in archidiaconatu Staffordie magistrum Johannem Wendesley, archidiaconum eiusdem, ac insuper in archidiaconatu Salopie magistrum Thomam Salesbury, archidiaconum eiusdem, et in archidiaconatu Cestrie – tam in comitatu eiusdem quam in comitatu Lankastrie in eodem archidiaconatu – magistrum Georgium Radclyff, archidiaconum eiusdem archidiaconatus Cestrie nostre diocesis sepedicte) collectores deputavimus; pariter et assignavimus, ac eis et eorum singulis firmiter dedimus in mandatis, quatinus de dictis sex solidos et octo denariis de singulis presbyteris (ut prefertur) juxta formam concessionis predicte in festo annunciacionis beate Marie Virginis quod erit anno domini millesimo CCCC^{mo} quinquagesimo dicto domino regi in scaccario suo plenarie satisfiat per eosdem, exceptis capellanis in dicto brevi preexceptis. Que omnia et singula vestris reverenciis patefacimus presentibus per tenorem sigillo nostro signatis. Datum in hospicio nostro apud le Stronde, London', quinto die mensis Decembris, anno domini millesimo CCCC^{mo} quadragesimo nono, et nostre consecracionis anno tercio.

Memorandum quod abbas de Cumba, abbas de Miravall, abbas de Haghmond et abbas de Valle regali certificati fuerunt in scaccario domini regis pro personis exemptis infra diocesim Coventrensem et Lichfeldensem, etc.

249. [Fo. 42v] Assignment of a life pension of 5 marks p.a. in four equal portions to be paid in Quatt church by Thomas Crowther, now vicar of Quatt, to Richard Russheton, formerly vicar (*ad submovenda opbrobria* etc). Eccleshall, 20 February 1450.

250. [Fo. 43] Dispensation, pursuant to letters, recited, of Dominicus, cardinal-priest, title of the Holy Cross, Jerusalem, dated at St Peter's, Rome, 24 January 1450 (9 Kalends February) to John Parkyn and Felicity Azakec to marry within the fourth degree of consanguinity. Leicester, 24 April 1450.

251. Dispensation, pursuant to letters, recited, of Dominicus, cardinal-priest, title of the Holy Cross, Jerusalem, dated at St Peter's, Rome (as in 250), to William Makoc and Felicity Campion to marry within the fourth degree of consanguinity (*duplici quarto consanguinitatis gradum*). Leicester, 24 April 1450.

252. [Fo. 43v] Dispensation, pursuant to letters, recited, of Dominicus, cardinal-priest, title of the Holy Cross, Jerusalem, dated at St Peter's, Rome, 28 July 1449 to Thomas Kendale, clerk, to proceed to all holy orders and to receive a benefice notwithstanding the fact that he has a defect of birth and is the son of a priest. Leicester, 31 May 1450.

253. [Fo. 44] Dispensation, pursuant to letters, recited, of Dominicus, cardinal-priest, title of the Holy Cross, Jerusalem, dated at St Peter's, Rome, 8 December 1449, to John Berdmore and Joan Lokwode to marry within the fourth degree of consanguinity. Leicester, 6 June 1450.

254. Assignment of a life pension of 10 marks p.a. in four equal portions to be paid in Grappenhall church by Thomas Byrom, now rector of Grappenhall, to William del Heth formerly rector, who has resigned because of old age and infirmity (*senio et adversa valitudine in dies plus solito laboranti et ad regimen animarum prefate ecclesie ut asserit penitus impotenti*). Clayton, 26 June 1450.

255. [Fos 44v–45v] 20 September 1450. Certificate of the bishop naming those appointed to collect the tenth and other subsidies granted to the king.

CERTIFICATORIUM COLLECTORUM INTEGRE DECIME ET SUBSIDIORUM DOMINO REGI CONCESSI, ETC. Reverendissimis in Christo patribus et dominis Johanni [Kempe], miseracione divina sancte Romane ecclesie tituli sancte Balbine presbytero cardinali, Eboracensis archiepiscopo, Anglie primati, et apostolice sedis legato; et Johanni [Stafford], permissione divina Cantuariensis archiepiscopo, tocius Anglie primati, et apostolice sedis legato; necnon reverendis in Christo patribus et dominis Thome, Londoniensi, et Willelmo, Wyntoniensi episcopis; Willelmus, permissione divina Coventrensis et Lichfeldensis episcopus, reverencias debitas cum honore. Breve regium nobis directum nuper reverenter recipimus in hec verba: Henricus, dei gracia, cuius datum est apud Westmonasterium, primo die Augusti anno regni regis, etc., vicesimo octavo.[159] Cuius brevis auctoritate in archidiaconatu Coventrensi abbatem et conventum monasterii de Cumba, et in archidiaconatu Derbie abbatem et conventum monasterii beate Marie de Pratis Leycestr' (proprietarios ecclesiarum parochialium de Bulkynton, Clifton, et Cruddeworth dicte nostre diocesis), et in archidiaconatu Staffordie abbatem et conventum monasterii de Hulton, in archidiaconatu eciam Salopie abbatem et

---

[159] *CPR 1445–52*, 139.

conventum de Lilleshull, et in archidiaconatu Cestrie (tam in comitatu eiusdem quam in comitatu Lancastrie eiusdem archidiaconatus) abbatem et conventum de Valle Regali dicte nostre diocesis, ad levandum et colligendum dictas duas medietates dicte integre decime de quibuscumque bonis, beneficiis, et possessionibus ecclesiasticis prefate nostre diocesis eidem domino regi ad festa predicta solvendas, salvis infrascriptis, juxta formam predictam collectores deputavimus; et assignavimus, ac eisdem firmiter dedimus in mandatis, quod tam prima medietas dicte integre decime ad festum annunciacionis beate Marie Virginis quod erit anno domini millesimo CCCC^{mo} quinquagesimo secundo, quam altera secunda medietas dicte integre decime eodem festo ad annum de post (quod erit anno domini millesimo CCCC^{mo} quinquagesimo tercio) vobis reverendissimis et reverendis in Christo patribus antedictis thesauraris et receptoribus per prelatos et clerum (ut predicitur) in hac parte limitatis et assignatis fideliter persolvantur per eosdem. Necnon in archidiaconatu Coventrensi predictum abbatem et conventum de Cumba, in archidiaconatu Derbie priorem et conventum de Greseley, in archidiaconatu vero Staffordie dictum abbatem et conventum de Hulton, et in archidiaconatu Salopie abbatem et conventum de Lilleshull predictum, ac in et per totam archidiaconatum Cestrie (tam in comitatu eiusdem quam in comitatu Lancastrie dicti archidiaconatus Cestrie) abbatem et conventum de Norton diocesis nostre predicte, ad statim levandum et colligendum tam dictos duos solidos de libra secundum taxam de bonis et possessionibus abbatum, priorumque et ceterorum clericorum secularium vel regularium infra diocesim nostram ad beneficia electiva (ut premittitur) promotorum, quam dictos duos solidos de libra prefato domino regi per dictum archiepiscopum Cantuariensem concessis, ac eciam quartam partem integre decime de quibuscumque personis dicte nostre diocesis per litteras regias a colleccione decimarum exemptis juxta formam dicti brevis regii collectores eciam deputavimus; et assignavimus, ac eisdem eciam firmiter dedimus in mandatis, quod tam de dictis duobus solidis de libra secundum taxam de bonis et possessionibus abbatum, priorum et ceterorum clericorum secularium vel regularium ad beneficia electiva infra diocesim nostrum (ut premittitur) promotorum, quam de dictis duobus solidis de libra de quibuscumque bonis et possessionibus religiosorum virorum et aliorum dicte nostre diocesis qui se per litteras regias ad contribucionem decime cum aliis de clero non teneri optinuerunt, et eciam de quarta parte integre decime de quibuscumque bonis et possessionibus quarumcumque personarum prefate nostre diocesis per litteras regias a colleccione decimarum exemptarum juxta formam predictam vobis thesaurario et receptoribus supradictis statim et integraliter satisfiat per eosdem. Exceptis a concessione et solucione dicte integre decime bonis, beneficiis, et possessionibus ecclesiasticis pauperum monalium de Pollesworth, Nuneton, Brewode, Derbie, Cestrie, hospitalis sancti Johannis Cestrie, ac hospitalis de Denwall et ecclesie parochialis de Burton in Wirall eidem hospitali annexe, per ruinam et alios casus fortuitos depauperatorum et diminutorum; monasteriorumque de Whalley, de Bello Capite, de Bildewas (per inundaciones aquarum), et de Dala (per incendium), ac prioratus de Stone cum ecclesiis parochialibus de Stone, Melwich, et Madeley eidem prioratui appropriatis, et prioratuum de Trentham, Erdebury, Tuttebury, Repyngdon, sancti Thome martiris juxta Stafford, Ronton, Callewich, Burscogh, et de Braydeshall Parke, dicte nostre diocesis, per diversos casus fortuitos nimium destructorum ac depauperatorum et nimium diminutorum. Exceptis eciam a concessione et solucione dicte decime beneficiis ecclesiasticis (videlicet ecclesia de Tachebroke in archidiaconatu Coventrensi et ecclesia de Sallowe in archidiaconatu Derbie) que per incendum ruinam et alios casus fortuitos depauperatis et nimium diminutis existunt; ac eciam beneficiis ecclesiasticis de Grenborgh (prioratui de Ronton appropriata), Bedworth, Compton Mardak, Stretton, Bathekynton, Stokton, Arley, Dercet parva, Lalleford, Borughton et Sheldon in archidiaconatu Coventrensi; et beneficiis de Longley, Clowne,[160] Shirland, Normanton, Whytyngton, Sutton in Dall, Barleburgh, Irton, Benteley, Bradeley, Rodeburn, Derley in alto pecco, Morley, Trusseley, Hertishorn, Bondeshale, Ravenston, Swerkeston, ac vicariis de Duffeld, Spondon,[161] Dovebrugge et de Mershton in archidiaconatu Derbie; ac insuper beneficiis de Draycote, Kyngeley, Wolstanston, Rideware, Alrewich, Norbury, Blymmehull et Quatte in archidiaconatu Staffordie; excepta eciam vicaria de Preez in archidiaconatu Salopie; necnon exceptis beneficiis ecclesiastis sancte Trinitatis in Cestria, Cristelton, Codyngton, Nerworthyn, Prestwich, Dodelaston, Gropenhale, Mottrom in Longdendale et Brereton in archidiaconatu Cestrie, eciam nimium depauperatis et diminutis, ac taxatis et ad decimam solvere consuetis, quorum singulorum verus valor annuus modernis temporibus ad summam xij marcarum se extendit et non ultra, quorum rectores et vicarii personalem fecerunt et faciunt residenciam in eisdem. Beneficia vero non taxata nec ad decimam solvere consueta, verusque valor annuus juxta estimacionem eorundem in et per totam nostram diocesim secuntur in hunc modum; videlicet archidiaconatus Coventrensis (xx marcas), archidiaconatus Derbie (xx marcas), archidiaconatus Staffordie (x libras), archidiaconatus Salopie (xiiij marcas), archidiaconatus Cestrie (xx marcas); et in archidiaconatu Coventrensi vicaria sancte Trinitatis ibidem (xiiij marcas), vicaria de Kirkby (xiij marcas), vicaria de Newbalde (xiij marcas), vicaria de Dercet magna (xij marcas et dimidia), vicaria de Aston (xiij marcas), vicaria de Hampton (xij marcas et dimidia), et cantaria de Copeston Coventrensi (xij marcas et dimidia); et in archidiaconatu Derbie vicaria de Glossop (xii marcas et dimidia), et vicaria de Hertyngton (xiij marcas); et in archidiaconatu Staffordie vicaria de Bromley Abbatis (xiij marcas), vicaria de Leeke (xiij marcas), vicaria de Astonesfeld (xiij marcas) et vicaria de Walsale (xiij marcas); et in archidiaconatu Salopie vicaria de Wellyngton (xiij marcas), et vicaria sancti Alkmundi Salop' (xiij marcas); et in archidiaconatu Cestrie vicaria de Bowdon (x libras), vicaria de Sondebache (x libras),[162] et vicaria de Prestbury (xiij marcas). Et de personis per litteras regias a collecione decimarum exemptis, ac eciam de religiosis viris et aliis qui se per litteras regias ad contribucionem decime cum aliis de clero non teneri impetrarunt et optinuerunt, infra diocesim nostram inquisicionem diligentem fieri fecimus; et per dictam inquisicionem compertum est, quod nulle persone infra diocesim nostram per litteras regias a collecione seu solucione decimarum sunt exempte; et quod infra dictam diocesim nostram non sunt aliqui religiosi viri nec aliqui alii qui per litteras regias ad contribucionem decime cum aliis de clero non teneri impetrarunt

---

160 Followed by a short gap filled with lines.
161 At this point occurs a marginal note, seemingly unconnected with the text: 'dominis suis qui sum'.
162 Following 'Sondebache' is 'vicaria de Croston' which has been struck through (and is in turn followed by a gap filled with lines), and 'vacat non estimatur' written above.

et optinuerunt. Que omnia et singula vestris reverenciis patefacimus per presentes sigillo meo signatas. Datum xx^mo die mensis Septembris, anno domini millesimo CCCC^mo quinquagesimo, et nostre consecracionis anno quarto.

R. Corrigitur in melius pro omnibus rasuris in littera prescripta per seipsum. R. W. Brand. Registrar.[163]

256. [Fo. 45v] List of the names of all who hold elective benefices within the diocese of Coventry and Lichfield.

NOMINA ABBATUM ET PRIORUM AC ALIORUM CLERICORUM SECULARIUM VEL REGULARIUM AD BENEFICIA ELECTIVA PROMOTORUM INFRA DIOCESIM NOSTRAM EXISTENCIUM.[164]

IN ARCHIDIACONATU COVENTR'
Ricardus prior ecclesie nostre cathedralis Coventrensis
Johannes abbas de Stoneley
Ricardus abbas de Cumba
Johannes abbas de Miravall
Thomas abbas de Kenilleworth
Robertus prior de Macstoke
Willelmus prior de Erdebury
Priorissa de Nuneton

IN ARCHIDIACONATU DERB'
Rogerus abbas de Derley
Johannes abbas de Dala
Willelmus abbas de Bellocapite
Johannes prior de Repingdon
Johannes prior de Greseley
Priorissa Derb'
Magister Johannes Macworth decanus Lincoln'

IN ARCHIDIACONATU STAFFORD'
Dominus Johannes Verney decanus Lichfeld'
Radulphus abbas de Burton
Johannes abbas de Dieuleucres
Ricardus abbas de Hulton
Radulphus abbas de Crokesden
Johannes abbas de Roucestre
Thomas prior de Stone
Ricardus prior sancti Thome martiris juxta Stafford' Johannes prior de Ronton

[163] This last phrase is contained towards the left of the page, extending over two lines. The layout is here imperfectly reproduced: the registrar's name seems to have been originally appended to the letter, with the phrase about correction then being added later and written around it.

[164] This list is arranged in three columns, the first containing the archdeaconries of Coventry and Derby; the second that of Stafford; the third those of Salop and Chester. The final note of certification occurs at the foot of the middle column.

Stephanus prior de Trentham
Johannes prior de Callewich
Prior de Duddeley
Prior de Wombrugg[165]
Abbatissa de Pollesworth

IN ARCHIDIACONATU SALOP'
Thomas abbas Salop'
Johannes abbas de Bildewas
Ricardus abbas de Haghmond
Johannes abbas de Lilleshull
Prior de Wombrugge

IN ARCHIDIACONATU CESTR'
Johannes abbas Cestr'
Thomas abbas de Norton
Nicholaus abbas de Whalley
Johannes abbas de Valle Regali
Rogerus abbas de Cumbermere
Ricardus prior de Birkheved
Johannes prior de Holand
Robertus prior de Burscogh
Priorissa monialium Cestr'

Et sub eadem forma certificatur thesaurario et baronibus de scaccario domini regis.

257. [Fo. 46] Commission to John Halyngbury, vicar of the prebendal church of Eccleshall, to receive the canonical compurgation of imprisoned clerk William Chaffar, late of Warrington, Lancashire, in the prebendal church of Eccleshall on 5 October 1450. 2 October 1450.[166]

258. Certificate of Richard Bretherton, vicar of Weaverham, Cheshire, and dean of Frodsham, reciting the bishop's mandate, dated at Eccleshall castle 7 August 1450, to make proclamation of the compurgation in Eccleshall prebendal church on 5 October 1450 of William Chaffar, late of Warrington, Lancashire, a wright. He certifies that proclamation has been made, and that details of William Chaffar, convicted after a trial by jury before William de la Pole, marquis of Suffolk, and Sir Thomas Stanley, justiciars of the king in the county of Chester, on the Tuesday following the feast of the Epiphany, for stealing '*vi et armis*' at Comberbach, Cheshire, on the Saturday after the feast of St Michael the archangel 1447 (26 Henry VI), three bulls and two cows, value 30s, the property of Henry Burghes of Comberbach, have been given in the parish church of Budworth and other surrounding churches, the market place at Northwich and other market

---

[165] This name is struck through: it reappears in its correct place under the archdeaconry of Salop.
[166] See **258–259**.

places, and other neighbouring places, citing opposers to appear at Eccleshall on the appointed day, that is, 5 October 1450. 28 September 1450.

259. [Fo. 46v] Certificate of John Halyngbury that on 5 October 1450 at Eccleshall prebendal church William Chaffar was admitted to canonical compurgation, no opposers appearing, in the presence of the following as compurgators; Thomas Wirley, chaplain, Ralph Wever, William Coton, David Kenrike, Stephen Kenrike, Ralph Henshagh, William Trente, William Hewster, John Nowell, Thomas Herte, Richard Hatherhorn, Thomas Trente, clerks and literates. Present; Mr William Brand, Roger Swyneshened and Geoffrey Pynyngton, literates and others. Eccleshall, 5 October 1450.

260. Assignment of a life pension of 6 marks p.a. in four equal portions to be paid in Doveridge church by Henry Russell, now vicar of Doveridge, to John Yeveley, formerly vicar (*ad submovenda opbrobria etc.*). Lichfield, 1 November 1450.

261. [Fo. 47] Assignment of a life pension of 40s p.a. in two equal portions, to be paid by Edmund Rediche, now rector of Taxal, to Robert Wightmon, formerly rector (*ad submovenda opbrobria etc.*). Eccleshall castle, 20 February 1451.

262. [Fo. 47–v] Assignment of a life pension of 13s 4d p.a. in two equal portions, to be paid in Carsington church by Richard Smyth, now rector of Carsington, to Thomas Porter, formerly rector (*ad submovenda opbrobria etc.*). Eccleshall castle, 27 March 1451.

263. [Fo. 48] Commission of the bishop to Thomas Byrom, canon of Lichfield cathedral,[167] to receive the canonical compurgation of imprisoned clerks Edward Lech of Uttoxeter, Staffs., and Christopher Smyth alias Smythyman, late of Cradley, Worcs., in the prebendal church of Eccleshall on 7 June 1451. Eccleshall castle, 5 June 1451.[168]

264. [Fos 48–49] Certificate of Richard Parlesven, vicar of Uttoxeter, Staffs., and Roger, chaplain of the church of Leigh, Staffs., reciting the bishop's mandate, dated at Eccleshall castle 5 May 1451, to make proclamation of the compurgation in Eccleshall prebendal church on 7 June 1451 of Edward Lech, late of Uttoxeter, Staffs., He certifies that proclamation has been made, and that details of Edward Lech, convicted after a jury trial before Thomas Arblaster and William Comberforde, justices of the peace for the county of Stafford, for the following crimes; (i) At Uttoxeter on the Thursday after the feast of the birth of St John the Baptist 1448 (27 Henry VI), stealing one 'gardievant' value 6s 8d and six caskets with divers muniments, the property of John Mynors senior. (ii) At Uttoxeter on the Saturday after the feast of St Michael the archangel 1449 (28 Henry VI), breaking into the chamber of the said John Myners senior and stealing therein one belt with contrasting silver bands, one rosary of coral and gold beads and two folds

---

[167] See note 60.
[168] See **264–265**. For an earlier compurgation for theft by Edward Leche, in 1448, see **226**.

of kerchiefs one of lawn, the other of wimple, total value 10 marks, property of the said John Myners senior. (iii) At Leigh on the Thursday after the feast of St Michael the archangel 1449 (28 Henry VI), stealing a chalice value 100s, the property of Robert Legh esq; have been given in the churches of Uttoxeter and Leigh and in the market place at Uttoxeter and other places, citing opposers to appear at Eccleshall prebendal church on the appointed day, that is, 7 June 1451. 2 June 1451.

265. [Fo. 49] Certificate of John Waller, rector of Tattenhill, Staffs., and Nicholas Cowper, chaplain of the chapel of Barton under Needwood, Staffs., reciting the bishop's mandate, dated Eccleshall castle, 5 May 1451, to make proclamation of the compurgation in Eccleshall prebendal church on 7 June 1451 of Christopher Smyth alias Smythyman, late of Cradley, Worcs., a labourer, convicted after a jury trial before Thomas Arblaster and William Comberforde, justices of the peace for the county of Stafford, for the following crimes; (i) At Barton under Needwood, Staffs, on the Thursday in the week of Pentecost 1448 (27 Henry VI), stealing a black cow and a sucking calf (*vitulo lactante*) value 10s the property of John Broke of Barton under Needwood. (ii) At Barton under Needwood, Staffs., on the Tuesday after the feast of St Bartholemew the apostle 1448 (27 Henry VI), stealing a black bull value 15s, the property of John Nuttynge, from a field called 'le Breche' at Barton under Needwood. Proclamation has been made in the church at Tattenhill and in the chapel at Leigh, and in the market places at Uttoxeter and Burton upon Trent and other places, citing opposers to appear at Eccleshall prebendal church on the appointed day, that is, 7 June 1451. Dated under the seal of the abbot and convent of Burton upon Trent, specially obtained for the purpose. 31 May 1451.

266. Certificate of Thomas Byrom[169] that on 7 June 1451 in the prebendal church of Eccleshall Edward Lech and Christopher Smyth *alias* Smythyman were admitted to canonical compurgation, no opposers appearing, in the presence of the following as compurgators: John Harway, Thomas Wirley, chaplains, Thomas Cronage, Edward Langton, Ralph Langford, Robert Warde, William Hewester, John Nowell, Robert Underwood, John Schirley, William Worthyngton and Ralph Heusthouse, literates. 7 June 1451.

267. [Fo. 50–v] Certificate of John Meyneley, vicar of Holy Trinity, Coventry, reciting the bishop's mandate, dated at Haywood, 20 August 1451, to make proclamation of the compurgation in Eccleshall prebendal church on the Monday after the feast of St Matthew the apostle of John Eton, late of Wem, Salop., a mercer, who was convicted on the Monday after the feast of St Gregory the pope before Richard Sharpe, Thomas Litilton and John Northwode, justices of the peace for the earl's part (*earle ville*) of the town of Coventry after a jury trial for 'At Coventry in the feast of the Epiphany 1450 (28 Henry VI), *vi et armis*, that is, cutlass and dagger, stealing the sum of £10 in money, the property of Henry Stone of Nothampton. After a long detention in the bishop's prison at Eccleshall' (*gaolam dicti ordinarii de Eccleshale*) John humbly desires the benefits of canonical compurgation. Proclamation has been made in the churches of Holy Trinity and St Michael the archangel,

169 See note 59.

Coventry, and in market places and neighbouring places in the city citing opposers to appear at Eccleshall prebendal church on the appointed day, that is, the Monday after the feast of St Matthew the apostle (21 September), 1451. Coventry, 7 September 1451, under the seal of the official of the archdeacon of Coventry.[170]

268. [Fo. 50v] Certificate of Thomas Byrom[171] that on the Monday after the feast of St Matthew the apostle, 1451, John Eton was admitted to canonical compurgation in the prebendal church of Eccleshall, no opposers appearing, in the presence of the following as compurgators; Peter Berdesley chaplain, John Harway chaplain, Thomas Wirley chaplain, Ralph Langford, Edward Langton, Thomas Tudor, Thomas Barbor, Ralph Henshawe, William Swyneshede, Roger Cowper, Thomas Cronage, Adam Smyth, literates and clerks.

269. Commission to Thomas Byrom, canon of Lichfield cathedral,[172] to receive the canonical compurgation of John Eton, late of Wem, Salop, mercer, in Eccleshall prebendal church on the Monday after the feast of St Matthew the apostle 1451 (as in nos 267 and 268). Eccleshall castle, 5 June 1451.

270. [Fo. 51] Assignment of a life pension of 4 marks p.a. in four equal portions to be paid in Walton church by Thomas Blakburne, now vicar of Walton, to John Iremonger, formerly vicar (*ad submovenda opbrobria etc.*). Eccleshall castle, 3 December 1451.[173]

271. [Fo. 51–v] Assignment of a life pension of 8 marks p.a. in four equal portions to be paid in Cheadle church by William Beek, now rector of Cheadle, to Mr William Hudale, formerly rector (*ad submovenda opbrobria etc.*). Eccleshall castle, 3 December 1451.[174]

272. [Fos 51v–52] 4 December 1451. Annexation and consolidation of the chantry of St Katherine in Lichfield cathedral with the chantry of the Blessed Virgin Mary in the parish church of Walton on Trent, both of which are poorly and insufficiently endowed to support a chaplain.

ANNECCIO ET CONSOLIDACIO CANTARIE IN ECCLESIA CATHEDRALIS LICHFELDENSI ET CANTARIE IN ECCLESIA PAROCHIALIS DE WALTON SUPER TRENT. Universis sancte matris ecclesie filiis ad quorum noticiam presentes lettere pervenerint Willelmus [etc.] salutem in Christo Jhesu omnium salvatore, ac fidem indubiam presentibus adhibere. Ad universitatis vestre noticiam deducimus et deduci volumus per presentes quod nos, matura deliberacione premissa et fide digno testimonio in hac parte requisito, accepimus quod cantaria sancte Katerine Virginis in ecclesia nostra cathedralis Lichfeldensi fundata, ad collacionem venerabilium confratrum nostrorum decani et capituli nostre cathedralis Lichfeldensis predicte pleno jure spectans, de se non sufficit ad plenam

---

170 See **268–269**.
171 See note 59.
172 See note 59.
173 See **218**.
174 See **116**.

exhibucionem [sic] capellani eiusdem et onerum supportacionem que ad eandem pertinent et incumbunt, nisi eidem aliquo modo aliunde succuratur; necnon in ecclesia parochiali de Walton super Trent, nostre diocesis, alia est cantaria ad altare beate Marie Virginis in eadem pro animabus domini Ricardi Waleis (quondam rectoris de Walton predicta) et omnium benefactorum suorum fundata, eciam ad collacionem eorundem confratrum nostrorum decani et capituli predictorum pertinens, vulgariter nuncupata cantaria de Walton super Trent, que ad tantam devenit pauperiem exilitatem et inopiam ut nullo modo de se suppetat ad plenam pro sacerdote ibidem in eadem celebrature, cuius valor annuus (onere reparacionis non deducto) quadraginta sex solidos et octo denarios non excedit. Ideo nos, volentes divini cultus stabile incrementum foveri ymmo (ut tenemur) et deo placere, ac ut fundatorum eorundem omniumque fidelium defunctorum animabus pocius succuratur, deum pre oculis nostris habentes, prehabitis in hac parte consensu et assensu venerabilium confratrum nostrorum decani et capituli ecclesie nostre cathedralis Lichfeldensis ac magistri Johannis Bryde, archidiaconi Derbie, et omnium quorum interest vel interesse poterit in hoc casu, juris ordine ac ceteris in hac parte requisitis in omnibus observatis, Christi nomine primitus invocato, ad honorem dei, beateque Marie Virginis genetricis sue, ac sancti Cedde episcopi et confessoris et patroni nostri, omniumque sanctorum, prefatam cantariam sancte Katerine virginis in ecclesia nostra cathedrali Lichfeldensi predicta ad altare eiusdem et cantariam vulgariter nuncupatam cantariam de Walton super Trent ad altare predicte beate Marie Virginis in ecclesia parochiali de Walton predicta fundata, ex causis premissis et aliis nos in hac parte moventibus, unimus, annectimus, incorporamus et consolidamus cum suis juribus et pertinenciis universis. Ipsum capellanum cantariarum predictarum in domino oneramus, quatinus ipse pro fundatoribus et benefactoribus earundem ac omnibus fidelibus defunctis misericordiam altitonantis devocius exoret perpetuis futuris temporibus. Insuper ordinamus et statuimus, quod capellanus cantariarum predictarum, qui nunc est et qui pro tempore fuerit, quolibet festo beate et gloriose virginis Marie singulis annis imperpetuum in ecclesia de Walton memorata ad altare prefate Marie missam celebret (seu per alium faciat celebrari) pro fundatore et ipsius cantarie et benefactoribus eiusdem sub pena t[r]esdecim solidorum et quatuor denariorum legalis monete Anglie fabrice ipsius ecclesie de Walton tociens quociens missam huiusmodi non celebraverit (vel celebrari non fecerit) applicandorum. Item volumus, ordinamus et statuimus, quod quilibet capellanus ad cantarias predictas imposterum admittendus in admissione sua, tactis per ipsum sacrosanctis dei evangeliis, corporale prestabit juramentum quod ipse ordinacionem nostram supradictam modo et forma supradictis fideliter observabit et sic faciet observari, prout capellanus qui nunc est simile prestitit coram nobis juramentum; et quod in collacione sua, institucione et admissione de huiusmodi juramento mencio fiat specialis, alioquin huiusmodi collacionem, institucionem et admissionem decernimus ipso jure fore vacuas et invalidas. In quorum omnium et singulorum testimonium atque fidem sigillum nostrum ac sigillum commune prefatorum confratrum nostrorum decani et capituli ecclesie nostre cathedralis Lichfeldensis fecimus et mandavimus hiis apponi. Datum in castro nostro de Eccleshale, quarto die mensis Decembris, anno domini millesimo CCCC^mo quinquagesimo primo, et nostre consecracionis anno quinto.

273. [Fo. 52] Indenture made between the bishop and William Smyth alias Lacemaker by which the bishop commits to Smyth for the duration of his life the custody of the bishop's hospice in the parish of St Mary outside Temple bar, London, together with the garden and the profits thereof, for an annual rent of 13s 4d at Easter and the nativity of St John the Baptist. Smyth concedes to the bishop and his successors fruits and herbs and other crops growing in the garden for the use of the bishop and his ministers providing that they are residing at the hospice. By the same indenture the bishop confirms to Smyth the lease of three tenements already held by him at an annual rent of 24s p.a. payable at the nativity of St John the Baptist, Michaelmas, Christmas, and Easter. If the payments are in arrears in part or in whole the indenture is null and void. 15 April 1452.

274. [Fo. 52v] Confirmation to William Gamull, notary, of the office of registrar and scribe in the consistory court at Lichfield with all fees and emoluments of the office.

DONACIO OFFICII SCRIBE CONSISTORII EPISCOPALIS LICHFELDENSIS. Willelmus [etc.] dilecto in Christo filio Willelmo Gamull, publico auctoritate apostolica notario, registratori scribeque nostre consistorii nostri Lichfeldensi, nostre diocesis, salutem, gratiam et benediccionem. Quia huiusmodi officium registrarii scribi nostri consistorii predicti, tibi per nos alias commissum, hactenus bene occupasti, rexisti, et laudabiliter gubernasti, ita quod ex tuo transacto regimine satis nobis datur intellegi quid de tua futura conversacione verisimiliter presumere valeamus; predictum igitur officium registrarii et scribe consistorii nostri Lichfeldensis predicti cum omnibus et singulis feodis et emolumentis eidem officio scribe et registrarii ab antiquo pertinentis, debitis et consuetis, hac presenti carta nostra tibi damus et concedimus quoadvixeris possidendum; ac te nostrum registratorem et scribam consistorii nostri Lichfeldensi predicti, librorumque et munimentorum existencium in dicto concistorio tenore presencium preficimus, ordinamus et constituimus; ad occupandum, exercendum et expediendum omnia et singula que dicto officio scribe et registrarii huiusmodi incumbere valeant seu debeant in futurum tibi plenam et liberam in domino concedimus potestatem. In cuius rei testimonium sigillum nostrum hiis apponi facimus. Datum quinto decimo die mensis Junii, anno domini millesimo CCCC^mo quinquagesimo secundo, et nostre consecracionis anno quinto.

275. Assignment of a life pension of 10 marks p.a., in two equal portions to be paid in St Paul's cathedral, London, by Mr Laurence Bothe, Lic. Leg.,[175] now canon and prebendary of Offley in Lichfield cathedral, to Thomas Pulter, formerly canon and prebendary of Offley,[176] who has resigned due to bodily weakness and loss of mind (*impotenciam and imbecillitatem*). 21 June 1452.

276. [Fo. 53v] Papal bull of Pope Nicholas V. dated at Rome 29 August 1450 confirming the recent petition of William bishop of Coventry and Lichfield, which sets out that there are, in the diocese of Coventry and Lichfield, many palaces,

---

[175] See note 52.
[176] Held by exchange from November 1449 (*Fasti* x, 48).

castles, manors, hospices, houses, and other buildings for the use of the bishop, many of which, due to the great expense to the episcopal mensa of maintaining them, have fallen into ruin. It is decreed that hereafter the following shall be deemed to be sufficient for the bishop for the purposes of habitation and for the keeping of hospitality, and shall be maintained: the palaces at Coventry and Lichfield, the castle and manor of Eccleshall, the manors of Haywood and Beaudesert, and the lodging (hospice) at Strand by the city of London. The remaining episcopal buildings in the diocese are hereby declared to be superfluous and useless, and may be destroyed and demolished, and the materials from them taken away and used elsewhere. The following documents are recited: (i) agreement to the above between the bishop and Richard Notyngham,[177] prior, and the chapter of Coventry cathedral, sealed in the chapter house at Coventry, 12 June 1448. (ii) the same between the bishop and John Verney,[178] dean of Lichfield cathedral, sealed in the chapter house at Lichfield, 15 June 1448. (iii) the confirmation of John, archbishop of Canterbury, sealed in the manor of Lambeth (*Lamhith*), 4 July 1448.[179]

[Folio 55v: blank.]

277. [Fo. 56] 11 October 1447. Following the recent visitation of Lichfield cathedral [2 October 1447] the bishop declares that the hospital of St Andrew, Denwall in Wirall, and the parish church of Burton in Wirall, annexed to the hospital and held by Mr Roger Walle,[180] archdeacon of Coventry, are compatible for the purposes of pluralism.

PRO HOSPITALI DE DENWALLE, QUOD SIT COMPATABILE. Willelmus, [etc.], universis sancte matris ecclesie filiis ad quos presentes littere pervenerunt, salutem, et fidem indubiam presentibus adhibere. Noverit universitas vestra quod cum nobis dudum visitacionem nostram ordinariam in ecclesia nostra cathedrali Lichfeldensi actualiter exercentibus, inter cetera detectum, delatum et denunciatum fuerit, quod magister Rogerus Walle, canonicus eiusdem ecclesie Lichfeldensis, hospitale sancte Andree de Denwall (nostrarum collacionis et diocesis) cum parochiali ecclesia de Burton in Wirehalle (eiusdem nostre diocesis) ab antiquo fuit et est unita, annexa et incorporata, ac archidiaconatu Coventrensi duo beneficia ecclesiastica sibi invicem (ut asserebatur) incompatibilia simul per nonnulla tempora retinuerat atque retinuit, illicite et contra canonicas sancciones. Nos deinde quod nobis in hac parte ex debito officii pastoralis incumbebat exequi volentes, tandem contra et adversus prefatum magistrum Rogerum Walle ex officio nostro rite in hac parte et legitime procedendo de et super premissis (et presertim super natura, statu et condicione predicti hospitalis) omnibusque et singulis ipsius circumstanciis diligenter inquisivimus veritatem. Et quia per inquisicionem huiusmodi probacionesque et informaciones legittimas reperimus, quod dictum hospitale a tempore et per tempus cuius inicii seu contrarii memoria

---

177 See note 56.
178 See note 79.
179 Calendared in *CPL* x, 471.
180 See note 16.

hominum non existit clericis secularibus in titulum conferri et assignari ac per eos regi et gubernari, ac cum quocumque alio beneficio ecclesiastico – eciam curato seu alias incompatibili – compatibiliter et absque quacumque dispensacione optineri et retineri, atque beneficium ecclesiasticum compatibile huiusmodi ex communi opinione et fama hominum atque communiter censeri, teneri et reputari consuevit. Nos, igitur, ex premissis et aliis veris, justis et legittimis causis nos et animum nostrum in hac parte moventibus, ad tollendum omnem dubitacionem et ambiguetatis scrupulum, circa premissa ad perpetuam rei memoriam, auctoritate nostra ordinaria et ex certa sciencia, tenore presencium, statuimus, decernimus et declaramus prefatum hospitalem sancti Andree cum (ut premittitur) dicta ecclesia de Burton fuit et est unita, annexa et incorporata, beneficium compatibile fuisse et esse, ac pro tali et ut tale censeri et reputari, atque per clericum secularem in eodem pro tempore intitulatum regi gubernari debuisse et debere, ac cum quocumque alio beneficio ecclesiastico – eciam curato vel alias incompatibili – compatibiliter et absque quacumque dispensacione obtineri et insimul retineri potuisse et posse libere et licite. In quorum omnium et singulorum fidem et testimonium premissorum presentes litteras nostras superinde fieri, nostrique sigilli fecimus appensione communiri. Datum et actum in capella palacii nostri episcopalis Lichfeldensis, undecimo die mensis Octobris, anno incarnacionis dominice millesimo quadringentesimo quadragesimo septimo, et consecracionis nostre anno primo.

LITTERA SUPER DIMISSIONE EXHUBICIONIS [sic] TITULORUM INCUMBENCIARUM PRO MAGISTRO ROGERO WALLE. Willelmus [etc.], universis et singulis sancte matris ecclesie filiis ad quos presentes littere nostre pervenerint, salutem, graciam et benediccionem. Universitati vestre notum facimus per presentes, quod cum nos nuper dictam ecclesiam nostram cathedralem Lichfeldensem jure nostro ordinario actualiter visitantes, confratrem nostrum magistrum Rogerum Walle, dicte ecclesie nostre canonicum ac prebendarium prebende de Offeley in eadem, archidiaconumque archidiaconatus Coventrensis ac magistrum sive custodem hospitalis de Denwalle una cum ecclesia de Burton in Wirehalle eidem hospitali annexa, Coventrensis et Lichfeldensis diocesis, titulos incumbenciarum suarum dictorum canonicatus et prebende ac archidiaconatus et hospitalis cum ecclesia prefata eidem annexa coram nobis exhibiturum certis die et loco fecimus evocari; quibus die et loco dictus confrater noster coram nobis sufficienter comparens, titulos dictorum canonicatus et prebende ac archidiaconatus et hospitalis cum ecclesia predicta eidem annexa nobis realiter exhibuit et sufficienter ostendit. Et quia per titulorum suorum huiusmodi recepcionem, inspeccionem et examinacionem diligentem per nos factas, dictum Rogerum Walle, confratrem nostrum, dictos canonicatum et prebendam archidiaconatum et hospitale cum prefata ecclesia de Burton eidem annexa rite et legitime ac canonice invenimus obtinuisse, retinuisse ac possidisse, ac sic obtinere, retinere et possidere debere in futuris; idcirco pro titulis ipsis et eorum sufficiencia pronunciavimus et declaravimus per decretum; ac sic pronunciamus et declaramus presencium per tenorem; ac dictum confratrem nostrum a visitacione nostra et a nostri officii impeticione, necnon ab ulteriori exhibicione et ostensione titulorum incumbenciarum suarum predictarum nobis seu officariis nostris quibuscumque occasione cuiuscumque visitacionis, inquisicionis, vocacionis ve nostre seu officiariorum nostrorum quorumcumque de cetero faciendum finaliter dimisimus et dimittimus per presentes. In cuius rei testimonium sigillum nostrum presentibus duximus apponendum. Datum in palacio nostro Lichfeldensi, undecimo die mensis Octobris, anno domini millesimo quadringentesimo quadragesimo septimo, et nostre consecracionis anno primo.

278. [Fos 56v–58v] Appropriation of the parish church of Newport, Salop, at the request of Thomas Draper, who had royal licence to found therein a college consisting of a warden priest and four chaplains to celebrate daily for the good state of Henry king of England, Humphrey duke of Gloucester, and the brethren of the gild of St Mary of Newport, Salop.

APPROPRIACIO ECCLESIE PAROCHIALIS DE NEWPORTE. Universis sancte matris ecclesie filiis ad quorum noticiam presentes littere pervenerint seu presens publicum instrumentum pervenerit Willelmus [etc.] salutem in Christo Jesu omnium salvatore ac fidem indubiam presentibus adhibere. Ad universitatis noticiam deduci volumus per presentes quod vicesimo quinto die mensis Septembris anno domini secundum cursum et computacionem ecclesie Anglicane millesimo quadragentesimo quadragesimo octavo indiccione duodecima pontificatus sanctissimi in Christo patris et domini nostri domini Nicholai divina providencia pape quinti anno secundo, coram nobis in capella principali manerii nostri de Heywode nostre diocesis judicialiter sedentibus comparuit personaliter dilectus nobis in Christo Thomas Draper de Newport dicte nostre diocesis ac quasdam litteras patentes metuendissimi in Christo principis et domini nostri domini Henrici dei gracia regis Anglie et Francie et domini Hibernie ipsius sigillo magno nobis bene noto sigillatas licenciam ipsius domini regis ad fundandum quoddam collegium de et in ecclesia parochiali de Newport predicta eidem Thome Draper graciose concessas exhibuit ac nobis realiter tradidit et liberavit, quarum tenor sequitur in hec verba: HENRICUS [etc.] omnibus ad quos presentes littere pervenerint salutem. Sciatis quod de gracia nostra speciali concessimus et licenciam dedimus pro nobis et heredibus nostris quantum in nobis est dilectis nobis in Christo abbati et conventui monasterii beate Petri Salopie quod ipsi advocacionem ecclesie parochialis de Newport in comitatu Salopie, que de nobis non tenetur in capite et que valorem decem et septem marcarum per annum non excedit ut dicitur, necnon advocaciones decimarum oblacionum proventuum et emolumentorum de villatis de Littel Aston et Michell Aston in parochia de Eggemanton, que de nobis similiter non tenetur in capite, dare et concedere possint dilecto nobis Thome Draper habendo et tenendo sibi heredibus et assignatis suis imperpetuum et eidem Thome quod ipse advocaciones predictas de predictis abbate et conventu recipere et eas tenere possit sibi heredibus et assignatis imperpetuum ut predictum est similiter licenciam dedimus specialem. Et ulterius de gracia nostra speciali concessimus et licenciam dedimus prefato Thome quod ipse ad dei laudem et beatissime virginis Marie matris sue gloriam et honorem quoddam collegium de et in dicta ecclesia parochiali de Newport in comitatu predicto ac de quadam cantaria de duobus capellanis divina singulis diebus in quadam capella ville predicte per prefatam Thomam licencia nostra sibi primitus superinde obtenta nuper constructa et fabricata imperpetuum celebraturis de uno custode sacerdote et quatuor capellanis, quorumquidem custodis et capellanorum capellam cantarie predicte sint duo divina singulis diebus in collegio predicto pro bone et salubri statu nostro et carissimi avunculi nostri Humfridi ducis Gloucestrie dum vixerimus ac fratrum et sororum fraternitatis sive gilde beate Marie in capella predicta vocata *seinte Marie gilde of Newport* pro tempore existencium et pro animabus nostris cum ab hac luce migraverimus ac anima carissimi domini et patris nostri defuncti ac animabus fratrum et sororum predictorum post eorum decessorum ac omnium aliorum fidelium defunctorum juxta ordinacionem eiusdem Thome in hac parte faciendam in collegio predicto perpetualiter celebraturi, facere erigere construere et stabilire possit quodque predicti custos et capellani collegii predicti cum sic factum erectum constructum et stabilitum fuerit custosque capellani de *seinte Marie college of Newport* pro perpetuo nominentur et nuncupentur ac pro nomine custodis et capellanorum collegii predicti in quibuscumque curiis et placitis nostris et aliorum quorumcumque in quibuscumque placitis realibus personalibus et mixtis implicare et implacitari respondere et responderi possint habeantque commune sigillum pro negociis suis peragendum, et quod quocienscumque collegium predictum de custode vacari contigerit infuturis capellani eiusdem collegii pro tempore existentes aliam personam sibi in custodem eiusdem collegii sacerdotem videlicet de tempore in tempus eligere valeant et perficere tam de sepius quam de aliis licite et impune, quo electo iidem capellani eum sic in custodem electum et factum dilecto nobis in Christo abbati monasterii beati Petri Salopie pro tempore existenti demonstrent. Et ulterius de gracia nostra speciali concessimus et licenciam dedimus pro nobis et heredibus nostris predictis prefato Thome quod ipse advocaciones predictas necnon terras tenementa et redditus, que de nobis non tenentur in capite ad valorem decem librarum per annum, quiquidem terras tenementa et redditus idem Thomas virtute licencie nostre predicte capellanis dicte cantarie pro eorum sustentacione data et assignata[181] eisdem custodi et capellanis collegii predicti dare possit et assignare habendum et tenendum sibi et successoribus suis in auxilium sustentacionis sue imperpetuum, et eisdem custodi et capellanis collegii predicti quod ipsi dictas advocaciones dicte ecclesie de Newport cantarie et decimarum oblacionam proventuum et emolumentorum predictorum una cum terris tenementis et redditibus predictis cum suis pertinenciis a prefato Thoma recipere et appropriare et ea sic appropriata in proprios usus suos tenere possint sibi et successoribus suis imperpetuum tenore presencium similiter licenciam dedimus specialem, statuto de terris et tenementis ad manum mortuam non ponendis edito non obstante, dumtamen per inquisiciones de terris tenementis et redditibus predictis capiendas et in cancellaria nostra rite retornandas sit compertum quod id fieri possit abseque dampno seu prejudicio nostri aut aliorum quorumcumque, nolentes quod predicti abbas et conventus seu successores sui aut predictus Thomam heredes vel assignati sui seu predicti custos et capellanis vel successores sui racione premissorum per nos vel heredes nostros justicios escaetores vicecomites coronatores ballivos officiarios aut alios ministros nostros vel dictorum heredum nostrorum quoscumque futuris temporibus impetantur inquietentur molestentur in aliquo seu graventur, proviso semper quod quilibet custos dicti collegii pro tempore existens curam animarum parochianorum dicte ecclesie de Newport habeat ac omnia et singula sacramenta ecclesiastica per se vel per unum capellanum dicti collegi quem idem custos ducet ad hoc deputandum eisdem parochianis de tempore in tempus debite ministrentur et fiant et quod quidem

---

[181] MS has 'dare possit et assignare'.

competens summa inter pauperes parochianos dicte ecclesie de Newport juxta formam statuti de appropriacionibus editi debita annuatim distribuantur. In cuius rei testimonium has litteras nostras fieri fecimus patentes. Teste me ipso apud Westmonasterium vicesimo nono die Marcii anno regni nostri vicesimo. Ac nobis humiliter supplicavit sepius et instanta quatinus dicti collegii fundacioni ereccioni et construccioni nostros assensum et auctoritatem probere et interponere dignaremur pariter et consensum. Nos vero perpensius attendentes qualiter et quantumcumque tam secundum et per celebre propositum prefati Thome in divini cultus cedit augmentum et incrementum manifesta, reputantes intencionem predicti Thome et causas per ipsum nobis expositas non tam racionabiles et justas quam deo placitas et ecclesie profuturas, ordinacioni fundacioni creacioni et ereccioni dicti collegii consensimus ac nostros consensum et auctoritatem eidem Thome prebuimus concessimus et interposuimus pariter et assensum. Et tunc ibidem incontinenti prefatus Thomas Draper vigore et auctoritate dictarum litterarum regiarum et regis predicti prefatisque nostris auctoritate et consensu ipsum collegium fecit erexerit fundavit et stabilivit sub ea que sequitur verborum serie: IN DEI NOMINE AMEN. Ego Thomas Draper de Newport de licencia domini regis Henrici sexti ac de expresso consensu et assensu ac auctoritate reverendi patris domini domini Willelmi Coventrensis et Lichfeldensis michi concessis et attributis, ad laudem dei et gloriose virginis Marie genetricis sue, collegium de et in ecclesia parochiali de Newport ac de quadam cantaria de duobus capellanis in quadam capella ecclesie predicte per me alias constructa et fabricata de licencia prefati domini regis de uno custode sacerdote et quatuor capellanis, quorumquidem custodis et capellanorum capellani cantarie predicte fuit et erunt duo divina singulis diebus in collegio predicto pro bono et salubri statu dicti domini Henrici sexti dum vixerit et fratrum et sororum fraternitatis sive gilde beate Marie in capella predicta vocata *Seintmarie gilde of Newport* pro tempore existencium et animabus prefati domini regis et bone memorie Humfridi nuper ducis Gloucestrie et anima Henrici quinti patris dicti domini Henrici sexti et animabus fratrum et suorum gilde predicte post eorum decessum et omnium aliorum defunctorum juxta ordinacionem meam prefati Thome Draper et statuta per me in hac parte edenda et facienda facio erigo fundo et stabilio perpetuis futuris temporibus duraturis. Insuper eidem Thome de concedendo et emendendo ordinaciones et statuta racionabilia in hac parte per vos seu successores vestros confirmanda licenciam concedimus et damus specialem presencium per tenore. Et consequenter idem Thomas nostris auctoritate et consensu statuit et ordinavit quod quociens dictum collegium vacare contigerit in futurum, abbas et conventus monasterii beati Petri Salopie alium custodem nominabunt et nobis seu successoribus nostris vel sede episcopali vacante custodi spiritualitatis eiusdem prestabunt ad huiusmodi collegium et ipsius regimen et eiusdem custodem canonice admittendum et instituendum. Quibus sic habitis et gestis, prefatus Thomas Draper quandam cartam sive licenciam donacionis et concessionis advocacionis et juris patronatus ecclesie parochialis de Newport predicte per venerabiles et religiosos viros abbatem et conventum monasterii beati Petri Salopie dicto Thome Draper factam ipsorum abbatis et conventus sigillo communi sigillatam ac aliam cartam donacionis et concessionis eiusdem advocacionis et juris patronatus eiusdem ecclesie de Newport per ipsum Thomam custodi et capellanis dicti collegii factam sigillo eiusdem Thome sigillatam exhibuit et nobis realiter liberavit, ac nobis humiliter supplicavit quatinus huiusmodi ecclesiam parochialem de Newport cum suis juribus et pertinenciis universis de consensu et licencia dicti domini nostri regis et omnium aliorum quorum interest eisdem collegio ac custodi et capellanis eiusdem incorporare unire annectere et appropriare ceteraque que nostro incumbunt officio pastorali peragere dignaremus; nosque laudabile propositum prefatorum domini nostri regis et Thome Draper pio consequi volentes effectum, ad instantem peticionem dicti Thome Draper, habito prius per nos cum venerabilibus viris priore et decano et capitulis ecclesiarum nostrarum cathedralium Coventrensis et Lichfeldensis super premissis tractatu diligenti et solempni, de ipsorum prioris et decani et capitulorum ac loci predicti archidiaconi consensu et assensu expressis, ad honorem dei et beate Marie virginis in quorum honore fundatur collegium predictum, Christi nomine primitus invocato ac solum deum oculis nostris preponentes, prehabita in hac parte licencia voluntate et consensu omnium quorum interest, juris ordine ac cetera in hac parte requisitis in omnibus observatis, prefatam ecclesiam parochialem de Newport in ecclesiam collegiatam seu collegium erecta ut prefertur ecclesiam collegiatam seu collegium beate Marie de Newport perpetuis futuris temporibus publice et communiter censandum et reputandum ac custodes et capellanos predictos imperpetuum custodem et capellanos de *Seintemarie gilde of Newport* nominandos et appellandos fore ac sic censeri reputari nominari et appellari debere pronunciamus declaramus et approbamus, ac eandem ecclesiam de Newport cum suis juribus et pertinenciis universis prefato custodi et capellanis collegii predicti et eidem collegio uninimus annectimus et appropriamus ipsamque ecclesiam de expresso consensu prefatorum abbatis et conventus monasterii beati Petri Salopie et prefati Thome Draper eisdem custodi et capellanis et ipsorum et dicti collegii in proprios usus perpetuo possidendam concedimus per decretum, eisdemque custodi habitis prius per eum ut est premissum canonicis institucione et induccione et capellanis et eorum successoribus eciam concedimus per presentes quod liceat eis per se vel eorum procuratorem legitimum dictam ecclesiam de Newport per mortem vel cessionem aut alio modo legitimo qualitercumque vacantem eaodem ecclesiam et ejus possessionem juriumque et pertinenciis suorum universorum ingredi et ipsam possessionem apprehendere et nancisci et eciam libere et licite retinere et continuare fructusquoque redditus et proventus eiusdem ecclesie et eidem qualitercumque pertinentes sive spectantes percipere et habere ac de eisdem ad opus et utilitatem eorum et dicti collegii disponere et distribuere nostra seu alterius cuiuscumque licencia seu auctoritate ad hoc non petita vel obtenta licenciam et auctoritatem imperpetuum. Et quia ex premissis unione et appropriacione nobis et ecclesiis nostris cathedralibus Coventrensi et Lichfeldensi ac loci archidiacono multa et varia incommoda pervenire possint in futurum, volumus statuimus decernimus et ordinamus quod in debitam recompencionem dampnorum et incommodorum huiusmodi custos et capellani predicti collegii quicumque pro tempore existentes nobis et successoribus nostris Coventrensis et Lichfeldensis episcopis duodecim denarios et archidiacono loco predicti sex denerios nomine indempnitatis huiusmodi ad festum sancti Michaelis archangeli singulis annis imperpetuum solvere teneantur, quasquidem pensiones racione indempnitatis predicte dicto termino ut prefertur solvendas per quascumque censuras ecclesiasticas exigi volumus et levari, dictique collegii custodem et socios capellanos eiusdem pro tempore existentes ad solucionem summarum huiusmodi racione indempnitatis predicte compelli et artari pronunciamus decernimus et declaramus. Volumus insuper et statuimus quod custos quiscumque dicti collegii post dicte ecclesie possessionem adeptam et dicti collegii capellani curam habeant animarum parochionarum eiusdem de Newport et parochianis eiusdem sacramenta et sacramentalia ecclesiastica quecumque per se vel unum capellanum dicti collegii per custodem assignandum ministrare teneantur, dictique custos et capellani [Fo. 58] duos solidos de bonis dicte ecclesie infra octo dies post festum annuniciacionis beate Marie virginis inter pauperes parochianos eiusdem eccleqie annuatim distribuere et erogare teneantur et quod sic distribuant perpetuis temporibus in futurum. Tenores vero dictarum litterarum regiarum cartarum sive litterarum prefatorum abbatis et conventus monasterii sancti Petri Salopie necnon litterarum concessionis dicti Thome de quibus supra sic mencio sequintur et sunt tales: OMNIBUS Christi fidelibus ad quos presens scriptum pervenerit Thomas abbas monasterii beati Petri Salopie et eiusdem loci conventus salutem in domino sempiternam. Cum serenissimus princeps et dominus noster rex nunc per litteras suas patentes quarum datum est apud Westmonasterium vicesimo nono die Marcii anno regni sui vicesimo licenciam suam pro se et heredibus suis nobis concessit quod advocacionem nostram ecclesie parochialis de Newport in comitatu Salopie que de domino rege non tenetur in capite et que valorem decem et septem marcarum per annum non excedit, dare et concedere possimus dilecto nobis Thome Draper habendum et tenendum sibi heredibus et assignatis suis imperpetuum, et eidem Thome Draper quod ipse advocacionem de nobis huiusmodi abbate et conventu recipere possit et tenere sibi heredibus et assignatis suis imperpetuum, et quod ipse Thomas Draper ad dei laudem et beatissime virginis Marie matris sue quoddam collegium de et in dicta ecclesia parochiali de Newport ac de quadam cantaria de duobus capellanis divina singulis diebus in quadam capella ecclesie predicte per prefatum Thomam Draper licencia dicti domini nostri regis primitus superinde sibi obtenta nuper constructa et fabricata imperpetuum celebraturis de uno custode sacerdote et quatuor capellanis, quorum capellani dicte cantarie sint duo divina singulis diebus in collegio predicto juxta ordinacionem prefati Thome Draper in hac parte faciendum perpetualiter celebraturo, facere erigere construere et stabilire possit, prout in eisdem litteris patentibus dicti domini nostri regis inde confectis plenius continetur: SCIATIS quod nos predicti abbas et conventus patroni ecclesie predicte de licencia regia nobis in hac parte sufficienter ut premittitur attributa et ad intencionem in regiis litteris patentibus supranominatis descripta dedimus concessimus et hac presenti scripto nostro confirmavimus ac pro nobis et successoribus nostris quantum in nobis est damus concedimus et confirmavimus per presentes prefato Thome Draper advocacionem nostram predicte ecclesie parochialis de Newport predicte et jus patronatus eiusdem habendum et tenendum predictam advocacionem et jus patronatus ecclesie predicte prefato Thome Draper heredibus et assignatis suis imperpetuum de capitalibus dominis feodi illius per servicia inde debita et de jure consuetis, et nos predicte abbas et conventus et successores nostri predicti advocacionem et jus patronatus ecclesie predicte prefato Thome Draper heredibus et assignatis suis contra omnes gentes warrantizabimus et defendemus imperpetuum. In cuius rei tesimonium hinc presenti scripto nostro sigillum nostrum commune apposuimus, hiis testibus: Phillipo Yong Ricardo Colet Willelmo Glover Ricardo Offeley Thoma Salter et aliis. Datum in domo nostra capitulari vicesimo die mensis Februarii anno domini millesimo quadragentesimo quadragesimo septimo et anno regni regis Henrici sexti post conquestum vicesimo sexto. SCIANT presentes et futuri quod ego

Thomas Draper patronus ecclesie parochialis de Newport in comitatu Salopie ex licencia speciali serenissimi in Christo principis et domini nostri domini Henrici sexti dei gracia regis Anglie et Francie et domini Hibernie illustris, prout per ipsius domini nostri regis litteras quarum datum est apud Westmonasterium vicesimo nono die Marcii anno regni sui vicesimo inde confectas plenius patet, michi graciose concessa et in hac parte sufficienter obtenta dedi concessi et hac presenti carta mea indentata confirmavi dilectis michi in Christo custodi collegi in ecclesia parochiali de Newport in comitatu Salopie ac capellanis eiusdem collegii advocacionem ecclesie parochialis de Newport predicte cum suis juribus et pertinenciis universis, habendum et tenendum predictam advocacionem cum suis juribus et pertinenciis universis prefatis custodi et [Fo. 58v] capellanis collegii predicti et successoribus suis in puram et perpetuam elemosinam pro divinis servicis et obsequiis secundum ordinacionem mei prefati Thome Draper heredum et executorum meorum ibidem faciendum et celebrandum et pro dotacione collegii predicti ac sustentacione custodis et capellanorum eiusdem collegii et successorum ibidem existencium imperpetuum. In cuius rei testimonium hinc presenti carte indentate sigillum meum apposui, hiis testibus Phillipo Yong Ricardo Colet Willelmo Glover Ricardo Offeley Thoma Salter et aliis. Datum apud Newport xx° die mensis Septembris anno domini millesimo CCCC^mo quadragesimo octavo et regni regis Henrici sexti vicesimo septimo. In quorum omnium et singulorum fidem et testimonium has litteras nostras fieri fecimus patentes quas per notarium publicum subscriptam scribam nostram in hac parte subscribi fecimus ac ipsius signo et nomine solitis signari nostrique sigilli appensione fecimus communiri. Data et acta sunt hec omnia et singula prout suprascribuntur et recitantur sub anno domini indiccione pontificatu mensis die et loco predictis, presentibus venerabilibus viris magistris Gregorio Newport canonico ecclesie cathedralis Lichfeldensis et Thoma Lye cononico ecclesie collegiate sancti Cedde Salopie dicte Coventrensis et Lichfeldensis diocesis testibus ad premissa vocatis specialiter et rogatis.

Et ego Willeimus Brande clericus Coventrensis et Lichfeldensis diocesis publicus auctoritate apostolica notarius premissarum litterarum presentacioni dictique Thome Draper supplicacioni prefati collegii ereccioni et fundacioni necnon prefate ecclesie parochialis de Newport translacioni et commutacioni in ecclesiam collegiatam eiusdem quoque ecclesie parochialis unioni et appropriacioni ceterisque omnibus et singulis, dum sic ut premittitur sub anno domini indiccione pontificatu mense die et loco predictis coram dicto reverendo patre domino episcopo et per eum agebantur et fiebant, una cum pronominatis testibus presens interfui eaque omnia et singula sic fieri vidi et audivi, ac aliunde occupatus per alium scribi feci publicavi et in hanc publicam formam redigi signoque et nomine meis signari rogatus et requisitus in fidem et testimonium omnium et singulorum premissorum. Et constat michi notario predicto de suprascripcione istius diccionis filiis supra prima linea et eciam de rasura istarum duarum diccionum manerii de Heywode in secunda linea, et eciam de interlinariis istius diccionis divina supra nomina et supra guadragesima septima lineas a capite processus presentis computandas, quos defectus approbo ego notarius antedictus.[182]

---

[182] The remainder of fo. 58v is blank.

279. [Fos 59–60] 30 October 1449. Appropriation of the parish church of Great Nesse (Nesse Straunge) to the monastery of St Peter, Salop, O.S.B., in order that a chantry may be erected in the conventual church from the fruits of the said church for a monk to celebrate daily for the soul of King Henry V, who had intended in his lifetime to found a chantry in the said conventual church to St Winifred the virgin, whom he venerated and whose relics are kept in the said conventual church. His intention, frustrated by his death, is completed by King Henry VI.[183]

APPROPRIACIO ECCLESIE PAROCHIALIS DE NESSE STRAUNGE. Universis sancte matris ecclesie filiis presentes litteras inspecturis seu quod presens tangit negocium Willelmus [etc.] salutem in Christo Jesu omnium salvatore et fidem indubiam presentibus adhibere. Quia ut accepimus et satis luculenter informamur excellentissimus in Christo princeps dominus Henricus dei gracia rex Anglie et Francie post conquestum quintus dum egit in humanis salutis anime sue memoris ad laudem omnipotentis dei et gloriose virginis Wenefrede quamplurimum venerabatur in terris, unam cantariam in ecclesie conventuali sancti Petri Salopie ordinis sancti Benedicti nostre diocesis de uno capellano seculari vel religioso divina celebraturus perpetuis futuris temporibus fundare et perpetuare firmiter proponebat, set antequam ad rei exitum suam intencionem finire potuerit mors amara ipsum tulit de medio, sed excellentissimus rex noster modernus filius et heres prefati domini Henrici regis quinti perpendens memorati patris sui devotam voluntatem sic ut est premissum minime fore completam, ipsam deducere peroptatum, inter alia carta confirmacionis sue magistro Thoma Ludlowe sacre pagine professori abbati et conventui monasterii sancti Petri Salopie contenta ut ipsi abbas et conventus ecclesiam parochialem de Nesse ipsis et eorum monasteri appropriare et unire ad effectum quod huiusmodi cantaria de fructibus et proventibus eiusdem erigatur et fundatur imperpetuum duraturam licenciam dedit et concessit sub ea que sequitur verborum series: quia dominus Henricus dominus nuper rex Anglie pater noster defunctus in vita sua ad laudem et honorem dei et gloriose virginis Wenefrede unum capellanum religiosum sive secularem perpetuum, qui ad altare dicte virginis in abbathia predicta singulis diebus divina pro anima ipsius patris nostri heredum et successorum suorum celebraret, devote proponebat et intendebat ordinasse quod antequam migravit non complevit, ut ex relacione predictorum abbatis et conventus certitudinaliter accepimus; nos piam et devotam intencionem predicti patris nostri effectui debito mancipari cupientes, et ut prefati abbas et conventus et successores sui firmiter teneantur unam personam ydoneam in commonachum ipsorum abbatis et conventus ultra suum numerum ante hec tempore consuetum accipere et acceptare et in eundem conventum admittere, qui pro salubri statu nostro dum vixerimus et pro anima prefati patris nostri ac pro anima nostra cum ab hac luce migraverimus et animabus heredum et successorum nostrorum et omnium fidelium defunctorum divina ad altare predictum de die in diem perpetuis futuris temporibus celebret, ad dictam intencionem prefati patris nostri perimplendum concessimus et licenciam dedimus pro nobis heredibus et successoribus nostris eisdem abbati et conventui et successoribus suis quod ipsi ecclesiam de Nesse Strange Coventrensis et Lichfeldensis diocesis que ad advocacionem et patronatum ipsorum abbatis et

[183] For the institution to the vicarage here see **183**.

conventus existit et que ad decem libras per annum taxatur, appropriare et eam sic appropriatam in proprios usus tenere possint sibi et successoribus suis in auxilium sustentacionis dicti commonachi pro statu et animabus predictis in forma predicta celebraturi in liberam puram et perpetuum elemosinam statuto de terris et tenementis ad manum mortuam non ponendis edite non obstante, proviso semper quod vicaria in ecclesia predicta sufficienter dotetur et debita pars fructuum et proventuum eiusdem inter pauperes parochianos ibidem annuatim distribuatur secundum ordinaciones et statuta inde edita ordinata. Unde ex parte eorundem abbatis et conventus nobis extitit humiliter supplicatum quatinus ex causis premissis prefatam ecclesiam de Nesse eis et eorum successoribus ac monasterio predicto unire annectere et incorporare ac in ipsorum proprios usus occasione premissa perpetuo possidendum concedere dignaremur. Unde nos Willelmus episcopus supradictus, quia per inquisicionem auctoritate nostra in hac parte rite et legitime captam et alias probaciones et informaciones legitimas comperimus et invenimus evidenter premissa fore notaria atque vera, parte prefatorum abbatis et conventus coram nobis legitime comparente ac pronunciacionem nostram super premissis interponi et fieri cum instancia debita humiliter supplicante et petente, habito per nos cum venerabilibus viris priore ecclesie nostre cathedralis Coventrensis ac decano ecclesie nostre cathedralis Lichfeldensis capitulisque earundem super hiis tractatu diligenti et solempni, ac de ipsorum prioris et decani et capitulorum necnon archidiaconi Salopie infra cuius archidiaconatus ambitum situatur ecclesia predicta consensu voluntate et assensu, ad honorem dei et prefate beate virginis Wenefrede cuius reliquie in ecclesie eorum conventuali predicta notorie sunt recondite, Christi nomine primitus invocato ac solum deum oculis nostris proponentes, juris ordine in hac parte ac ceteris de jure requisitis in omnibus observatis, causas premissas ad appropriacionem dicte ecclesie parochialis de Nesse prefatis abbati et conventui ac eciam eorum monasterio faciendam justas legitimas sufficientes et congruas fuisse et esse pronunciavimus declaravimus ac sic pronunciamus et declaramus per presentes, et prefatam ecclesiam parochialem de Nesse cum suis juribus et pertinenciis universis auctoritate nostra ordinaria prelibatis abbati et conventui et eorum monasterio unimus annectimus et approbamus et in ipsorum usus proprios ex causis premissis perpetuo possidendos concedimus per presentes, eisdemque abbati et conventui et eorum successoribus licenciam et facultatem imperpetuum quod liceat eis per se vel procuratorem suum legitimum ecclesiam parochialem de Nesse sepedictam vacantem et ejus possessionem apprehendere et nancisci ac eam libere et licete retinere et continuare fructusque redditus et proventus eiusdem percipere et habere et de eisdem ad usum eorum ac dicti monasterii prefateque cantarie sustentacionem et monachi eidem cantarie futuri exhibicione disponere et distrubuere licencia nostra seu successorum nostrorum et dicti loci archidiaconi aliter minime petita vel obtenta, porcione tamen congrua vicarii perpetui in eadem ecclesiam auctoritate nostra ad presentacionem prefatorum abbatis et conventus in dicta ecclesia instituendi introducendi imponendi et inducendi imposterum per nos legitime limitanda semper excepta. Cantariam insuper memoratam sic duximus in ecclesia conventuali predicta fore celebrandum, videlicet quod monachus presbyter de conventu predicto ebdomadatim tabulatur sive intituletur qui missas singulis diebus ad altare sancte virginis Wenefrede predicte juxta feretrum eiusdem situatum celebrabit seu per alium celebrari faciet pro salubri statu domini regis moderni ac pro anima prefati domini Henrici regis patris sui et pro anima dicti domini regis nunc cum ab hac luce migraverit et pro animabus heredum et successorum suorum ac animabus omnium fidelium defunctorum perpetuis futuris temporibus duraturis. Et pro remuneracione sua percipiat monachus huiusmodi celebraturus singulis ebdomadis duos solidos de fructibus et proventibus ecclesie memorate de Nesse per manus precentoris dicti monasterii qui pro tempore fuerit imperpetuum fideliter persolvendum. Et ad observanda prefatam cantariam bene et fideliter et premittitur singulis temporibus futuris abbas predictus et singuli conmonachi et confratres dicti monasterii qui nunc sunt ac singuli monachi et confratres in futuris admittendi seu recipiendi in eodem in professione sua corporale prestabunt juratum ad sancte dei evangelia per ipsos corporaliter tacta.

PENSIONES DOMINI EPISCOPI ECCLESIE CATHEDRALIS LICHFELDENSIS ET ARCHIDIACONI SALOPIE DE ECCLESIA DE NESSE STRAUNGE. Et quia ex predictis unione et appropriacione nobis ac successoribus nostris Coventrensi et Lichfeldensi episcopis ac ecclesiis nostris Coventrensis et Lichfeldensis necnon archidiacono Salopie plura et varia incommoda pervenire verisimiliter poterint in futuris, volumus statuimus et decernimus quod in debitam recompensacionem dampnorum et incommodorum huiusmodi prefati abbas et conventus nobis Willelmo episcopo predicto ac successoribus nostris Coventrensis et Lichfeldensis episcopis tresdecim solidos et quatuor denarios priorique et capitulo ecclesie nostre cathedralis Coventrensis sex solidos quatuor denarios ac decano et capitulo ecclesie nostre cathedralis Lichfeldensis sex solidos quatuor denarios necnon archidiacono loci tres solidos quatuor denarios in festo sancti Michaelis archangeli singulis annis futuris imperpetuum solvere teneantur, quasquidem pensiones racione indempnitatis predicte termino predicto ut premittitur solvendum per quascumque censuras ecclesiasticas exigi et levari volumus prefatosque abbatem et conventum monasterii sancti Petri predicti ad solucionem summarum huiusmodi racione indempnitatis predicte compelli et coartari decernimus insuper et ordinamus. Volumus eciam et declaramus ac abbati et conventui sepedictis imponimus quod ipsi de fructibus et proventibus dicte ecclesie de Nesse eis pertinentibus inter pauperes parochianos eiusdem ecclesie magis indigentes sex solidos et octo denarios infra mensem post festum annunciacionis beate Marie singulis annis futuris imperpetuum distribui et persolvi faciant cum effectu, premissaque omnia et singula modo et forma premissis recitat pronunciamus decernimus et diffinimus perpetuis futuris temporibus inviolabiliter observari. In quorum omnium et singulorum testimonium atque fidem sigillum nostrum presentibus apponi et has litteras nostras signo et subscripcione magistri Willelmi Brande clerici notarii publici scribe nostri in hac parte assumpti fecimus communiri. Data et acta sunt hec omnia et singula prout suprascribuntur et recitantur per nos Willelmum episcopum supradictum in capella nostra principali infra manerium nostrum de Heywode situata penultimo dio mensis Octobris anno domini millesimo CCCC^{mo} quadragesimo nono et nostre consecracionis anno tercio indiccione vero terciadecima sanctissimi in Christo patris et domini nostri domini Nicholai divina providencia papa quinti anno tercio, presentibus tunc ibidem venerabilibus viris magistris Johanne Reedhill et Thoma Lye canonicis ecclesie nostre collegiate sancti Cedde Salopie testibus ad premissa vocatis specialiter et rogatis. W. Brande. Constat. de interlinatur instarum diccionum in festo sancti Michaelis de rasura.

Et ego Willelmus Brande clericus Coventrensis et Lichfeldensis diocesis publicus auctoritate apostolica notarius prefate ecclesie de Nesse appropriacioni unioni et annexioni ac cantarie predicte ordinacioni et decreto ceterisque omnibus et singulis premissis, dum sic ut premittitur sub anno domini indiccione pontificatu mensis die et loco predictis coram dicto reverendo domino episcopo et per eum agebantur et fiebant, una cum pronominatis testibus presens personaliter interfui eaque omnia et singula sic fieri vidi et audivi scripsique et publicavi et in hanc formam redegi signoque et nomine meis solitis et consuetis ex mandato dicti reverendi patris una cum sigillo eiusdem signavi ac me hic subscripsi rogatus et requisitus in fidem et testimonium premissorum. Et constat michi notario predicto de interlinio istarum duarum diccionum patris sepedictam supra IX et XXV lineas a capite computando, quos defectus approbo ego notarius predictus, necnon de interliniacie istarum litteras nostras supra quarta linea a pede huiusmodi instrumenti computanda, quem defectum approbo ego notarius predictis.[184]

280. [Fos 61–63v] Appropriation of the parish church of Mancetter (*Mancestr*), now vacant, to the abbot and convent of the Cistercian house of Merevale (*Miravalle*), whose petition for the appropriation sets out that Thomas Arblaster senior and Alice his wife, Anne who was sometime the wife of Thomas Porter esq, Robert Armeburgh esq, Clement Draper, Joan who was sometime wife of William Harper, Ralph Holte and Eleanor his wife, have granted to the abbot and convent of Merevale the advowson of the church of Mancetter with a view to its appropriation, and that the fruits given to the monastery at its original foundation have decreased because of the barrenness of lands, flood, the dearth of cultivators, and the fewness of their servants on account of their excessive wages and other misfortunes, and that the house is much burdened with hospitality (*per terrarum sterilitatem aquarum inundaciones colonorum raritatem servicium paucitatem ob immoderata et excessiva eorum stipendia et alios casus fortuitos in tantum decreverint et inofficiatus fuit et diminut necnon hospitalitate*). The bishop, sitting in tribunal, having summoned Mr Roger Walle, archdeacon of Coventry,[185] and others concerned, examined the witnesses and other proofs produced by the abbot and convent, and the royal licence of King Henry VI for the appropriation having been issued, has appropriated the church to the abbot and convent and their successors. The appropriators are to endow a perpetual vicarage in the parish which the bishop assigns at 16 marks p.a., payable at the four terms of the year, that is, Easter, nativity of St John the Baptist, Michaelmas and Christmas. The first collation to the vicarage is reserved to the bishop, thereafter the abbot and convent shall present. The appropriators shall build at their own expense within two years a suitable manse for the vicar and his successors. The following pensions are reserved: to the bishop of Coventry and Lichfield and his successors 13s 4d; to the cathedral churches of Coventry and Lichfield 13s 4d each; to the archdeacon of Coventry 4s 4d payable at Michaelmas. The sum of 3s 4d in alms is to be distributed among the poor parishioners annually within a week after Lady Day at the discretion of the vicar and the churchwardens. The following documents are recited: (i) The charter of the patrons, as above, conceding to the abbot and convent the advowson of the church of Mancetter together with one acre of land, a parcel of the manor of Mancetter, as

184 The remainder of fo. 60r is blank. The whole of fo. 60v is blank.
185 See note 16.

glebe. Dated 25 November 1449 in the presence of William Ferrers knight, lord of Chartley, Richard Bagot, Robert Aston, William Newport esquires, William Cumberforde 'gentilman', and others. (ii) Letters patent (a royal licence for the grant in mortmain), tested at Westminster 20 November 1449. (iii) Letters of the abbot and convent of Merevale dated in the chapter house at Merevale, 12 December 1449, appointing Mr John Thurstan, B. Dec , Robert Kente, LL.B., and John Athureston, as proctors in the negotiations. (iv) Letters of Thomas Lyseux, dean and canon of St cathedral, London, keeper of the spiritualities, sede vacante, approving the negotiations so far as they affect his church. London, 26 January 1450. Dated 29 January 1450, in the dwelling house of Mr Laurence Bothe, canon residentiary of St Paul's cathedral, London,[186] in the presence of Mr John Thurstan, archdeacon of Colchester, Richard Hall, D. Dec., and Robert Kente, LL.B. (Canterbury, London, and Lincoln dioceses). Notarial attestation of William Brande, notary, scribe (Coventry and Lichfield diocese).[187]

281. [Fos 64–67v] Appropriation of the parish church of Prescot (*Prestcote*), Lancashire, to the college of the Blessed Virgin Mary and St Nicholas [King's College], Cambridge (Ely diocese), by Mr George Radclyff,[188] D. Dec., treasurer of Lichfield cathedral, John Wendesley, B. Dec., archdeacon of Stafford,[189] and Gregory Newport, appointed as commissaries by William, bishop of Coventry and Lichfield, by letters, recited, dated at Strand, London, 16 December 1447 (*quia aliis arduis negociis regem et regnum ac ecclesias nostras predictas concernentibus taliter sumus et verisimiliter erimus prepediti quod circa expedicionem negocii predicti attendere non possumus*). The commissaries, with the consent of the chapters of the cathedral churches at Coventry and Lichfield, and of the archdeacon of Chester, having examined the witnesses and other proofs produced by the appropriators, and the licence of King Henry VI having been issued for the appropriation, have appropriated the church to the provost and scholars of the said college who may enter into and take possession of the church, vacant by the consecration (*per munus consecracionis*) of William Bothe as bishop of Coventry and Lichfield. The appropriators are to endow a perpetual vicarage within the parish with a sufficient portion for the support of the vicar and his successors to be assigned by the bishop. The following pensions are reserved: to the bishop of Coventry and Lichfield and his successors, 13s 4d p.a., and to the archdeacon of Coventry 6s 8d p.a. payable at Michaelmas. The sum of 10s in alms is to be distributed annually among the poor parishioners within one month following Lady Day at the discretion of the vicar and the provost of the said college. The following documents are recited: (i) Letters patent under the seal of the duchy of Lancaster dated at Westminster 6 August 1444, conceding to the provost and college the advowson of the church of Prescot, subject to the usual provisions, the Statute of Mortmain notwithstanding; (ii) Letters patent under the great seal dated at Westminster 6 November 1445 confirming the above; (iii) Letters of the prior and convent of Coventry cathedral dated in the chapter house, Coventry, 3 January 1448 appointing Roger Felford and Thomas Northbrig,

---

186 See note 52.
187 See **44**. The remainder of folio 63v is blank.
188 See note 11.
189 See note 144.

monks, and Mr John Jolyff, canon of Lichfield cathedral,[190] and Mr John Twyss, LL.B. as proctors in the negotiations; (iv) Letters of the dean and chapter of Lichfield cathedral, dated in the chapter house, Lichfield, 22 December 1447, appointing Mr Thomas Chestrefeld and Mr John Jolyff, canons residentiary of Lichfield cathedral, as proctors in the negotiations; (v) Letters of Mr John Burdett, B. Dec., archdeacon of Chester,[191] dated at London, 12 December 1447, appointing Mr John Wendesley and Mr John Jolyff, canons of Lichfield cathedral, as proctors in the negotiations; (vi) Letters of John Chedworth, provost of the college of the Blessed Virgin Nary and St Nicholas, Cambridge, dated at Cambridge, 8 October 1447, appointing Mr Nicholas Cloos, S.T.P., William Brig, Thomas Decon, John More, and John Brokenhawe, clerks, as proctors for the college in the negotiations. Dated 16 January 1448 in the consistory at Lichfield under the seal of the official of the consistory. Present: Mr William Calton, notary public, and William Brand, clerk, Coventry and Lichfield diocese. Notarial attestation of William Gamull, Coventry and Lichfield diocese. Ratification of the above by William, bishop of Coventry and Lichfield, dated at Haywood, 1 October 1448.[192]

282.   [Fo. 68–v] 2 October 1448. Instrument endowing a vicarage at Prescot, Lancashire, which has been recently appropriated to the college of the Blessed Virgin Mary and St Nicholas, Cambridge (Ely diocese), and to which the provost and scholars of the said college have presented Mr Ralph Dukworth, S.T.P.

DOTACIO VICARIE DE PRESTCOTE. Universis sancte matris ecclesie filiis ad quos presentes littere pervenerint et quos infrascripta tangunt seu tangere poterint in futurum Willelmus [etc.] salutem [etc.] ac fidem indubiam presentibus adhibere. Ad universitatis vestre noticiam deduci volumus per presentes quod venerabiles viri prepositus et scolares collegii regalis beate Marie et sancti Nicholai de Cantabrigia Eliensis diocesis proprietarii ecclesie parochialis de Prestcote nostre diocesis ad vicariam perpetuam eiusdem ecclesie eis nuper per commissarios nostros in hac parte sufficienter deputatos legitime appropriate venerabilem virum magistrum Radulphum Dukworth sacre theologie professorem nobis rite et legitime presentarunt, congrua[193] porcione de decimis fructibus et proventibus ecclesie predicte pro ipsius et successorem suorum victu et vestitu ac onerum eidem incumbencium supportacione primitus assignata, per nos canonice admittendum et instituendum in eadem; nosque volentes sustentacioni vicarie predicte ecclesie cuiuscumque in futurum ut tenemur canonice providere, porcionem vicarii eiusdem limitamus assignamus in et de decimis oblacionibus fructibus et obvencionibus eiusdem ecclesie inferius declaratis, ac huiusmodi decimas oblaciones fructus et proventus infrascriptos dicte ecclesie vicario cuicumque in futurum existenti et ipsius porcioni de voluntate consensu et assensu expressis predictorum prepositi et scolarium proprietoriorum predictorum et predicti vicarii

---

[190]   Prebendary of Dasset Parva, admitted 17 May 1435, died before 8 August 1455 (*Fasti* x, 31).
[191]   Collated 6 March 1433. Died before 26 April 1449 (*Fasti* x, 13).
[192]   See **282.** The remainder of folio 67v is blank.
[193]   MS has 'presentarunt ad ipsam perpetuam vicariam congrua'.

pertinere et spectare debere pronunciamus decernimus et declaramus, videlicet feni totius parochie de Prestcote predicti. Item dicte ecclesie vicarius quiscumque percipiet et habebit decimas molendinorum bosci et subbosci agistamentorum piscariarum agnorum lane vaccarum bovum vitulorum pullorum porcellorum aucarum collumbarum apiariorum cignorum canabi lini allei ceparum herbarum pomorum et fructuum quorumcumque ac omnes alias decimas minutas cum omnibus oblacionibus et decimis personalibus ac mortuariis quibuscumque. Item volumus ordinamus et decernimus quod prepositus et scolares proprietorii supradicti infra duos annos proximo jam futuris ordinabunt seu ordinari et edificari facient dicte ecclesie vicario cuicumque in futuris unam mansionem sive habitacionem decentem et competentem pro se et familiaribus suis in loco congruo et eminenti infra parochia dicte ecclesie et prope eandem. Item dicti proprietorii subibunt onus reparandi cancelli ecclesie parochialis de Prestcote predicte. Item dicte ecclesie vicarius reparabit capellam de Farneworth si et quatenus reparaciones eiusdem ab antiquo pertinebant ad rectorem ecclesie de Prestcote predicte et eiusdem ecclesie vicarius erit exoneratus a solucione decimarum seu alicuius partis vel quote earum alicuius subsidii si forte talia pape aut regi seu episcopo solvi contigerit in futuris. Item dicte ecclesie vicarius inveniet omnes capellanos infra parochiam dicte ecclesie debite inveniendos ac visitacionem episcopi Coventrensis et Lichfeldensis cum ipsum visitare contigerit et visitacionem archidiaconi Cestr' singulis annis fieri consuetam subibit, et agnoscet procuraciones racione visitacionum predictarum debitas et solvi consuetas una cum synodalibus et indempnitatibus tresdecim solidorum et octo denariorum archidiacono Cestr' singulis annis racione appropriacionis ecclesie de Prestcote predicte solvendis realiter solvet cum effectum, et alia jura tam episcopalia quam archidiaconalia per dicte ecclesie rectorem solvi consueta vicarius ecclesie de Prestcote supradicte et successores sui supportabunt. In quorum omnium fidem et testimonium sigillum nostrum presentibus litteris nostris apponi fecimus una cum subscripcione magistri Willelmi Brand notarii publici scribe nostri in hac parte assumpti in fidem premissorum. Datum in manerio nostro de Heywode secundo die mensis Octobris anno domini millesimo quadragentesimo quadragesimo octavo et nostre consecracionis anno secundo.

Et ego Willelmus Brande clericus Coventrensis et Lichfeldensis diocesis publicus auctoritate apostolica notarius premissis assignacioni et limitacioni porcionis vicarii predicti ceterisque omnibus et singulis, dum sic ut premittitur sub anno domini mense die et loco predictis indiccione vero unodecima pontificatus sanctissimi in Christo patris et domini nostri domini Nicholai divina providencia pape quinti anno secundo coram dicto reverendo patre domino episcopo et per eum agebantur et fiebant, presentibus discretis domino Thome Wolsall presbytero et Ricardo Croke literato dicte Coventrensis et Lichfeldensis diocesis testibus ad premissa vocatis specialiter et rogatis, presens personaliter interfui eaque omnia et singula sic fieri vidi et audivi, ac aliunde occupatus per alium scribi feci publicavi et in hanc publicam formam de mandato reverendi patris redegi signoque et nomine meis solitis una cum sigillo dicti reverendi patris signavi et communivi rogatus et requisitus in fidem et testimonium premissorum.

283. [Fos 68v–71v] Appropriation of the parish church of Leigh (*Leght*), Lancashire, now vacant, to the prior and convent of the Augustinian house of Arbury (*Erdebury*), whose petition for the appropriation sets out that William, lord of Lovell, Burnell and Holland, whose ancestor Ralph Botiller, knight, baron of Sudeley and treasurer of England, founded the monastery, had granted the said monastery the advowson of the church of Leigh with a view to its appropriation, and that the fruits of the monastery given at its original foundation and endowment have decreased because of the barrenness of the lands, floods, the dearth of cultivators and the fewness of their servants on account of their excessive wages, and other misfortunes, and that the house is much burdened with hospitality (as in 280). The bishop, sitting in tribunal in the chapel of the castle of Eccleshall, with the consent of all the parties concerned, and the licence of King Henry VI for the appropriation having been issued, has appropriated the church to the said monastery, saving the right of Hugh de Lawe to a tenement lately held of the bishop when he was rector of Leigh (*salvo tenemento quod Hugo de Lawe nuper de nobis tenuit dum rector sumus*). The appropriators are to endow a perpetual vicarage in the parish which the bishop assigns at 16 marks p.a. payable at the festivals of the nativity of St John the Baptist, Michaelmas, Christmas and Lady Day, with the aforesaid tenement. The first collation to the vicarage is reserved to the bishop, thereafter the prior and convent shall present. The appropriators shall build at their own expense within a year a suitable manse for the vicar and his successors. The following pensions are reserved: to the bishop of Coventry and Lichfield and his successors, 6s 8d, and to the archdeacon of Chester, 3s 4d, annually at Michaelmas. The sum of 6s 8d in alms is to be distributed among the poor parishioners annually within fifteen days after Lady Day at the discretion of the vicar and the church wardens (*custodum bonorum eiusdem ecclesie*). The following documents are recited: (i) Letters patent tested at Westminster 13 April 1445, a licence for the prior and convent of Arbury, of the foundation of the king's knight Ralph Botiller, baron and lord of Sudeley, and of his patronage, poorly endowed and impoverished and burdened through the improvident government of late priors so that divine service and the number of canons is diminished, to acquire in mortmain rents and advowsons to the annual value of 100 marks without fee or fine; (ii) Letters patent tested at Westminster 26 November 1447, a licence for the grant in mortmain to the prior and convent of Arbury of one acre of land a parcel of the manor of Westleigh, and the advowson of the church of Leigh subject to the usual provisos; (iii) Letters patent under the seal of the duchy of Lancaster 16 November 1447, as above; (iv) Charter of William, lord of Lovell, Burnell and Holland, conceding to William Catton, prior of Arbury, and the convent of the same, one acre of land a parcel of the manor of Westleigh and the advowson of the church of Leigh. Westleigh, 20 August 1447. Present; Geoffrey Shakerley esq, Gilbert Hilton, Thurstan Rodley, Thomas Chardok, Geoffrey Aynesworth and others; (v) Letters of the prior and convent of Arbury dated at the chapter house at Arbury 15 March 1450 appointing Thomas Byrom, canon of Lichfield cathedral,[194] and Robert Baguley, chaplain, as proctors in the negotiations. Dated in the chapel of the castle of Eccleshall, 17 March 1451. Present: Thomas Byrom, chaplain, canon of Lichfield cathedral, and Seth Worsley, literate, Coventry and Lichfield diocese.[195]

---

[194] See note 59.
[195] See **212**. The remainder of folio 71v is blank.

284. [Fos 72–73v] Statutes made by Thomas Draper for the college or perpetual chantry for a master and four chaplains founded by him in the parish church of Newport, Salop. (as in 278). The master is to receive 10 marks p.a., the chaplains 7 marks p.a., and their servant 13s 4d p.a., from the fruits of the said college. The sum of 10s p.a., is allowed for the common hearth (*pro commune focali*). They shall observe the morning divine office of the day, all the canonical hours with the service of the Blessed Virgin Mary according to the use of Sarum with the mass of the dead, that is, placebo, Dirige and commendation, and they shall celebrate with skill, without haste or shortening of the service (*non transcurrendo sincopando set cum debita intencione et devocione*). On Sundays and feast days they shall be present, wearing their surplices, in the chancel of the parish church, at matins, vespers, and mass; and not only present, but reading, singing and psalm singing. On Sundays and feast days one of the chaplains shall observe the seventh hour, and on ferial days the sixth hour, beginning mass at the altar of St Mary in the chapel, earlier if he wishes, provided there is no legitimate impediment. The other chaplains are to celebrate straight after in the chapel or at an altar. Chaplains are obliged to reside continually in a house provided by the founder next to the college, to table together, and to abstain from idle talk. The master and each of the chaplains shall have his own room in the college. Neither the master nor any of the chaplains shall be outside the college at night. No chaplain shall absent himself from the chantry without reasonable or legitimate cause and then only with the consent of the master. The master of the college may absent himself from the college on its business with the consent of the master and stewards of the gild (of St Mary, Newport), and on no other instance unless approved by them. Neither the master nor any of the chaplains shall accept any other benefice, office, or service incompatible with the college or chantry, which, by virtue of its being accepted, would impede personal residence in the college; and if the master or any chaplain should accept any such office he must within fifteen days of such acceptance be dismissed from the college in deed and word. The master and chaplains should, as far as human frailty permits, be pure in life and conversation, mature and circumspect in behaviour, and when they go outside they should wear robes of one piece, like friars. They should avoid taverns and dishonest women. They shall not play dice, and similar games forbidden to clerks, which would disturb the peace and cause discord and hatred. Women and young men shall not enter the rooms of the master or the chaplains only or secretly, but if a women who is of blood relationship or honest wishes to see them let it be in the hall or the parlour, or in some other honest place in the presence of another chaplain, lest scandal arise. Chaplains should not be outside their own dwelling house after the seventh hour from Michaelmas to Easter, and after the ninth house from Easter to Michaelmas, unless for some reasonable cause explained, and then such occasions to be rare and not frequent. If the master or any of the chaplains should be convicted for theft, robbery, murder, rape, or any other felony and for any felony be outlawed or forced to abjure the realm, he shall, *ipso facto*, be deprived of his benefice and office. A chest under three keys of diverse pattern shall be provided in which the charter, indentures, muniments, and jewels and treasures of the college shall be kept. One key shall be kept in the possession of the master of the college, the second by the master of the gild, and the third by one priest of the place, and every year the residue remaining over and above the salaries of the master and chaplains shall be placed in the chest for safe keeping. It is ordained that the treasure of the college shall not be spent otherwise than on buildings or repair of houses or other property of the college, or for the defence of the rights of the college or other use of the college. All goods, rents, and profits, and any other income of the college shall be kept and distributed by the common counsel and the assent of the master of the college and the master and two stewards of the gild. Accounts shall be rendered twice annually, namely in the month after Easter and the month after Michaelmas, by the master of the college and the master and stewards of the gild in the presence of the chaplains. Three copies of the audit shall be made, one of which is for the master of the college, the second for the master of the gild, and the third to be preserved in the chest. The immoveables of the college shall not be alienated in any way and the moveables alienated only with the consent and assent of the master of the college and his fellow chaplains and of the master and stewards and fellows of the gild. In any vacancy of the mastership of the college the abbot and convent of St Peter, Shrewsbury, shall present a fit and suitable person to the ordinary for admission to the college: at the time of his admission he will take a corporal oath that he will faithfully observe the statutes of the college. In any vacancy of a chaplaincy caused by death, cession, deprivation, or any other reason, the master of the college and the master, stewards, and fellows of the gild shall, within fifteen weeks of the vacancy nominate a successor. If they fail to do so then the abbot and convent of St Peter, Shrewsbury, shall, within a further fifteen weeks, nominate a successor. Should they fail to do so, then the bishop of Coventry and Lichfield shall nominate a successor, and this method of selection shall be competent in itself and sufficient without any institution or induction by the bishop or archdeacon of the place, and the chaplain thus elected should have letters testimonial sealed by the person appointing him. Breaches of the statutes shall result in deprivation and exclusion. The statutes shall be read in full twice annually, on the day after Michaelmas and the day after Low Sunday. The founder reserves to himself the right to interpret, alter, add to the statutes, or to make new statutes. Neither the statutes, nor the confirmations of the master and the bishop, which follow, are dated.

285. [Fos 76–78v] 5 December 1450. Following quarrels within the community of the Augustinian house of St Wulfard, Stone, giving rise to scandals 'offensive to God and man' and also leading to 'great expenses and losses', the abbots of Darley and Lilleshall, and the priors of Arbury and Ranton visited the house on 3 December 1450 'by the express wish, mandate and authority' of Humphrey, duke of Buckingham, patron of the priory, and the bishop. They framed ordinances and statutes for the reform of the spiritual and temporal government of the priory. These were later ratified by the archbishop of Canterbury, the duke of Buckingham, and the bishop.

ORDINACIONES ET STATUTA IN PRIORATUM DE STONE. In dei nomine amen. Nos Rogerus et Johannes de Derley et de Lilleshull abbates, et nos Willelmus et Johannes de Erdebury et de Ronton priores, ordinis sancti Augustini Coventrensis et Lichfeldensis diocesis, dilectis in Christo fratribus fratri Thome Wyse priori prioratus sancti Wulphadi martiris de Stone, ordinis et diocesis predictorum, et conventui eiusdem loci salutem in eo qui est filius virginis et ea que dei religionis sunt sapere salubris ad salutem. Sane quia inter vos satore zizaniorum in agro dominico ipso videlicet diabolo instigante orta fuit noviter materia dissenssionis gravis et brigarum, ex quibus scandala et obliquia deo et piis auribus offensiva necnon et dispendia grandia atque dampna non modica vobis et prioratu vestro succreverunt, et verisimiliter nisi remedium provideretur opportunum clerius majora succrescerent in futuris, et nos igitur abbates et priores antedicti de expressa voluntate mandato et auctoritate tam nobilis et graciosi domini nostri domini Umfridi ducis Bukynghamme dicti prioratus de Stone fundatoris devoti quam reverendi in Christo patris et domini domini Willelmi dei gracia Coventrensis et Lichfeldensis episcopi de quibus satis constat ad dictum prioratum vestrum de Stone dic videlicet tercio mensis Decembris jam praeteriti juxta mandatum a dictis dominis nostris nobis datum pro reformacione reformandorum ibidem in propriis personis nostris attendentes, et de hiis quibus videbatur nobis inquisicionem fore fiendum ad intentum secundum discrecionem nobis adtunc inspiratam juxta canonica ac regularia instituta diligencia possibili inquisicionem facientes, invenimus inter vos tam in capite quam in membris inconveniencias varias et defectus a calle caritatis et a tramite recto religionis multum discrepiances, pro quorum reformacione et ut noxius appetitus eorum quia inter vos ambulare cuperit vias non bonas nec religioni consonas sed post carnalia et secularia desideria sua sub religionis et juris regula limitetur, injuncciones et ordinaciones subscriptas vobis et prioratui vestro ut speramus multum utiles et salubres auctoritate nobis in hac parte demandata fecimus et eas decrevimus a vobis observari. Quarumquidem in injunccionum et ordinacionum singule velud medi-cine morbis singulis inconvenienciis et defectibus predictis sunt apponende, et eas mandamus apponi eisdem ut sic ille vetus homo peccati inter vos sanetur et gracia ducie uberius crescat in agendis. Quiquidem injuncciones et ordinaciones nostre sequitur et sunt tales: IN PRIMIS quia non bene colitur auctor pacis nisi in loco et inter homines pacis unanimes habitantes in domo, idcirco ordinamus injungumus et injungendo mandamus quatinus extunc cessant inter vos scismata rixe contumelie et verba dura atque injuriosa et fermento veteri malicie et nequicie deposite ac remoto regnent, et vigeant inter vos de cetero caritas vera pax et concordia et sonent verba dulcia ac benigna que amicos multiplicant et sic vobis erit unitas animorum, et hoc est quod sanctus pater noster Augustinus percipiendo tradit filiis suis dicens eis in regule sue pricipio sic, 'vobis anima una et cor unum in deim nam ubi est unitas caritas et dileccio, ibi sanctorum est congragacio, ibi nec ira nec indignacio sed firma caritas imperpetuum'. ITEM quia quod est quisque appareret, ideo injungimus quod vos omnes tam prior quam canonici atque vestrum singuli deo et religioni vestre, ad cuius observacionem vinculo professione solempne estis astricti, intendatis studio diligenti et diligentius ac melius in futuris quam retroactis temporibus intendistis, advertentes et memoriter retinentes quod scriptum est 'venire ad religionem perfectio est sed non perfecte unire in eadem dampnacio est', et studeatis ac studeat unusquisque vestrum interpretari nomen suum et in re esse quod vocatur nomine cum nomina rebus et res nominabus debeant convenire vocamini et enim canonici et canon Grece quod regulam sonat latine nil quod regulare de cetero reperiatur in vobis nil religione aut regule dissonum nichil que fiat quod cuiusquam offendat aspectum sed quod vestram deceat sanctitatem, ut sic conversacio vestra inter gentes videatur bona et ab hiis qui hoc viderint deus glorificetur, et tunc coram deo et hominibus laud crescet cum honore. ITEM quia obediencia est inter regni dei, injungimus quod vos omnes et singuli dicti prioratis de Stone canonici sitis in futuris patri et priori vestre obedientes et benevoli prout ex professione vestra tenemini, ne tum in obediencia actuali que est utum hiis que dei et religionis sunt quando imperantur re et facto

propter deum et obediencie meritum alacriter ac humiliter obediatis, sed eciam in
obediencia reverenciali hoc est quando et quociens vos vel aliquem vestrum ad ejus
presencium ob aliquam causam accedere vel ad eadem recedere seu per ipsum
transire contigerit in futuris, non dorse non vultu turgido nec fronte erecta ut solite
ipsum respiciatis sed reverenciam congruam sibi exhibeatis prout observancie
docent regulares nam sicud impudicus oculis impudiccie sic et oculis superbus
superbie nuncius esse perhibitur, et hoc edibile est psalmiste dicenti 'superbo oculo
et insaciabili corde cum hoc non edebam'. Attendentes quod hoc quod sibi factum
est in iste pocius ipsi deo qui retribuit bona bonis quam sibi creditur esse factum.
Attendentes eciam quod ipse vice dei supra vos constituntur et quod pro vobis
districtam deo reddet racionem, injungimus eciam quod vos domine prior inter
dictos canonicos fratres et filios vestros sitis amodo benevolus benignus ac
modestus, plus appetens ab eis amari quam licet utrumque sic necessarium, quia ea
ex amore magis quam et timore procedunt melius sauvine atque dulcius sonant in
aure dei. ITEM quia propter officium datur beneficium, injungimus ut vos omnes
tam prior quam canonici vestrum qui singuli laudibus et obsequiis divinis diurnis
pariter et noctibus diligenter et diligencius amodo quam temporibus retroactis sitis
intendentes temporibus congruis et re ac facto intendatis eisdem, videlicet missis
matutinis vesperis completoriis et aliis horiis consuetis, et vos domine prior ac
vester celararius seu is qui extra pro utilitate communi sub vobis administrat omni
dei dominicali ac festiva et solempni adminus justo impedimento cessante, inter
sitis personaliter in matutinis vesperis atque missis una cum fratribus vestris
divinum officium debite prout decet pro patre vestra exequendo et dictos fratres
vestros ad consimile exemplo et facto devocius exitando. Et quod vos domine prior
omni festo solempni divinum officium ad magnum altare justo impedimento non
detentus in propria persona vestra exequi studeatis. Et quod omnes et singuli
confratres claustrales dicti prioratus et canonici dictis divinis officiis postposita
vagacione confabulacione et occasione quacumque dissoluta singulis temporibus
simul intersitis personaliter et intendatis, nam principaliter propter hoc officium ad
dei laudem et honorem debite exequendum a piis et devotis fundatoribus et
benefactoribus vestris vobis largiuntur et dantur que habetis; et siquis
canonicorum in matutinis deficerit, si semel in septimana hoc fecerit et justam
causam excusacione non habuerit, duos denarios perdet de salario suo quia teste
ewanglis 'laborantibus in vinea et non ociosis debetur denarius' et si bis in
septimana sic deficerit, quatuor denarios perdet de salario ei pro habitu assignato.
Et nichil ominus sexta feria tunc sequente in capitulo coram fratribus publice
proclamatur pro dicta culpa sua, et ab eo qui capitulo post sibi immergatur pro illo
die in pane et aqua jejunimus pro eadem, nam dignum est ut qui cum aliis laborare
recusat cum illis non manducet, ut sic delinquens corrigatur et aliis audacia
auferatur similia perpetrandi. Et si in missis vesperis et aliis horis canonicis aliquis
defuerit, die sequente in capitulo proclamatur et secundum discressionem
presidentis prout qualitas culpa exigerit pro culpa sua sumus puniatur. Injungimus
eciam quod vos domine prior et canonici vestris in ordine sacerdotali constituti in
consciencie puritate castitate et devocione missas vestras singulis diebus prout
congruis justam causam impedimenti non habentes celebrare curetis fundatoribus
et benefactoribus vestris pro temporalibus bonis vobis ab eis collatis spiritualia
prout tenemini jugiter repedentes. Et siquis vestrum sanus in celebrando missam
per duos dies insimul defecerit, a priori aut ab eo qui ordini preest causa inquiratur
propter quam abstinuit, et si racionabilis fuerit admittatur sin autem

emendacoriam subeat vindictam et celebrare missam ut tenetur et decet devote doceatur, et ut honestas regularis inter vos crescat et vigeat in futurum et in odore bone fame ad dei laudem gaudere valeatis et valeant vestri dilectores. Injungimus ut a personis et locis suspiciosis et suspectis abstineatis ac confabulaciones injurias cum secularibus et presertim notatis aut suspectis et colloquia prava omnino fugatis nam scriptam est 'corrumpunt bonos sepius colloquia prava'. ITEM quia dignum est quod hiis qui in monasterio deo devotius famulantur de proventibus et redditibus monasterii victui necessaria congrue ministrentur, et ut proviso pro huius necessariis fiat melius et certius in futuris quam facta fuit temporibus retroactis ut cessant litigia occasione huius prius habita, injungimus et ordinamus quod omnes canonici et confratres prioratus predicti divinis obsequiis et religioni sue debite intendant ut tenentur et modo quo premissum est et quod unusquisque canonicus in prioratu predicto professus et in ordine sacerdotali constitutus jam existens in futuris quinque nobilia in pecunia numerata pro salario habitu et vestitura suis de communibus redditibus et proventibus annuatim percipiet et habebit, de quibusquidem nobilibus quatuor nobilia fideliter persolvantur equis porcionibus ad quatuor festa subscripta videlicet annunciacionis beate Marie nativitatis sancti Johannis baptiste sancti Michaelis et sancti Thome apostoli vel infra mensem ad ultimum extunc proximo securitas per manus prioris vel canonici ad hoc per priorem deputati, et quintum nobile solvetur per manus sacriste ad festum sancti Wulphadi martiris vel infra octo dies postea absque dispendio moris longioris. Habebunt eciam singuli canonici denarios ex rewardo hiis qui legunt epistulam et Evangelium in Festis principalioribus ex antiqua curialitate dari consuetis una cum datis et legatis ac denariis in exequiis mortuorum cum acciderint. De quibus quinque nobilibus modo predicto percipiendos una cum predictis denariis in missis dari consuetis ac cum datis et legatis ac denariis in exequiis mortuorum cum contigerint pro porcione annua competente singuli canonici prioratus predicti pro salario habitu vestitura et necessariis suis pro anno et annuatim amodo futuris temporibus debent contentari prout in aliis monasterii majoribus et dignioribus, videlicet Derley Lilleshull Kenylleworth et aliis ut accepimus consimili porcione canonici contenantur, cessante extunc exaccione quacumque ulteriori et peticione alicuius denarii de aliquo loco speciali vel in specie limitato, non obstante quacumque concessione aut donacione inepta et religioni contraria per aliquem priorem seu priores in hac parte prius facta et quantum ad ulteriorum exaccionem seu peticionem ultra quinque nobilia cum aliis specificatis ut premissum per aliquem canonicorum fiendum in futuris pretextu alicuius concessionis seu donacionis inepte per priorem seu priores facte ut premissum est, predictis canonicis et eorum singulis silencium pro perpetuo duximus imponendum, nam docet omnis policia quod commune comodum est merito preferendum et a communi subtrahere et bursas canonicorum privatum inpinguare voluptati et dissolucioni pocius quam virtuti aut religioni fomenta ministrat et nutrit hiis diebus, et ideo dicit sanctus pater Augustinus in Regula per ipsum filiis suis tradita 'melius est minime egere quam plus habere' et in psalmo scriptum est 'incrassatus inpinguatus dereliquit deum' novitius autem medietatem porcionis quam canonicus sacerdos percipit pro habitu vestituris et necessariis quis percipiet et habebit. ITEM pro rasura canonicorum et lotura vestum eorundem de communibus redditibus domus modo congruo et honesto prior providebit, et injungendo districte mandamus quod nullus canonicus habeat lotri in particulari cum sic regule dissonum ne ex tali nacta mundacia pannorum oriantur et crescant sordes animorum, sed laventur omnes in communi et siquis eorum in isto culpabilis reperiatur per regularem disciplinam canonicus compescatur. ITEM pro esculentis et potulentis pro eisdem canonicis sic duximus ordinandum: canonici omnes et eorum singuli habebunt panem et potum necessarium prout congrue sufficiet de communi honestum et competentem et prout congruet racioni bene preparatum, et fiet panis eorum de farina non sicut venit a molendino ut perantea prout dicebatur sed de farina purafurfure ab ea separato et in diebus dominicalis feriis terciis atque quintis servietur duobus canonicis in prandio de coquina de duobus generibus carnium recente coctarum et super unum discum pro ferculo coram eis honeste ponendarum et de uno genere carnium assatarum in quantitate prout honeste convenit pro pietencia sua. Et in cena de uno genere carnium perantea coctarum et de uno genere carnium recenter assatarum ita quod de utroque simul posito fiat ferculum competens pro refeccione in cena et feriis vero secundis atque quartis servietur duobus canonicis in prandio de porciuncula carnium unius generis coctarum cum viij ovis pro refeccione. Et in cena servietur eis de sex ovis cum una porciuncula carnium bovinarum perantea coctarum anglice *a leche of cold beef*. Diebus autem Veneris servietur duobus canonicis in prandio de quatuor allecis et de uno ferculo piscie duri anglice *stokkefyshe* sive piscis salsi simul appositi lacticiniis dum durant, et si allecia deficiant in loco illorum servietur eis de ferculo competente piscis duri atque salsi aut de uno eorum si alterum deficerint, et modo consimlli servietur eis diebus sabbati excepto quod illo die habebunt unam pietanciam oppositam de piscibus marinis cum congrue et comode haberi poterint, et si festum duplex contigerit feria secunda seu quarta aut in die Veneris habebunt pietanciam oppositam sicut in aliis diebus ob honorem festi. In quadragesima vero servietur duobus canonicis de coquina diebus videlicet dominicalis seriis terciis et quintis de quatuor alleciis et de uno ferculo piscis durus frix cum porcumcula competente piscis marini sive salmonis salsis. Feriis autem secundis quartis et sextis servietur duobus canonicis de quatuor alleciis et de uno ferculo piscis duris sive piscis salsis, et modo consimili servietur eis diebus Sabbati excepto quod illo die habebunt ferculum competens et honestum de piscibus marinis ad ferculum predictum appositum cum piscis marini comode haberi poterunt. In Adventu nempe dum servietur eis de victualibus tan tempori quam personis convenientibus et modo consimili quo premittitur et de talibus quales pro tempore poterunt communiter reparari. Et volumus quod canonici omnes et singuli contententur de servicio suo de coquina modo predicto coram eis apponendo. Et quod fragmenta quo superfuerint cum manducaverit transeant ad usus pios et prioratui eorum utiles ac honestos, et quod nulla per canonicos nec per canonicum fiat missio ad extra de eisdem nisi ob justam causam prius cognitam et per eum qui ordini pre est pro tempore approbandam. Et congrua refeccione sic accepta, gracias agant deo et studeant omnes et singuli gaudere in deo et consciencie puritate pocius quam in nimio aut in ventre excessive repleto seu crapula vel ebrietate ex quibus multa solent evenire mala. Injungimus eciam quod conventus et canonici singuli claustrales dum sunt sani, comedant simul in uno loco videlicet in aula prioris quosque refectorium fuerit congrue reparatum, cuius reparacionem fieri cum festinacione et diligencia possibili mandamivus et fieri mandamus per priorem postposita omni mora, quiquidem refectorio congrue reparato canonici manducabunt et bibent in illo, quia sine refectorio ubi fuerit religiosorum multitudo non bene ut noverunt qui experti sunt servatur religio et ideo refectorium a canonicis claustralibus in refeccione et insimul servatibur omni die, nisi prior aliquos bene meritos ob reverenciam alicuius festi aut aliam justam causam ad presenciam suam pro refeccione sua capienda ibidem duxerit evocandos et quod in refectorio dum canonici fuerint ibi in refeccione biblia vel leccio alia de scriptura sacra aut devocione legatur ibidem, cuicum silencio dum fuerint in prandio postpositis confabulacionibus vanis et ineptis omnes intendant diligenter, et sic reficietur uterque homo corpus videlicet cibo et potu et anima verba dei et hoc est quod sanctus pater Augustinus docet filios suos dicens eis 'Cum acceditis ad mensem non solum sances sumant sed aures efuriant verbum dei'. ITEM injungumus quod in choro claustro et dormitorio servetur silencium et religionis honestas secundum ordinem atque modum prout liber ordinis ad quem vos referimus vos docet manifeste. Et ne profectum spiritualem laboribus assiduis et occupacionibus fructuosis per totam diem adquisitum brevis hora sero factum fuerit in potacionibus et vanis confabulacionibus male impensa dissipet et trucidet, ac eciam ut canonici gui media nocte surgere sunt astricti ad impendendum deo debite famulatum melius aut dispositi, injungumus districte et ordinamus quod canonici claustrales in refectorio comendentes hora completori in choro laudibus divinis tunc ibidem deo exsolvandis simul intersint nullo deficiente, et quod completorio dicto et completo omnes simul dormitorium ingrediantur, et quod postquam dormitorium sic fuerint ingressi, nullus dormitorium exeat sed unusquisque callam suam reputat et cum silencio ibidem oracionem devote meditationi sancte et contemplacione pie jugiter vacans prout decet sanctos paret se ad lectum, et siquis canonicus post completorium completum dormitorium sic ingredi recusaverit aut inde postquam ingressus fuerit sine speciali licencia ob justam causam petita et optenta exierit, die sequente in capitulo publice coram fratribus pro culpa sua huiusmodi proclematur et secundum discrecionem presidentis puniatur graviter pro eadem. Injungumus eciam quod canonici omnes et singuli in lectis suis seorsum quiescant, et quod seculares ad colloquia ibidem non admittant praeter quam servientes et in hiis tantomodo que necessaria fuerint, ac eciam quod in dormitorio causa infirmitatis gravis non excusante neque bibant, et siquis eorum in aliquo istorum reperiatur culpabilis, pro offensa huiusmodi in capitulo proximo proclematur et pro tanto excessu injungatur sibi ieiunium pane et aqua feria sexta proximo tunc sequente ut motu pene a talibus excessibus abstinere distat in futuris. ITEM pro recreaccione solacio et sportis canonicorum ordinamus prout ordinavimus quod qualibet septimana feria videlicet secunda tercia atque quinta, nisi aliquo dierum illorum duplex festum occurat, omnes canonici claustrales hora recreaccionis consueta transeant insimul ad extra in clausum infra septa monasterii constitutum vocatum *le orchard* modo honesto et religioso simul speciando leccionibus scripture sacre ac devocionis partum intendendo. Et ludis honestis ac religiosis consonis partum tunc vocando, et quod ad huiusmodi recreaccionem inter eos prout premittitur et decet habendum non admittant sed ad eis abstineant tunc omnino, et quod extra septa monasterii non exeant sine licencia speciali. Et quod erga horam vesperis ad ecclesiam parando se divertant ut eum signum per campanam ad vesperas informerit in claustrum ad divinum servicium redire sunt parati et simul redeant sicud simul exierunt, et siquis canonicorum secularem personam ad ludendum inter eos in huiusmodi solaciis et recreaccionibus suis admiserit aut extra septa monasterii exieri sine licencia ab eo qui preest specialiter petita et optenta, ad huiusmodi recreaccione et solacio separetur et ut puniatur in eo quo deliquit ea careat et claustrum custodiat et illud non exeat per septimanam integram tunc sequentem, ut quem timor a malo non recovat pena cohibeat ut est justum. Volumus eciam ut aliis quatuor diebus in septimana videlicet diebus Dominicale feriis quartis sextis et sabbatis canonici claustrales omnes et singuli in claustro et in ecclesia sedeant et permeant deo et religioni sue in humilitate cordis et devocione leccionique studio et contemplacioni jugiter intendentes a confabulacionibusque ibidem abstineant et extra claustrum et ecclesiam non exeant nisi ex licencia ob justam causam petita et optenta attendentes quod metrice nomine Christi crucifixi bono religioso legitur esse dietum 'O mi claustralis professe sub ordinais alis Respice devote passus sum qualia pro te In claustro mecum residens sic sum quia tecum Per claustrali sedem celi mercaberis edem'. ITEM quis pro gardinis et croftis inter priorem et canonicos fuit ut accepimus noviter litigatum ut in futuris omnis occasio et materia cesset pro huiusmodi litigandum ordinamus quod conventus habebit in communi vestrum gardinum illud videlicet quod jacet propinquis et juxta cimiterium conventuale, salvo spacio pro via habenda Hugoni Erdeswyke pro se et familiaribus suis ab hospicio in quo manet ad et in ecclesiam prout antea consuevit, et quod nullus canonicus aliquem locum dicti gardini sibi proprium vendicabit sed gardinum illud totum excepta via in ecclesiam ut premissum est conventus habebit in communi, vocabitur de cetero gardinum conventuale ita quod licitum erit conventui ex consensu eorum communi dictum gardinum singulis annis inter se dividere per partes et parcellas, sic ut singuli canonici partes suas habeant in eodem pro anno tunc sequente et quod unusquisque canonicus partem gardini sic sibi limitatam fodeat et colat herbasque speciales et meliores sic in ea plantare studeat ut unusquisque se partem habere honestiorem magis herbegeram gaudeat atque meliorem ad usus coquine communes et quod occupacione in fodendo et colendo dictum gardinum per canonicos facienda et plantando in eodem inpendatur et fiat temporibus congruis et modo quo decet cum religionis honestate et dei servicio propter hoc non lese neque diminuto, et quoad ad alia gardina sive crofta petenda pro usu privato conventus silebit in futurum. Apes vero in cimiterio conventuali et in gardinis predictis jam existentes et per canonicos nutritas una cum proficus proveniente de eisdem ad officium sacriste assignavimus pro usibus ecclesie ad dei honorem provedendam et volumus quod nullus canonicus ad usus privatos de cetero talia vendicabit sed ad usus communes hoc bene licebit dummodo divinum officium per hoc non minuatur in aliquo nec inpediatur. ITEM quia ubi mainse iminet periculum ibi cautius est agendum, injungumus quod commune sigillum dicti prioratus vestri sub tribus diversis clavibus ac seruris securo et fideliter custodiatur, quarquidem clavium una remaneat in custodia prioris alia supprioris et tercia in custodia sacriste, et quod sub sigillo communi nulla liberacio seu corrodium alicui ad terminum vita sive longum tempus concedatur neque alienacionem bonorum dicti prioratus neque impignoraciones seu obligaciones absque consensu conventus seu sanioris et discrecio partis eiusdem fiant seu quovisimodo concedantur, firme vere et cetera ad modicum tempus concedenda non aliter cum communi sigillo predicto quam in domo capitulari semper tractatu diligenti perhabito cum conventu sigillentur. ITEM quia quod a pluribus queritur facilius invenitur, injungumus quod licet prior onum vestrum curam gexat et prioratus vestri ac omni que pertinent ad eiusdem administracio pertineat et sibi commitatur in solidum gubernanduus et propter hoc eligitur proficitur et capud appellatur, tamen cum in partem solitudine et cure sibi commisse officiarii consueti in conventu pro communi utilitate inter vos fuerint deputandi ipsos in officiarios huius assignat et proficiat qui discreciores et magis apti ad huius officia reputantur et hoc cum consilio conventus vel sanioris et discrecioris partis eiusdem et quod singuli officiarii huius singulos proventus et receptiones ad huius officia pertinentes recipeant et per supervisum prioris in usus utiles officiorum huius et prioratus sui convertant ita quod ipsi officiarii in fine anni de receptis et expensis huius reddere racionem et compotum sunt parati et reddant cum effectu et similiter quod prior de receptis et singulis administratis per ipsum in fine anni racionem et compotum reddat et de statu sui prioratus doceat modo et forma quibus per jura et ordininis instituta ad hoc faciendum .... obligatur. ITEM quia pro infirmis canonicis ibidem non fuit congrue provisum per annos aliquos ut refertur, injungumus et injungendo mandamus quod proviso congrua fiat pro huiusmodi infirmis temporibus pro futuris ita quod provideatur locus congruus in infirmaria in quo lectus et altare poterint honeste et congrue collocari in quibus canonicus infirmus tempore infirmitatis suo requestere possit cum quiete et missam audire prout decet et quod deputetur unus canonicus qui canonicus infirmis tempore infirmitatis eorum intendat divinum officium cum eis dicat aut per se ipsum et in presencia infirmi ut ipso infirmus hoc audire posit cum per se ipsum pro debilitate dicere non valeat et ulterius provideat quod ipsis infirmus debite ministretur in hiis que eis necessaria fuerint ad salutem attendens quod casus consimilis ei evicino verisimiliter poterit evenire et ideo alteri faciat quod sibi vellet fieri et hoc juris naturalis est et ideo metrice scribitur quod tibi vis fieri michi quod non tibi noli sic potes in terris unire jure poli. Injungumus itaque et injungendo mandamus quod vos et omnes vestrum singuli prior quam canonici premissas et prescriptas injuncciones et ordinaciones nostras ymmo verius duorum nostrorum supradictorum quorum auctoritate mandato et voluntate facte sunt prout superius in serie recitantur pro dei honore et religionis incremento ac vestrum et prioratus vestri predicti salute felici et utilitate diligenter et studiose observare curetis et curet vestrum unusquisque temporibus pro futuris et sub penis gravioribus quas religio pro magis excessibus delinentibus dictat infligendas et ne per incuriam aut oblimionem aliquid negligatur volumus quod bis in anno die videlicet sabbati ante dominicalis in ramus psalmarum et in vigilia omnium sanctorum iste nostre ymmo verius dictorum dominorum nostrorum injuncciones et ordinaciones prescripte que regule sancti patris nostri Augustini sunt executive in capitulo et hora capitulari postquam leccio de regula lecta fuerit ut moris est legantur publice et aperte et ubi vos .... everitis ea que scripta sunt facientes, agite gracias Domino bonorum omnium largitori, ubi autem sibi quicumque vestrum videt aliquid deese doleat de praeterito caveat de futuro orans ut ei debitum dimittatur et in temptacionem ulterius non inducatur. Et hinc pagine injunccionum et ordinacionum nostrarum ymmo verius dictorum dominorum nostrorum ut predictum est. Sigilla nostra duximus apponenda et sigilla dictorum nostrorum una cum subscripcione eorum hiis apponi similiter imploraminus in confirmacionem et robus eorundem. Datum quoad nos abbates et priores predictos apud Stone quinto die mensis Decembris anno domini millesimo CCCC^{mo} quinquagesimo.

Et nos JOHANNES, permissione divina Cantuariensis archiepiscopus tocius Anglie primas et apostolice sedis legatus volentes predictorum prioris et conventus indempnitatibus prospicere et quieti attendentes premissas provisiones ordinaciones et injuncciones racionabiles deo gratas et dictiis priori et conventui utiles fuisse et esse quamplurimum necessarias ipsis omnibus et singulis, nostras probamus consensum pariter et assensum ac premissa omnia et singula auctoritate nostra opprobamus auctorizamus et confirmamus per presentes.

Et nos HUMFIDUS dux Bukynghamme fundatorque supradicti prioratus de Stone attendentes ordinaciones et injuncciones superius recitatas et de voluntate ac mandata nostro sic ut premittitur factas religioni ac virtuti fore satis consonas dictoque prioratui de Stone ac priori et canonicis ibidem per utiles valde et salubres, ipsas injuncciones et ordinaciones omnes et singulas approbamus et pro quanto in nobis est ratificamus per presentes, volumusque et mandamus quod prior et canonici dicti prioratus de Stone oratores nostri tam presentes quam futuri ipsas injuncciones observent et secundum eas de cetero componant vitam suam et vivere studeant cum effectu, ut sic per vitam religiosam pia suffragia et oraciones devotas eorundem in quibus non modicum confidimus tam nobis quam aliis pro quibus orare tenentur gracia proveniat obserius et crescat in agendis. In cuius rei testimonium presentibus sigillum nostrum fecimus apponi. Datum in hospicio nostro London' sexto die mensis Aprilis anno domini millesimo CCCC^{mo} quinquagesimo primo et anno regni regis Henrici sexti post conquestum Anglie vicesimo nono.

Et nos Willelmus permissione divina episcopus Coventrensis et Lichfeldensis premissas ordinaciones et injuncciones omnes et singulas prout superius recitantur per supradictos abbates et priores ex mandato nostro in hac parte factas et nobis per eosdem oblatas auctoritate nostra ordinaria roborandas, attendentes eas religioni consonas et priori ac conventui dicti prioratus de Stone et prioratui eorum predicto per utiles fore et salibres, pro bono tam pacis et quietis quam religionis habendo ac regnaturo inter eos temporibus pro futuris tenore presencium approbamus ratificamus et eas pontificali auctoritate nostra confirmamus, damusque in mandatis prefatis priori et canonicis de Stone qui nunc sunt et qui futuri sint in eodem quod ipsi et eorum singuli predictas ordinaciones et injuncciones omnes et singulas quatenus eos et eorum singulos concernerint et concernere poterint in futurum observent diligenter, et quocumque ac omnia excusacionis insepte seu tergiversacionis velamine postposito penitus et remoto re et facto studeant efficaciter adimplere sub pena excommunicaionis majoris necnon et sub penas quas religio sancti Augustini pro excessibus gravioribus infligeri solet delinquentibus in eisdem, per quasduidem penas contrafacientes seu contravenientes ordinacionibus et injunccionibus predictis priorem videlicet si ipsum pro parte sua quod absit contrafacere seu contravenire contingat per nos et officium nostrum canonicos vero et singulos eorum si causas exposcat per priorem volumus coherceri; Et ad observacionem earudem ordinacionum et injunccionem decernimus fore compellandos temporibus perpetuis in futurum. Et in testimonium et fidem omnium premissorum ac ad perpetuam rei memoriam eorundem sigillum nostrum presentibus duximus apponendum. Datum sub sigillo nostro in castro de Eccleshale vicesimo primo die mensis Maii anno domini millesimo CCCC^{mo} quinquagesimo primo et nostre consecracionis anno quarto.

286.   [Fo. 79] 18 October 1448. Commission to Mr George Radclyff, D. Dec.,[196] treasurer of Lichfield cathedral, to act as vicar general in spirituals during pleasure.[197]

---

[196] See note 11.
[197] The commission differs only slightly from the first commission, **11.**

COMMISSIO VICARII GENERALIS. Willelmus [etc.] universis et singulis Christi fidelibus prefertim civitatum et diocesis nostrarum Coventrensis et Lichfeldensis presentes litteras inspecturis salutem in auctore salutis. Noveritis nos de circumspeccionis industria et fidelitate ac vite et morum honestate dilecti nobis in Christo venerabilis viri magistri Georgii Radclyff decretorum doctoris thesaurarii ecclesie nostre Lichfeldensis antedicte ac eiusdem ecclesie canonici et confratris nostri specialiter confidentes, eundem in nostra absencia in remotis agente in et per totam nostram diocesim Coventrensem et Lichfeldensem ad causarum spiritualium seu negociorum que ad forum pertinere consueverint ecclesiasticum cognicionem decisionem et terminacionem ac sentenciarum execuccionem, criminumque et excessuum spiritualium et ecclesiasticorum seu eorum que ad forum consueverint pertinere ecclesiasticum inquisicionem correccionem et punicionem, administracionem ammocionem beneficiorum privacionem, juramentorum canonice obedience ac fidelitatis recepcionem, censurarum eciam suspencionis excommunicacionis vel interdicti fulminacionem, clerum ad synodum convocandum, visitacionem ordinariam exercendam, eleccionesque quascumque confirmandas seu infirmandas, necnon cuicumque episcopo catholico potestatem et execucionem sui officii obtenti ad celebrandum et conferendum ordines majores et minores generales et speciales infra diocesim nostram predictam ac eciam benediciendum ecclesias altaria cimiteria calices et alia ornamenta ecclesiastica quecumque consecranda et reconsilianda et benedicenda ac quecumque alia que ad ordinem episcopalem spectant facienda exercenda et expedienda nostris vice et nomine facultatem et licenciam danda et concenda, penitentiariosque unum seu plures ut moris est deputandos, clericosque convictos quoscumque de judicibus secularibus quibuscumque petendos et et recipiendos, jurisdiccionemque omnimodam ecclesiasticam et spiritualem in dictis nostris civitatibus et diocesi cum omnibus et singulis suis emergentibus dependentibus et connexis quibuscumque exercendam expediendam et gerandam, nostrum vicarium generalem et specialem ita quod generalitas specialitati non deroget nec contra deputasse proficesse constituisse et ordinasse quem sic ut prefertur deputamus preficimus constituimus et ordinamus ad beneplacitum nostrun duraturum cum potestate unum vel plures prout eidem melius videbitur expedire ad predicta omnia et singula jurisdiccionalia (collacionibusque dignitatum et prebendarum ac aliorum beneficiorum ecclesiasticorum quorumcumque nostri patronatus ac eciam jure devoluto, necnon presentacionibus beneficiorum ecclesiasticorum nostri patronatus extra nostram diocesim existencia et aliorum quorumcumque beneficiorum ecclesiasticorum cuiuscumque seu quorumcumque patronatus existat et institucionibus eorundem, et confirmacionibus eleccionum abbathiarum et prioratuum quorumcumque infra nostram diocesim, necnon potestate de non residendo in beneficiis beneficiis huiusmodi ac litteris dimissoriis et pro oratoriis ac aliis dispensacionibus huiusmodi quibuscumque dumtaxat exceptis et nobis in hac parte specialiter reservatis) sustituendi delegandi et committendi ceteraque agendi et faciendi ac si nos in propria persona facere possumis si personaliter interessimus. In cuius rei testimonium sigillum nostrum presentibus apposuminus. Datum in manerio nostro de Heywode decimo octavo die mensis Octobris anno domini millesimo CCCC^{mo} quadragesimo octavo et nostre consecracionis anno secundo.

287. 10 July 1448. Grant to Mr John Wendesley,[198] canon of Lichfield cathedral, and prebendary of Prees, of the house in the close by the chantry priests' building, lately occupied by Mr William Admondeston,[199] and before him Robert Wolveden, with the onus of maintenance and repair.

DONACIO DOMORUM INFRA CLAUSUM LICHFELDENSEM. Willelmus [etc.] dilecto in Christo filio magistro Johanni Wendesley canonico ecclesie nostre cathedralis Lichfeldensis ac prebendario prebende de Prees in eadem salutem graciam et benediccionem. Domos et edificia que dudum inhabitarunt magistri Willelmus Admondeston et ante eum Robertus Wolveden dicte ecclesie nostre cathedralis Lichfeldensis canonici residenciarii infra clausum ecclesie nostre antedicte juxta edificia cantariarum eiusdem ecclesie nostre cathedralis Lichfeldensis proximo futuris vacantes et ad nostram donacionem sive collacionem spectantes tibi cum onere reparacionis et congrue sustentacionis eorundem concedimus per presentes juribus et pertinenciis universis possidendo. In cuius rei testimonium sigillum nostrum fecimus hiis apponi. Datum in manerio nostro de Heywode decimo die mensis Julii anno domini millesimo CCCC^mo quadragesimo nono et nostre consecracionis anno tercio.

288. 17 April 1449. Letters dimissory to John Bothe[200] and William Worsley of Coventry and Lichfield diocese to receive the first tonsure from any catholic bishop.

LITTERA DIMISSORIAS PRO JOHANNI BOTHE ET WILLELMO WORSLEY. Willelmus [etc.] dilectis in Christo filiis Johanni Bothe et Willelmo Worsley nostre diocesis salutem graciam et benediccionem. Ut a quocumque episcopo catholico graciam sedis apostolice et execuccionem sui officii obtinenti vobisque aut alteri vestrum sacras manus apponere volenti primam tonsuram clericalem recipere valeatis et uterque vestrum recipere sic valeat, eo non obstante quod in dicta diocesi nostra oriundi existis, tam vobis et uterque vestrum quam quicumque episcopo huiusmodi liberam in domino concedimus facultatem et licenciam specialem per presentes. In cuius rei testimonium sigillum nostrum fecimus hiis apponi. Datum in manerio nostro de Heywode xvij^to die mensis Aprilis anno domini millesimo CCCC^mo quadragesimo nono et nostre consecracionis anno tercio.

289. [Fo. 79v] Grant to Henry Inse,[201] canon of Lichfield cathedral, prebendary of Wolvey, of the house in the close situated by the east gate, recently occupied by Mr William Kynwolmersh,[202] with the onus of maintenance and repair (as in 287). Haywood, 20 October 1449.

---

[198] See note 144.

[199] Prebendary of Dasset Parva and of Gaia Minor. Archdeacon of Stafford from 1 March 1422 until his death, by 4 July 1432 (*Fasti* x, 19, 31, 42).

[200] Later treasurer of Lichfield, 1459 to 1495 (*Fasti* x, 12).

[201] See note 16.

[202] M.A. and B.Th. Completed lectures on the Sentences in 1443 and the next year was fined 100 shillings for not incepting within a year of receiving his licence in theology. Held prebends in Lichfield, and was also canon of St Martin le Grand, London, and treasurer of

290. Commission to Mr George Radclyff, D. Dec.,[203] archdeacon of Chester, canon of Lichfield cathedral, to act as vicar general in spirituals during pleasure (as in 286). 4 November 1449.

291. 2 November 1450. The commission to Mr George Radclyff, D. Dec.,[204] as vicar general in spirituals during pleasure is renewed.

DEPUTACIO VICARII GENERALIS. Item prefatus reverendus pater Coventrensis et Lichfeldensis episcopus constituit predictum magistrum Georgium Radclyff archidiaconum Cestr' suum vicarium generalem in et per totam diocesim suam in ejus absencia per suas litteras speciales superinde confectas tenorem proximo suprascriptum continentes ad beneplacitum domini duraturum cuius commissionis datum est sub sigillo domini secundo die mensis Novembris anno domini millesimo CCCC^mo quinquagesimo et consecracionis anno tercio.

292. [Fo. 80] 6 April 1450. Grant for life to Henry Wryghtyngton, literate, of the office of apparitor general for the whole diocese of Coventry and Lichfield.

DONACIO OFFLCII APPARATORIS PRO DIOCESI. Willelmus [etc.] dilecto in Christo filio Henrico Wryghtyngton literato graciam et benediccionem. De tuis fidelitate experta et industria ad plenum informati concessimus tibi pro nobis et successoribus nostris officium generalis apparitoris nostri totius nostre diocesis Coventrensis et Lichfeldensis ad termium vite tue, ac te in apparitorem nostrum generalem per dictam totalem nostram diocesim Coventrensem at Lichfeldensem pro nobis et successoribus nostris ad terminum vite tue creamus facimus ordinamus et preficimus per presentes, dantes et concedentes tibi potestatem citacionis in quantum de jure seu consuetudine per apparitorem in eadem diocesim nostra fieri poterint et debebunt ac certificatoria inde rite et legitime citacionibus huiusmodi conveniencia debite faciendi quociens et quando opus erit ulteriusque exercendi omnia et singula cum suis juribus et emolumentis et pertinenciis universis que per apparitorem generalem in eadem diocesim nostram antedictam fieri et expidiri fuerint et sunt consueta, mandantes omnibus et singulis nobis subditis quatinus tibi in hiis que ad ipsum pertinent officium debite obediant pariter et intendant ut tenentur. In cuius rei testimonium sigillum nostrum presentibus duximus apponendum. Datum sexto die mensis Aprilis anno domini millesimo CCCC^mo quinquagesimo et nostre consecracionis anno tercio.

293. Grant for life to Henry Wryghtyngton of the office of clerk of all the bishop's [secular?] courts in the counties of Stafford and Salop.[205]

Abergwlli as well as rector of Castor in Northamptonshire and of Bosworth in Lincolnshire. Had papal dispensation to hold all of these in plurality in 1435. After this admitted to rectories in Berkshire, Somerset and Yorkshire. Chaplain to John, duke of Bedford in 1433. Died by August 1469. (Emden iii, 1077).

203 See note 11.
204 See note 11.
205 See **292**.

DONACIO OFFICII CLERICI CURIARUM INFRA COMITATUS STAFFORDIE ET SALOPIE. Universis sancte matris ecclesie filiis presentes litteras inspecturis Willelmus [etc.] salutem in domino omnium salvatore. Cum bone memorie Willelmus Hayworth nuper Coventrensis et Lichfeldensis episcopus predecessor noster dederit et concesserit dilecto et fideli servienti suo Willelmo Brocton filio Johannis Brocton de Longdon officium clerici omnium curiarum suarum et successorum suorum infra comitatus Staffordie et Salopie habendum et tenendum predictum officium cum omnimodis feodis emolumentis et proficiis eidem officio spectantibus sive pertinentibus predicto Willelmo Brocton ad terminum vite sue ad occupandum per se seu tempore infirmitatis vel causa necessitatis per sufficiente deputatum suum, percipiendo inde annuatim de se et successoribus suis sextaginta solidos et octo denarios ad festa annunciacionis beate Marie et sancti Michaelis equis porcionibus per manus collectoris redditus manerii sui de Longdon et successorum suorum qui pro tempore fuerint infuturis; noveritis nos dedisse et concessisse Henrico Wryghtyngton predictum officium omnium curiarum predictarum ad terminum vite ipsius Henricu habendum et tenendum predictum officium. Et si contingat predictos sextaginta solidos et octo denarios eretro fore in parte vel in toto ad aliquod festum quo solvi debeant per quadraginta dies, quod tunc bene liceat prefato Henrico pro dictis sextaginta solidos et octo denariis in predicto manerio de Longdon distringere et districciones sic captas asportare abducere effugare et imparcare et penes se retinere quousque de predictis sextaginta solidis et octo denariis et ejus arreragiis sique fuerint plenarie fuerit ei satisfactis. In cuius rei testimonium sigillum nostrum apponi fecimus. Datum in manerio nostro de Heywode penultimo die mensis Julii anno domini millesimo quadragentesimo quinquagesimo primo et nostre consecracionis anno quinto.

294. Commission to Mr George Radclyff, D. Dec.,[206] archdeacon of Chester, canon of Lichfield, to act as vicar general in spirituals during pleasure (as in **286**). Daventry, 23 January 1451.

295. [Fo. 80v] Letters dimissory to Robert Wyche, Henry Wygan, John Malbon, and Matthew Cawnffeld, canons regular of Norton, to receive all sacred orders from John, bishop of Sodor and Man (*Sodoriensis*).[207] Eccleshall castle, 2 November 1451.

And on the same day, at the request of Henry Halshale and William Faryngdon, letters dimissory were issued to Robert Blakelaw to receive orders from the same bishop.

296. 26 November 1451. Commission to Christopher Harnage to collect the fruits of the parish church of Shenstone (*Sheynton*), now in the hands of illicit farmers, and to use them for the support of a suitable priest in the parish.

---

[206] See note 11.
[207] John Seyre/Feyre, bishop of Sodor and Man. Consecrated 11 November 1435. Deceased by 25 September 1455 when his successor was provided (*Handbook of British Chronology*, 273).

COMMISSIO AD COLLIGENDUM FRUCTUS ECCLESIE DE SHEYNTON VACANTIS.
Willelmus [etc.] dilecto in Christo filio Christoforo Harnage armigero nostre
diocesis salutem graciam et benediccionem. Quia ecclesia parochialis de Sheynton
dicte nostre diocesis propter deterioracionem et exilitatem eiusdem a diu viduata
extitit prout existit in presenti, ac ipsius parochi intervenientes quorumcumque
diminorum destituuntur auxiliis ac universi fructus et proventus eiusdem per
manus illicitorum occupatorum ut informantur dilapidantur ac eciam
dampnabilibus consumuntur quorum reformacio disposicio et gubernacio ad nos
et nostrum officium de jure et consuetudine noscuntur notorie pertinere; ad
colligendum igitur ac sublevandum disponendum et custodiendum dictos fructus
et proventus ecclesie predicte pro comodo et sustentacione unius presbyteri
parochialis dicte ecclesie de Sheynton divina continue celebraturi ac sacramenta et
sacramentalia eisdem administraturi tam tibi quam cuicumque presbytero
committimus et licenciam specialem concedimus ad nostrum beneplacitum
duraturum per presentes, proviso eciam quod nostra episcopalia ac alia onera
eidem ecclesie medio tempore incumbencia debite facias supportari, reddendo
inde nobis fidelem compotum cum per nos aut ministros ad hoc fueris congrue
requisitus. Datum sub sigillo nostro in castro nostro de Eccleshale xxvj^{to} die mensis
Novembris anno domini millesimo CCCC^{mo} quinquagesimo primo et nostre
consecracionis anno quinto.

297.   [Fo. 81] Letters dimissory to Edward Massy of the parish of Coddington
(Codyngton) to receive all orders from John, bishop of Sodor and Man
(*Sodoriensis*).[208] Haywood, 15 March 1452.

298.   Dispensation to William Dounne, Coventry and Lichfield diocese, who
had received acolyte's orders from John, bishop of Sodor and Man,[209] without
having first obtained letters dimissory. Haywood, 7 April 1452.

299.   2 May 1452. Memorandum that the bishop has commissioned Mr George
Radclyff, archdeacon of Chester,[210] as vicar general in spirituals during pleasure.

Item memorandum quod ii^o die mensis Maii anno domini millesimo CCCC^{mo}
quinquagesimo secundo apud Daventr' dominus Coventrensis et Lichfeldensis
episcopus constituit prefatum magistrum Georgium Radclyff archidiaconum
Cestrie vicarium suum generalem ipso absente per suas litteras patentes simili
modo prout in commissione sua proximo suprascripta ex altero latere satis liquet.

300.   Grant to Mr John Thurstan, L. Dec., canon of Lichfield cathedral, of the
house within the close recently occupied by James Langton, lately canon
residentiary of Lichfield cathedral, with the onus of repair and maintenance (as in
287). 6 May 1452.

301.   Grant to Thomas Byrom, chaplain, canon of Lichfield cathedral,[211] of the
house within the close recently occupied by Mr William Berforde, lately canon

208 See note 207.
209 See note 207.
210 See note 11.
211 See note 59.

residentiary of Lichfield cathedral, with the onus of repair and maintenance (as in **287**). 7 May 1452.

302. [Fo. 81v] Letters of Vincent Clement, S.T.P., papal referendary, subdeacon, collector and nuncio in England, citing faculty of Pope Nicholas V (dated at St Peter's, Rome, 17 August 1451) to grant dispensations for fifty marriages in the third and fourth degrees of consanguinity. He grants dispensation to Thomas Redeche and Cecilie Prestwiche of Coventry and Lichfield diocese, the sixth in the number he is allowed. London, 8 May 1452.

Memorandum quod ex mandato domini premissa inseruntur. W. Brand. RR.

303. [Fo. 82] Decree appropriating the parish church of Southam, Warwicks., from the next vacancy, to the prior and convent of Coventry cathedral (O.S.B.), whose petition sets out that the fruits of the cathedral have decreased through the barrenness of the lands, floods, dearth of cultivators, and the fewness of their servants on account of their excessive wages and other misfortunes, and because they are burdened with hospitality (as in **280**). The bishop, sitting in tribunal in the chapel of the manor of Haywood, decrees as follows: The prior and convent are to have the church of Southam in perpetuity and to take possession on the vacancy caused by the death, resignation, or cession of William Sugge, the present rector, or in any other way. They are to institute a perpetual vicarage with an annual portion of 12 marks to be paid in four equal portions at Christmas, Lady Day, the birth of St John the Baptist, and Michaelmas. They are also to provide, at their own expense, a suitable manse for the vicar. The following pensions are reserved: to the bishop of Coventry and Lichfield, 2s p.a., and to the archdeacon of Coventry, 20d. The sum of 2s from the fruits of the church is to be distributed to the poor parishioners in the month after Lady Day. The following documents are recited: (i) Letters patent (a license for the grant in mortmain) tested at Westminster 4 July 30 Henry VI (1452). (ii) Letters of the prior and chapter of Coventry cathedral appointing Br. Thomas Doram, monk and steward (*senescallum*) of Coventry cathedral, Mr Thomas Lye, archdeacon of Salop,[212] Mr John Twysse, LL.B., and Robert Baguley, chaplain, as their proctors in the negotiations. Chapter house at Coventry, 20 April, 1450, under the seal *ad causas*. Dated 15 July 1452, in the chapel of the manor of Haywood, in the presence of Mr John Reedhill, B.Cn.L. and B.C.L., Peter Berdesley, chaplain, and others, with subscription by Mr William Brande, notary and scribe of the bishop.

304. [Fo. 83v] Grant to Mr Roger Lye, D. Dec., vicar of Wellington (*Wellyngton*), canon of Lichfield cathedral, prebendary of Weeford,[213] of the house within the close by the east gate, recently occupied by Mr Thomas Chestrefeld,[214] lately canon residentiary of Lichfield cathedral, with the onus of repair and maintenance (as in **286**). Haywood, 24 August 1452.

---

[212] Collated 22 May 1450, died before 1 June 1464 (*Fasti* x, 18). See note 18.
[213] Held the prebend of Weeford from 6 May 1437 to his death, by 4 March 1475 (*Fasti* x, 64).
[214] See note 2.

305. Licence to John Iremonger, chaplain, to marry James Harebroun and Elizabeth Glover, daughter of William Glover, of Liverpool (*Lyverpoll*), in the chapel or oratory of his house within the parish of Toxteth (*Toxstath*), banns having been called and no canonical objection forthcoming. Haywood, 8 July 1452.

306. [Fo. 84–v] 22 July 1450. Certificate of Mr John Reedhill, B.Cn.L. and B.C.L., canon of the collegiate church of St Chad, Salop., citing the bishop's mandate dated 30 April 1450 at Leicester, to hold an inquest with a jury to discover the true value of the vicarage of Leek, Staffs.[215]

CERTIFICATORIUM INQUISICIONIS PRO VICARIA DE LEKE. Reverendo in Christo patri et domino domino Willelmo dei gracia Coventrensi et Lichfeldensi episcopo vester humulis et devotus orator Johannes Reedhill in utroque jure bacallarius ecclesie vestre collegiate sancti Cedde Salopie canonicus obedienciam reverentiam omnimodas tanto patri debitas cum honore. Mandatum vestrum reverendum nuper recepi sub eo qui sequitur verborum tenore: Willelmus [etc.] dilecto in Christo filio magistro Johanni Reedhill in utrique jure bacallario canonico ecclesie nostre collegiate Salopie salutem graciam et benediccionem. Presentarunt nobis religiosi viri abbas et conventus monasterii de Dieuleucres dilectum sibi in Christo dominum Galfridum Massy presbyterum ad vicariam perpetuam ecclesie parochialis de Leke nostre diocesis per liberam resignacionem domini Hugonis Wetrenes ultimi vicarii eiusdem in manibus nostris factam et per nos admissam vacantem et ad eorum presentacionem spectantem. Set quia ex relacione fidedigna ad nostrum nuper pervenit auditum quod fructus et proventus dicte vicarie ad competentem et congruam exhibicionem vicarii huiusmodi in eadem minime sufficiunt hiis diebus cum debita supportacione singulorum onerum eidem incumbencium, nos igitur cupientes prout ad officium nostrum pastorale pertinere dinoscitur indempnitatem prefate proficere ac eciam certificari qui et quales sunt fructus et proventus vicarie predicte et ad quam summam annuatim se extendunt, vobis committimus et mandamus quatinus per rectores et vicarios predicte ecclesie convicinos in numero sufficienti presenti in forma juris iuratos fidelem et diligentem faciatis inquisicionem, videlicet de vero valore fructuum et proventuum prefate vicarie de Leke pertinencium et ad quam summam annuatim se extendunt necnon de oneribus ordinariis et extraordinariis eiusdem et quantum se eciam extendunt, vocatis ad hoc genere et in specie de jure vocandis. Et quod in premissis feceritis ac per inquisicionem huiusmodi inveneritis, nos cum omnia celeritate ac comoda distincte et aperte certificare curetis per litteras vestras patentes harum seriem ac dicte inquisicionis formam nominaque et cognomina inquisitorum huiusmodi plenius in se continentes auctentice sigillatas. Datum Leycester sub sigillo nostro ultimo die mensis Aprilis anno domini millesimo CCCC^mo quinquagesimo et nostre consecracionis anno tercio. CUIUS auctoritate mandati in ecclesia parochiali de Leke xxij° die mensis Julii anno domini millesimo CCCC^mo quinquagesimo super vero valore fructuum et proventuum vicarie prefate ecclesie de Leke pertinencium et ad quam summam se annuatim extendunt necnon de oneribus ordinariis et extraordinariis eiusdem vicarie et ad quantum eciam se extendunt ac aliis articuliis in dicto mandato vestro

---

[215] See **101**.

reverendo continentibus, vocatis ad hoc in genere et in specie abbate et conventu monasterio de Dieuleucres necnon Galfrido Massy ad dictam vicariam per prefatos abbatem et conventum presentato in pleno loci capitulo, videlicet per magistrum Ricardum Falchrest rectorem ecclesie parochialis de Kyngesley, dominum Willelmum Rufford rectorem ecclesie parochialis de Grendon, dominum Willelmum Walker rectorem ecclesie parochialis de Swetnam, dominum Humfridum Harrison perpetuum vicarium ecclesie parochialis de Alstonffeld, dominum Johannem Briggham, perpetuum vicarium ecclesie parochialis de Bedulf, et dominum Henricum Cole vicarium temporale de Ipstone presentes in forma juris juratos diligentem feci inquisicionem qui dicunt quod dicta vicaria de Leke est dotata in vj marcas pecunie numeratis per dictos abbatem et conventum solvendas ad tres annui terminos ut in composicione dicte vicarie liquet manifeste; Item in decimis personalibus et aliis tempore quadragesimali soluciones que extendunt se annuatim ad valorem ix marcarum vj solidorum viij denariorum; Item in oblacionibus quatuor festorum principalium que extendunt se ad quinque marcas et x solidos; Item in fructibus et proventibus capellanorum videlicet Chedulton Ipstone et Horton ac denariis panis benedictis et aliis valentibus annuatim viij marcas vj solidos; Item in cera oblata die purificacionis beate Marie annuatim valente v solidos; Item in decima lini et canabi valenti viij solidos iiij denarios; Item in decima aucarum valenti annuatim xx solidos; Item in decima porcellorum et ovorum annuatim valenti vj solidos viij denarios; Item in decima granorum et feni proveniente de ortis curtilagiis omnium ruralium et aliorum una cum decima feni de Grendon valente annuatim x solidos; Item in omnibus perquisitis casualibus ut de legatis sponsalibus vigiliis mortuorum testamentis et consimilibus annuatim valentibus xl solidos. Dicunt eciam quod perpetuus vicarius quicumque ecclesie parochialis de Leke predicte qui pro tempore fuerit obligatur ad exhibicionem unius capellani continue celebrantis in capella de Chedulton hoc anno recipientis pro salario suo et sic annuatim viij marcas, et ad exhibicionem continuam unius capellani celebrantis in capella de Ipstone qui recipit hoc anno nomine stipendii sui centum solidos ac ad exhibicionem continuam unius capellani celebrantis in capella de Horton percipientis pro salario suo hoc anno septem marcas. Et sic onera dicte vicarie extendunt se ad summam quatuordecim marcas. Que omnia et singula patrem vestrum reverendum certifico per presentes sigillo officii mei et sigillis dictorum inquisitorum consignatis. Datum apud Leke predicta xxij° die mensis Julii anno domini millesimo CCCC^mo quinquagesimo.

Memorandum quod premissa hic inseruntur ex mandato domini videlicet apud Heywode x° die mensis Augusti anno domini.

307. [Fo. 84v] 21 April 1452. Ratification by the bishop of a confession made by Humphrey Swynnerton of his marriage to Joan Cotes, daughter of Humphrey Cotes, while he was under age.

CONFESSIO HUMFRI SWYNERION. Item memorandum quod xxj die mensis Aprilis anno domini millesimo quadragentesimo quinquagesimo secundo indiccione quinta decima pontificatus sanctissimi in Christo patris et domini nostri domini Nicholai divina providencia pape quinti anno sexti apud Heywode in capella principali manerii ibidem comparuit coram domino Coventrensi et Lichfeldensi episcopo voluntarie ut apparuit Humfridus Swynerton juvenis de Isewall etatis xix annorum, non ad hoc compulsus set ut apparuit voluntarie sponte et non deliberato, coram domino Willelmo Coventrensi et Lichfeldensi episcopo predicto erumperat ac publice fatebatur quod ipse alias impubes contraxit solempnizavit et optinuit matrimonium inter se et Johannam filiam Humfridi Cotes armigeri per rectorem nunc de Hamstall Ridware videlicet citra festum natalis sancti Johannis baptiste quod erat anno domini millesimo CCC^{mo} quadragesimo ix^{no} infra hospicium dicti Humfridi Cotes in capella ibidem, ac ipse huiusmodi matrimonium sic contractum expresse adtunc coram dicto reverendo patre gratificavit oretenus ratificavitque et approbavit ac in dictam Johannam ut in conjungem ducere consensiit precise et expresse pre ceteris mulieribus viventibus in mundo nec eam mutare aut per aliud derelinquire volebat nec intendebat. Et incontinenter post prefatus reverendus pater Coventrensis et Lichfeldensis episcopus confessionem suam huiusmodi judicialiter factam acceptavit approbavit et ratificavit in hec verba: In dei nomine amen. Nos Willelmus permissione divina Coventrensis et Lichfeldensis episcopus justam confessionem per te coram nobis factam acceptamus approbamus ratificamus et auctorizamus ac pro matrimonium ex parte tua occasione confessis tue predicte decernimus et declaramus in hiis scriptis. Presentibus tunc ibidem dominis Thoma Byrom canonico ecclesie cathedralis Lichfeldensis et Johanne Averall literato testibus.

308. [Fo. 85] 5 January 1451. Manumission by the bishop, with the ratification of the dean and chapter of Lichfield cathedral, and the prior and convent of Coventry cathedral, of John Sallowe.

MANUMISSIO JOHANNIS SALLOWE. Omnibus Christi fidelibus ad quos presens scriptum pervenerint Willelmus [etc.] salutem in domino sempiternam. Noveritis nos manumisse et liberum fecisse Johannem Sallowe filium Willelmi Sallowe in comitatu Derbie nativum nostrum cum totis sectis et sequelis suis procreatis et procreandis ac omnibus bonis et catallis suis mobilibus et immobilibus, ita quod nec nos predictus Willelmus episcopus nec successores nostri aliquod juris seu clamei in corpore predicti Johannis Sallowe vel se vel sequilis suis bonis seu catallis eiusdem deceter exigere seu vendicare poterimus in futurum, qui per presens scriptum nostrum ab omni jugo vetustatis bondagii et servitutis sumus exclusi imperpetuum. In cuius rei testimonium hinc presenti scripto sigillum nostrum apponendum. Datum in castro nostro de Eccleshale quinto die mensis Januarii anno domini MCCCCL^{mo} regno vero regis Henrici sexti post conquestum Anglie vicesimo nono.

CONFIRMACIO DECANI ET CAPITULI LICHFELDENSIS SUPER MANUSSIONE PREDICTO. Universis sancte matris ecclesie filiis presentes litteras visuris vel audituris Johannes Verney decanus et capitulum ecclesie cathedralis Lichfeldensis salutem in omnium salvatore. Noveritis universitas vestra litteras reverendi in Christo patris et domini domini Willelmi dei gracia Coventrensis et Lichfeldensis episcopi nuper inspexisse in hec verba: Omnibus Christi fidelibus et cetera, quibus litteras per nos inspectis nos Johannes decanus et capitulum supradictum habitis super premissis deliberacione provida et matura eas que ratas et gratas habentes quantum ad nos attinet auctoritate nostra capitulari acceptamus approbamus ratificamus et tenore presencium confirmamus. In cuius rei testimonium sigillum nostrum commune presentibus apponi fecimus. Datum Lichfeld' in domo nostra capitulari vicesimo die mensis et anno predictis.

CONFIRMACIO PRIORIS ET CAPITULI COVENTRENSIS SUPER EADEM. Universis sancte matris ecclesie filiis presentes litteras visuris vel audituris Ricardus prior et capitulum ecclesie cathedralis Coventrensis (as in the preceding confirmation). Datum Coventr' in domo nostra capitulari vicesimo primo [die] mensis et anno predictis.[216]

309. [Fo. 86] Indult of Pope Boniface IX dated 12 November 1402, allowing the prior of Lenton, O.Clun., [Notts.] to farm the priory's appropriated churches to clerks or laymen.[217]

COPIA BULLA PRO PRIORE DE LENTON. Bonifacius episcopus servus servorum dei dilectis filiis priori et conventui prioratus sive monasterii de Lenton ordinis Cluniacensis Eboracensis diocesis salutem et apostolicam benediccionem. Quociens illud a nobis petitur quod sacre religioni et honestati convenire videtur, animo nos decet libenti concedere et petencium desideriis congruam suffragium impartiri. Hunc est quod nos vestris in hac parte supplicacionibus inclinati ut tu fili prior et successores tui priores vestri prioratus sive monasterii qui erunt pro tempore et vos filii conventus omnes fructus et proventus decimas oblaciones ecclesiarum capellarum porcionum pensionum aliarumque possessionum ad vos vestrumque prioratum sive monasterium modo spectancium vel imposterum spectaturarum clericis sive laicis conjunctim vel divisim prout vobis magis videatur expediens, et eciam antequam huiusmodi fructus redditus et proventus decime porciones ac penqiones a solo vel a novem partibus seperentur se oblaciones offerantur, arrendare locare et ad firmam dare seu vendere libere et licete valeatis, necnon prefatis clericis sive laicis ut fructus redditus et proventus decimas pensiones et porciones colligere et ad firmam recipere ac in fundo clericali sive laicali libere et licete imponere et de eis disponere possint per ipsorum libito voluntatis, auctoritate apostolica tenore presencium indulgemus, ordinariorum vestrorum vel aliorum quorumque licencia super hoc minime requisita seu obtenta, apostolicis necnon bone memorie Ottonis et Ottoboni dudum in regno Anglie sed apostolice legatorum ac provincialibus et synodalibus ac aliis constitucionibus ac statutis ordinis vestri contrariis juramento confirmacione apostolica vel quacumque firmitate alia roboratis non obstantibus quibuscumque. Et si forte contingat quod venerabilis frater noster archiepiscopus Eboracensis pro tempore vel quivis alius litteras a sede apostolica vel ejus legatis contra huiusmodi indultum nostrum impetraverit aut in futurum impetrare contigerit in genere vel in specie litteras ipsas nisi in illis de presentibus plena et expressa ac de verbo ad verbum mencio habeatur nullum penitus obtinere volumus robur firmitatis decernentes exnunc irritum et inane si secus super hiis a quoquam quavis auctoritate scienter vel ignoranter contigerit attemptari nulli ergo omnino hominum liceat hanc paginam nostre concessionis voluntatis et constitucionis infringere vel ei ausu temerario contrarie. Siquis autum hoc attemptare presumpserit, indignacionem omnipotentis dei et beatorum [Petri] et Pauli apostolorum ejus se noverit incursurum. Datum Rome apud sanctum Petrum ij idus Novembris pontificatus nostri anno quarto decimo.

216 Fo. 85v is blank.
217 Calendared *CPL* v, 545.

310. Indult of Pope Boniface IX dated 17 January 1403, allowing the prior of Thurgarton, O.S.A., [Notts.] to farm the priory's appropriated churches to clerks or laymen.[218]

[The tenor of the bull is practically identical to that of 309 above with very slight difference in word order.]

311. [Not dated.] Ralph Yong, chaplain of the chantry in Lichfield cathedral appointed by King Edward I petitions the bishop to appoint some certain altar for his chantry, which he holds at 6 marks p.a. in two portions. The bishop, with the consent of Master George Radclyff, assigns the altar which Master George has newly constructed, and Master George undertakes to assign to the chaplain and his successors land and tenements to the value of 13s 4d p.a.

LIMITACIO ET ASSIGNACIO ALTARIS DOMINO RADULPHO YONG CAPELLANO CANTARIE DOMINI EDWARDI REGIS IN ECCLESIA LICHFELDENSI PER EPISCOPUM FACTA. Willelmus [etc.] dilecto in Christo filio Radulpho Yong capellano cantarie pro regibus in ecclesia nostra cathedralis Lichfeldensi et omnibus successoribus dicti Radulphi salutem graciam et benediccionem. Cum sancte laudabilis memorie serenissimus princeps dominus Edwardus filius Henrici regis Anglie et dominus Hibernie illustris inter cetera magnificencie seu regalis beneficia quadam cantariam in dicta ecclesia nostra cathedrali Lichfeldensi pro salute sua et progenitorem suorum tam vivorum quauum mortuorum fundavit ordinavit et stabilivit ad valorem sex marcarum per venerabiles et religiosos viros abbatem et conventum monasterii sancti Petri Salopie annuatim fideliter persolvandas, videlicet quadraginta solidos ad festum sancti Michaelis archangeli et quadraginta solidos ad festum annunciacionis beate Marie in plenariam solucionem summe predicte, cuiusquidem cantarie collacio nobis et successoribus nostris pertinet; hinc est quod idem dominus Radulphus Yong presbyter predictus nobis pro se et successoribus suis cum debita instancia humiliter supplicavit quatinus certum altare in ecclesia nostra cathedrali Lichfeldensi predicta pro deo et caritatis intuitu dicte cantarie limitari et assignari dignaremus. Unde nos desiderium ipsius Radulphus justum reputantes, quoddam altare per venerabilem confratrem nostrum magistrum Georgium Radclyff in ecclesia nostra cathedrali predicta ex expensis predicti magistri Georgii constructum ex consenu dicti confratris nostri predicto Radulpho et successoribus suis cantarie predicte assignamus et limitatus imperpetuum ad celebrandum divina in altari predicto, et predictus venerabilis confrater noster magister Georgius Radclyff promisit dare et assignare dicto Radulpho et successoribus suis divina celebrantibus ad altare predictum terras et tenementa ad valorem annuum tresdecim solidorum et quatuor denariorum. In cuius rei testimonium sigillum nostrum fecimus hiis apponi. Datum [*blank*].

312. [Fos 87–8] 30 September 1447. Certificate of John Verney,[219] dean of Lichfield cathedral, reciting the bishop's mandate dated 14 August 1447, that he

---

[218] Calendared in *CPL* v, 510.
[219] See note 79.

has warned the dignitaries and canons of Lichfield cathedral of the bishop's visitation on 2 October 1447, and appending schedules of vicars and chantry chaplains serving in the cathedral.

CERTIFICATORIUM CITACIONIS PRO VISITACIONE IN ECCLESIA CATHEDRALI LICHFELDENSI. Reverendo in Christo patri et domino, domino Willelmo dei gracia Coventrensi et Lichfeldensi episcopo paternitatis vestre commissariis quibuscumque vestre in hac parte obediencie filius Johannes Verney decanus ecclesie vestre cathedralis Lichfeldensis xviijo die mensis Augusti anno domini millesimo quadragentesimo quadragesimo septimo mandatum vestrum reverendum michi in hac parte directum exequendum cum ea qua decint reverencia in hec verba recipimus: Willelmus etc. dilecto in Christo filio domino Johanni Verney decano ecclesie nostre Lichfeldensis salutem graciam et bendiccionem. Cum ex incumbenti nobis solicitudine officii pastoralis gregis nobis commissa actualis visitacio tam de jure quam consuetudine laudabili legitime prescripta ad nos ut loci diocesanus jure ordinario pertinere debeat et pertinere consuevit, nos eiusdem gregis mores reformare extirpare vicia et in eo plantaria virtutum enferetro cupientes ne eiusdem gregis sanguis in districtio examine de nostris manibus requiratur, visitacionem nostram ordinariam in dicta nostra ecclesie Lichfeldensi inchoare ac ipsam ecclesiam nostram vosque decanum et capitulum ac certos ministros eiusdem favente domino canonice decrevimus visitare. Vos igitur decanum predictum tenore presencium premunimus peremptorie quem citamus ac per vos decanum antedictum omnes et singulos dignitates in dicta ecclesia nostra habentes ac alios canonicos et confratres vestros in dicta ecclesia nostra tam presentes quam absentes ac vicarios capellanos ceterosque dicte ecclesie nostre ministros quoscumque debite premuniri peremptorieque citari volumus et mandamus, quod compareatis et compareant ac eorum quilibet compareat coram nobis seu nostris in hac parte commissarius in domo capitulari ecclesie nostre predicte secundo die mensis Octobris proximo jam futuro cum continuacione et prorogacione dierum tunc sequenciun visitacionem nostram ordinari huiusmodi canonice et humiliter subituros, ac vestre et ipsorum dignitatum canonicatuum et prebendarum ac officiorum et administracionum huiusmodi titulos necnon vestrorum suorum ordinum atque pluritatum litteras prout vestri et ipsorum singulorum dignitas status officium vel administracio exigit et requiret exhibituros et ostensuros, ulteriusque facturos et recepturos quod huiusmodi visitacionis nostre ordinarie negocium in et de se exigit et requirit et in hac parte canonice dictaverint sancciones. Terminum vero brevem et peremptorio predictam propter imminencia animarum pericula et alias causas legitimas in hac parte nos moventes, sic duximus statuendum de die vobis recepionis presencium necnon quid feceritis in premissis nos aut dictos commissarios nostros dictis die et loco per litteras vestras patentes harum seriem ac premunicionis citacionis vestre huiusmodi modum et formam nominaque et cognominum per vos in hac parte citatorum una cum expressis designacionibus dignitatum prebendarum officiorum et administracionum huiusmodi plene in se continentes distincte et aperte certificetis sigillo auctentico sigillatas. Datum in manerio nostro de Heywode xiiijo die mensis Augusti anno domini millesimo quadragentesimo quadragesimo septimo et nostre consecracionis anno primo.

CUIUS quidem mandati vestri reverendi auctoritate omnes et singulos dignitates in dicta ecclesia vestra obtinentes ac alios canonicos et confratres meos in prefatam ecclesiam vestram tam absentes quam presentes, videlicet magistrum Georgium Radclyff decretorum doctorem et dicte vestre cathedralis thesaurium ac prebendarium prebende de Sallowe, magistrum Willelmum Berford prebendarium prebende de Bishophill, magistrum Thomam Chestrefeld prebendarium prebende de Tervyn, magistrum Johannem Jolyff prebendarium prebende de Darset et dominum Jacobum Langton prebendarium prebende de Stotfold, canonicos et confratres meos ac dicte ecclesie vestre cathedralis Lichfeldensis residentiariis per me personaliter approhensos peremptorie citavi et premunivi, ac eciam magistrum Rogerum Wall archidiaconum Coventrensem ac prebendarium prebende de Offeley, magistrum Johannem Wendesley archidiaconum Stafford' et prebendarium prebende de Pryce, magistrum Thomam Heywode prebendarium prebende de Handesaker et magistrum Gregorium Newport prebendarium prebende de Flixton eciam personaliter peremptorie citavi et premonui, necnon certos canonicos absentes videlicet magistrum Thomam Thowe eiusdem ecclesie vestre cathedralis precentorum et prebendarium prebende de Ichyngton, magistrum Vincencium Clement prefate ecclesie vestre cathedralis cancellarium ac prebendarium prebende de Allerwas in eadem, magistrum Johannem Burdet archidiaconum Cestr' et prebendarium prebende de Bolton, magistrum Johannem Bryde archidiaconum Derb' et prebendarium prebende de Whityngton, magistrum Thomam Lane prebendarium prebende de Freeford, magistrum Thomam Clerke prebendarium prebende de Wolvey, magistrum Walterum Shiryngton prebendarium prebende de Tachebroke, magistrum Willelmum Grey prebendarium prebende de Longdon, magistrum Johannem Faukes prebendarium prebende de Parva Pipa, magistrum Rogerum Lye prebendarium prebende de Wyford, magistrum Willelmum Kynwolmersh prebendarium prebende de Gaye minori, magistrum Ricardum Lyot prebendarium prebende de Eccleshale, Johannem Higford prebendarium prebende unius medietatis de Ulfeston, dominum Thomam Maxfeld prebendarium prebende ulterius mediatatis de Ulfeston, magistrim Walterum Blaket prebendarium prebende de Gaye majori, magistrum Johannem Werkeworth prebendarium prebende de Sandiaker, magistrum Gregorium Browne prebendarium prebende de Curburgh, magistrum Johannem Arundell prebendarium prebende de Darneforth, Thomam Whitgreve prebendarium prebende de Colleywich, magistrum Ricardum Dikkelon prebendarium prebende de Bobynhill, et dominum Thomam Mawnchill prebendarium prebende de Ruyton in eadem, citacionibus stallis eorum choralibus sigillo officii mei decanatus affixatis eciam premunivi peremptorie citari: necnon omnes et singulos vicarios capellanos ceterosque dicte ecclesie vestre cathedralis antedicte ministros per me personaliter eciam apprehensos, quorum nomina et cognomina in quadam cedula presentibus annexata nominata subscribuntur, eciam premunivi et peremptorie citavi quod compareant et quilibet eorum compareat coram vobis die et loco in dicto mandato vestro reverendo contentis cum continuacione et prorogacione dierum sequencium visitacionem vestram ordinariam huiusmodi canonice et humiliter subdituros ac suos et eorum dignitatum canonicatuumque et prebendarum ac officiorum et administracionum huiusmodi titulos necnon suorum ordinum atque pluralitatum litteras prout sui et ipsorum singulorum dignitatas status officium vel administracio exigit et requirit exhibituros et ostensuros ulteriusque facturos et recepturos quod huiusmodi visitacionis vestre ordinarium negocium in et de se exigit et requirit, et sic mandatum vestrum reverendum humiliter sum executus. In cuius rei testimonium sigillum officium mei decanatus presentibus apposui. Datum apud Lichfeld' predicta ultimo die mensis Septembris supradicto anno domini supradicto.

NOMINA VICARIORUM.
Dominus Petrus Berell
Dominus Ricardus Brown
Dominus Willelmus Godybour
Dominus Rogerus Billeston
Dominus Johannes Yuglond
Dominus Ricardus Merbury
Dominus Ricardus Knyght
Dominus Willelmus Bokelond
Dominus Ricardus Trewe
Dominus Johannes Alderwas
Dominus Ricardus Hervy
Dominus Willelmus Manchest'
Dominus Willelmus Savage
Dominus Nicholas Coventr'
Robertus Batemon
Willelmus Bate
Johannes Sowresby
Magister Willelmus Gamull

NOMINA CAPELLANORUM CANTARIARUM
Dominus Willelmus Alton
Dominus Thomas Lyot
Dominus Ricardus Wade
Dominus Johannes Michell
Dominus Johannes Leycester
Dominus Thomas Bromley
Dominus Radulphus Yonge
Dominus Johannes Forton
Dominus Edward Croke
Dominus Johannes Okeley
Dominus Thomas Blangram
Dominus Petrus Bagshawe
Dominus Jacobus Radclyff

QUO die adveniente predictus decanus ceterique omnes et singuli confratres sui canonici et prebendarii supranominati adtunc tam presentes quam absentes per procuratores suos sufficienter et legitime comparentes necnon prefati vicarii omnes et singuli ac cantariarum capellani huiusmodi in domo capitulari prefate ecclesie cathedralis Lich' capitulariter congregati unanimi consensu et assensu in alto et in basso correccionibus statutis ordinacionibus laudis et decretis quibuscumque canonice per prefatum reverendum Willelmum Coventrensem et Lichfeldensem episcopum in visitacione sua huiusmodi factis et faciendis se et quemlibet eorum sigillatim subierunt et submiserunt ac predicte visitacioni sic habendum et tenendum ceterisque correccionibus statutis et ordinacionibus huiusmodi in eadem factis et faciendis ut predictur consensierunt ac humiliter et expresse ut tenentur obedierunt.

313. [Fo. 88] Letters testimonial of Andreas de Montecchio (*Monticulo*), D. Dec., vicar general in spirituals to Pope Eugenius IV, bishop of Osimo (*Auximum*), certifying that William Outlad of London diocese, vicar of Chilverscoton (*Coton*), had conferred on him the following holy orders, after due examination, in the chapel of the palace of St Appollinaris during general orders celebrated there: Subdeacon on the Saturday of the four times after the feast of Pentecost, 21 May 1440. Deacon on the Saturday of the four times after the feast of the exaltation of the Holy Cross, 24 September 1440. Priest on the Saturday of the four times after the feast of St Lucy, 17 December 1440.[220]

314. [Fos 89–94v] 28 July 1450. Foundation by William Bothe, bishop of Coventry and Lichfield, Sir John Byron,[221] Richard Bothe, Laurence Bothe clerk and Seth Worsley, of a chantry for two chaplains in the parish church of Eccles, Lancashire, to celebrate daily for the good estate of King Henry VI and the bishop while they live and for their souls after death, and for others named. The chaplains are to have lands, rents, tenements, services and other possessions to the value of 24 marks p.a. and to be capable of impleading and being impleaded by others under the name of 'the chaplains of St Katherine' in the parish church of Eccles. The royal licence for the foundation, tested by King Henry VI. is dated at Westminster on 22 January 1450. [The statutes are obviously the model for those for the chantry of Jesus and the Blessed Virgin Mary (**315**).][222]

FUNDACIO CANTARIE IN ECCLESIA PAROCHIALI BEATE MARIE DE ECCLES. Universis sancte matris ecclesie filiis ad quod et quorum noticiam presentes littere pervenerint, Willelmus Bothe episcopus Coventrensis et Lichfeldensis, Johannes Byron miles Ricardus Bothe Laurencius Bothe clericus et Seth Worsley, salutem in domino sempiternam et fide, indubiam et perpetuam presentibus adhibere. Universitatis vestre noticie notum facimus per presente quod nos Willelmus Bothe episcopus Johannes Byron miles Ricardus Bothe Laurencius Bothe clericus et Seth Worsley, licencia primitus christianissimi in Christo principis et domini nostri domini Henrici sexti regis Anglie et Francie et domini Hibernie illustrissimi nobis Willelmo Bothe Coventrensi et Lichfeldensi episcopo predicto Johanni Byron militi Ricardo Bothe Laurencio Bothe clerico et Seth Worsley predictis graciose data in hac parte et concessa et per nos obtenta, prout in litteris regiis patentibus

---

[220] It is clear that this entry does not belong to the register of William Bothe but to that of his effective successor, Reginald Boulers. It is addressed to 'Reginaldi Coven' et Lich' episcopi'. The register of Boulers shows that on 26 September 1454 William Outlade was instituted to the vicarage of Chilverscoton, Warwickshire (Lichfield Record Office, B/A/1/11 (Register of Reginald Boulers), fo. 21). For a previous institution to Chilverscoton, see **68**.

[221] Bothe's brother in law, see **110**.

[222] In 1368, Bothe's grandfather, Thomas, had left 100 marks for two priests to celebrate for King Edward III, his feudal overlord and others (R. Hollingworth, *Mancuniensis: or An History of the Towne of Manchester and what is most memorable concerning it* (Manchester, 18239), p. 52).

dicti domini regis Henrici sexti inferius conscriptis plenius est contentum, quarum litterarum regiarum tenor sequitur in hec verba: HENRICUS dei gracia rex Anglie et Francie et dominus Hibernie omnibus ad quos presentes littere pervenerint salutem. Sciatis quod nos dei gracia nostra speciali ob reverenciam dei et divini cultus augmentacione concessimus et licenciam dedimus pro nobis et heredibus nostris quantum in nobis est Willelmo Bothe episcopo Coventrensi et Lichfeldensi Johanni Byron militi Ricardo Bothe Laurencio Bothe clerico et Seth Worsley quod ipsi quatuor tres vel duo eorun quandam cantariam perpetuam de duobus capellanis in ecclesia parochiali beate Marie Virginis de Eccles in comitatu Lancastrie divina in eadem ecclesia pro salubri statu nostro ac ipsius episcopi dum vixerimus, et pro animabus nostris cum ab hac luce migraverimus, ac pro animabus certarum aliarum personarum per ipsos episcopum Johannem Ricardum Laurencium et Seth nominandarum et omnium fidelium defunctorum singulis diebus juxta ordinacionem ipsorum episcopi Johannis Ricardi Laurencii et Seth quatuor tercium vel duorum eorum in hac parte faciendam celebraturis facere fundare creare erigere et stabilire possint imperpetuum; et quod capellani predicti et eorum successores capellani cantarie sancte Katerine in ecclesia parochiali beate Marie Virginis de Eccles nuncupentur, quodque capellani predicti et eorum successores capellam cantarie predicte sint persone capaces et habiles ad omnimoda terras et tenementa redditus et servicia ac alias possessiones quascumque de quibuscumque personis adquirendi capiendi et recipiendi, tenendum sibi et successoribus suis capellanis cantarie predicte imperpetuum, necnon quod ydem capellani et eorum successores capellam cantarie predicte persone habiles ad alios implacitandos et ab aliis implacitari existant ac ad defendendum in quibuscumque placitis et querelis per nomen capellanorum cantarie sancte Katerine Virginis in ecclesia parochiali beate Marie de Eccles. Et ulterius de uberiori gracia nostra concessimus et licenciam dedimus pro nobis et heredibus nostris quantum in nobis est prefato episcopo Johanni Ricardo Laurencio et Seth quod ipsi quatuor tres vel duo eorun terras tenementa redditus et servicia ac alias possessiones quascumque cum pertinenciis ad valorem viginti quatuor marcarum per annum ultra reprisas, tam ea que de nobis tenentur in burgagio vel socagio quam ea que de nobis non tenentur, adquirere et ea prefatis capellanis cantarie predicte cum eadem cantaria sic facta fundata creata erecta et stabilita fuerit dare concedere et assignare possint, habendum et tenendum eisdem capellanis et successoribus suis capellanis cantarie predicte imperpetuum divina in ecclesia predicta pro statu et animabus predictis singulis diebus celebraturis in auxilium sustentacionis sue ac in supportacionem aliorum onerum juxta ordinacionem ipsorum episcopi Johannis Ricardi Laurencii et Seth quatuor tercium vel duorum eorum in hac parte faciendum imperpetuum. Et insuper de uberiori gracia nostra concessimus et licenciam dedimus pro nobis et heredibus nostris quantum in nobis est predictis capellanis cantarie predicte cum eadem cantaria sic facta fundata creata erecta et stabilita fuerit a prefatis episcopo Johanno Ricardo Laurencio et Seth quatuor tribus vel duobus eorum recipere possint terras tenementa redditus et servicia ac alias possessiones quascumque cum pertinenciis ad valorem viginti et quatuor marcarum per annum ultra reprisas, tam ea que de nobis tenentur in burgagio vel socagio quam ea que de nobis non tenentur, habendum et tenendum eisdem capellanis et successoribus suis capellanis cantarie predicte imperpetuum si militis licenciam dedimus specialem, statuto de terris et tenementis ad manum mortuam non ponendis edito non obstante. In cuius rei testimonium has litteras nostras fieri fecimus testimoniales. Teste me ipso apud Westmonasterium vicesimo secundo die mensis Januarii anno regni nostri vicesimo octavo. Ad fundacionem ereccionem creacionem et stabilimentum unius cantarie duorum capellanorum in ecclesia parochiali beate Marie Virginis de Eccles in comitatu Lancastrie juxta ordinacionem vim formam et effectum huiusmodi licencie regie suprascripte nobis in hac parte concesse procedimus in hunc modum. IN PRIMIS nos Willelmus episcopus Coventrensis et Lichfeldensis predictus Johannes Byron miles Ricardus Bothe Laurencius Bothe clericus et Seth Worsley predicti de dei omnipotentis unam summi confisi dicti domini regis Henrici sexti licencia ac certororum quorum interest consensu et assensu prehabitis, fulciti facimus creamus erigimus stabilimus et fundamus unam perpetuam cantariam duorum capellanorum in ecclesia parochiali beate Marie Virginis de Eccles in comitatu Lancastrie pro salubri statu dicti domini regis Henrici sexti nostrique predicti Willelmi episcopi dum vixerimus, et pro animabus dicti regis Henrici sexti nostrique Willelmi episcopi predicti cum ab hac luce migraverimus, animabusque certarum aliarum personarum per nos Willelmum episcopum predictum Johannem Byron militem Ricardum Bothe Laurencium Bothe clericum et Seth Worsley predictos inferius nominatarum ac omnium fidelium defunctorum singulis diebus juxta ordinacionem nostram inferius descriptis perpetuo celebraturorum. QUAM cantariam perpetuam capellanorum cantarie sancte Katerine in ecclesia parochiali beate Marie Virginis de Eccles nuncupari et esse volumus ordinamus creamus stabilimus et fundamus per presentes. Volumus quoque insuper ordinamus creamus stabilimus et fundamus ex licencia dicti regis Henrici quod capellani predicti et eorum successores dicte cantarie capellani quicumque in vim licencie regie predicte sint persone capaces et habiles ad omnimoda terras et tenementa redditus et servicia ac alias possessiones quascumque de quibuscumque personis adquirendum capiendum et recipiendum tenendum sibi et successoribus suis capellanis cantarie predicte imperpetuum. QUOD CAPELLANI SINT HABILES AD IMPLACITANDUM ET AB ALIIS IMPLACITARI. Et quod ijdem capellani eorumque successores in capellam dicte cantarie quicumque persone habiles ad alios implacitandum et ad alios implacitari existant ac ad defenendendum in quibuscumque placitis et querelis per nomen capellanorum cantarie sancte Katerine in ecclesia parochiali beate Marie Virginis de Eccles. DE JURE PATRONATUS CANTARIE VIVENTIBUS FUNDATORIBUS. Item volumus statuimus et ordinamus quod jus patronatus sive conferendum sive presentandum personas idoneas ac capellanias predictas tam in primaria sua incorporacione quam eciam postea, quociens ipsas capellanias eorum aliquam vacare contigerit, semper atque solum et in solidum pleno jure ad nos prefatum Willelmum Bothe episcopum predictum dum vixerimus, et post decessum nostri Willelmi episcopi ad nos prefatos Johannem Byron militem Ricardum Bothe Laurencium Bothe clericum et Seth Worsley durante vita nostra dumtaxat pertineat, ita quod post mortem nostri prefati Willelmi episcopi predicti Johannes Byron miles Ricardus Bothe Laurencius Bothe clericus et Seth Worsley illos qui in capellanos cantarie predicte fuerint proficiendos episcopo diocesano vel ejus vicario in spiritualibus generali seu sede ibidem vacante custodi spiritualitatis eiusdem presentare teneantur. DE JURAMENTO PRESENTANDI IN ADMISSIONE ET INSTITUCIONE. Ac quilibet eorundem capellanorum postquam per eundem episcopum seu ejus vicarium in spiritualibus generalem seu sede ibidem vacante custodem spiritualitatis eiusdem ad dictas capellanias admissum et canonice institutus fuerit, tactis per eum sacrosanctis dei evengeliis, ad ea juret quod dicte cantarie debite et honeste quatenus in ea est deserviet in divinis. DE FORMA INDUCENDI CAPELLANI IN POSSESSIONE. Et quod fundacionem et ordinacionem dicte cantarie ac omnia et singula in ipsis fundacione et ordinacione contenta quatenus ad ipsum attinet observabit, alioquin huiusmodi admissio et institucio ad capellanias huiusmodi nullius sint momenti vigoris vel virtutis, habitasque litteras episcopi diocesani seu ejus vicarii in spiritualibus generalis seu sede ibidem vacante custodis spiritualitatis eiusdem super huiusmodi admissione et institucione, tunc episcopus diocesanus qui pro tempore fuerit vel ejus vicarius in spiritualibus generalis seu sede ibidem vacante custos spiritualitatis eiusdem dirigat litteras suas vicario ecclesie parochialis de Eccles qui pro tempore fuerit ad inducendum ipsos capellanos in cantariam predictam et realem possessionem eiusdem, ac easdem litteras coram vicario de Eccles predicte qui pro tempore perlegi faciant atque petant se in capellanos cantarie predicte et ad eorum possessionem admitti secundum vim formam et effectum litterarum suarum, quibus perlectis ipsos in capellanos cantarie predicte ac ad possessionem pacificam cantarie predicte cum suis juribus et pertinenciis universis vicarius de Eccles qui pro tempore fuerit benigne recipiat et inducat, et huiusmodi admissio institucio et induccio sint eis titulus competens et sufficiens absque aliqua alia admissione institucione vel induccione episcopi seu archidiaconi loci cuiuscumque. DE JURE PRESENTANDI POST MORTEM FUNDATORIS. Et quod post mortem nostrum prefati Willelmi episcopi Johannis Byron militis Ricardi Bothe Laurencii Bothe clerici et Seth Worsley jus patronatus sive presentandi personas idoneas ad dictas capellanias Roberto Bothe militi et Nicholai Byron filio Johannis Byron militis et eorum heredibus masculis de corporibus suis legitime precreatis, quociens aliquem capellani dicti cantarie obire privari vel alio modo a dicta cantaria recedere ipsius aut beneficium vel officium in eadem cantaria resignare et dimittere contigerit in futurum, pertineat videlicet quod dictus Robertus Bothe miles et eius heredes masculi de corpore suo legitime procreati presentabunt idoneam personam ad capellaniam quamcumque dicte cantarie primo vacante infra sex septimanas post mortem privaccionem ammocionem cessionem resignacionem seu dimissionem huiusmodi capellani, et si predictus Robertus Bothe miles et eius heredes masculi ut predicti infra sex septimanas huiusmodi personam idoneam ad capellaniam huiusmodi sic primo vacante presentare neglexerit seu neglexerint, quod tunc ad Nicholaum Byron et eius heredes masculos ut prefertur in pena negligencie huiusmodi pro illa tantum jus presentandi ad huiusmodi capellaniam devolvatur et pertineat. Et si dictus Nicholaus Byron et eius heredes masculi de corpore suo ut prefertur legitime procreati idoneam personam presentare ad capellaniam huiusmodi primo vacante per alias sex septimanas neglexerit seu neglexerint, quod tunc in pena negligencie sue huiusmodi ad episcopum diocesanum vel eius vicarium in spiritualibus generalem seu sede ibidem vacante ad custodem spiritualitatis eiusdem jus conferendi capellaniam huiusmodi persone idonee devolvatur ea vice tantum et pertineat, et prefatus Nicholaus Byron et eius heredes masculi de corpore suo legitime procreati presentabunt idoneam personam ad capellaniam quamcumque dicte cantarie secundo vacante infra sex septimanas post vaccacionem huiusmodi capellanie. Et si predictus Nicholaus Byron et eius heredes masculi de corpore suo legitime procreati ut premittitur infra sex septimanas huiusmodi personam idoneam ad capellaniam huiusmodi secundo vacantem presentare neglexit seu neglexerint, quod tunc ad Robertum Bothe militem et eius heredes masculos ut prefertur in pena negligencie huiusmodi pro illa tantum jus presentandi ad huiusmodi capellaniam devolvatur et perineat. Et si dictus Robertus Bothe miles et eius heredes masculi ut prefertur idoneam personam presentare ad capellaniam huiusmodi secundo vacantem per alias sex septimanas neglexerit seu neglexerint, quod tunc in pena negligencie sue huiusmodi ad episcopum diocesanum seu eius vicarium in spiritualibus generalem seu sede ibidem vacante custodem spiritualitatis jus conferendi capellaniam huiusmodi persone idonee devolvatur ut prefertur vice tantum et pertineat. Et sic alterni vicibus successive ad capellanias predictas modo et forma predictis presentabunt et non aliter nec alio modo. Et si contingat predictum Robertum Bothe militem et Nicholaum Byron sine heredibus masculis de corporibus suis legitime procreatis obire, tunc volumus ordinamus et statuimus quod jus patronatus sive presentandi personas idoneas ad dictas capellanias heredibus et assignatis nostri Willelmi episcopi antedicti pertineat, ita quod heredes et assignati nostri Willelmi episcopi predicti illos qui [in] capellanos predicte cantarie fuerint preficiendos episcopo diocesano vel ejus vicario in spiritualibus generali seu sede ibidem vacante custodi spiritualitatis eiusdem infra sex septimanas quociens aliquam capellaniam cantarie predicte vacare contigerit presentare personam idoneam teneantur, et si infra sex septimanas huiusmodi personam idoneam presentare neglexerint tunc jus conferendi capellaniam huiusmodi ad episcopum diocesanum vel eius vicariam in spiritualibus generalem seu sede ibidem vacante ad custodem spiritualitatis eiusdem devolvatur pro ea vice tantun et pertineat. DE ABSENCIA CAPELLANORUM A CANTARIE PER TOTUM ANNUM. Item volumus statuimus et ordinamus quod nullus capellanorum cantarie predicte a dicta cantaria ultra spacium triginta dierum quolibet anno continue vel per vices capiendum se absentabit, nisi cum certis capellanis cantarie predicte in vita nostra per nos nominatorum seu nominandorum per nos Willelmum episcopum predictum viva voce seu alio modo dispensatum fuerit, et si aliquis eorundem capellanorum cantarie predicte contrarium fecerit ipso facto a dicta cantaria sit privatus et ammotus. DE NON RECIPIENDO BENEFICIUM AUT OFFICIUM CUM DICTA CANTARIA. Et quod nullus capellanorum predictorum pro tempore intitulacionis sue in ipsa cantaria aliquod beneficium ecclesiasticum incompatabile nec aliquod officium extra parochiam de Eccles predictam nec servicium ubicumque habeat recipiat aut aliquo modo occupet, nisi cum certis capellanis cantarie predicte in vita nostra per nos nominatis seu nominandis ut prefertur per nos Willelmum episcopum predictum viva voce seu alio modo dispensatum fuerit. Et si in contrarium aliquis capellanorum predictorum aliquod beneficium vel servicium habuerit receperit seu occupaverit, ipso facto a dicta cantaria sit privatus et ammotus. DE DISPENSACIONE NON PROCURANDA AUT OPTINENDA. Ac insuper siquis capellanorum cantarie predictum secum de non residendo in dicta cantaria contrarium effectum presentis ordinacionis nostre dispensari procuraverit aut obtineat, eo ipso eundem capellanum a dicta cantaria privatum et ammotum perpetuo esse volumus statuimus et ordinamus per presentes. DE HORIS CANONICIS DICENDIS INFRA ECCLESIAM DE ECCLES. Necnon volumus statuimus et ordinamus quod dicti duo capellani cantarie predicte et eorum successores ac alii capellani per eosdem conducti seu conducendi dum presentes fuerint in parochia de Eccles predicte singulis diebus, legitimo impedimento cessante, divinum officium matutinas scilicet de die et omnes horas canonicas secundum usum Sarum' et missam si commode valeant infra ecclesiam sive capellam de

Eccles predictam horis et temporibus debitis et congruis ac officium mortuorum, videlicet PLACEBO et DIRIGE cum novem leccionibus ac COMMENDACIONEM, pro animabus dicti regis Henrici sexti et prefati nostri Willelmi episcopi cum ab hac luce migraverimus et animabus certarum personarum inferius nominatarum quantum eis deus dederit cum debita intencione et devocione horas canonicas et missam huiusmodi in dicta ecclesia sive capella studiose dicent et devote celebrabunt. DE HORA DICENDI MISSAS DIEBUS FESTIVIBUS. Et quod presertim diebus dominicalibus et festivis non ante horam octavam per estimacionem seu saltem ante adventum plurimarinus parochianorum ad dictam ecclesiam de Eccles confluencium et tunc non simul sed successive missas celebrabunt. DE VESTIMENTIS CONPLICENDIS POST MISSAM CELEBRATAM. Et quod capellani predicti seu unus eorum post missam celebratam seu missas celebratas in dicta ecclesia vestes sacerdotales decenter et honeste complicent seu complicet, ac eas vestes libros et calices ac alia ornamenta ad altare spectantia quecumque in mansa cantarie predicte quam cito edificata fuerit et medio in vicaria ibidem portent et reponant seu portet et reponat, linthiaminibus altaris aliisque ornamentis circa altare pendente dumtaxat exceptis et ibidem dimissis, et in crastino die reportent seu reportet tales calices vestes libros et alia ornamenta que eisdem capellanis pro illo die videbuntur necessaria; et si aliquo dicti capellani cantarie predicte seu unus eorum huiusmodi libros calices vestes et alia ornamenta predicta in mansum quam cito ut prefertur edificatum fuerit et medio tempore in dicta vicaria de Eccles non portaverint seu portaverit, quadraginta denarios tociens quociens ipso facto de porcionibus suis amittant, et vicarius dicte ecclesie de Eccles qui pro tempore fuerit libros calices vestesque et alia ornamenta huiusmodi in mansum sive in vicariam predictam in forma prescripta reportavit, et huiusmodi quadraginta denarios labore recipiet dictique capellani cantarie huiusmodi quadraginta denarios porcionibus suis ut prefertur vicario persolvant. Et si contingat aliquem calicem librum vestem vel aliud ornamentum quodcumque cantarie predicte et in futurum eidem cantarie qualitercumque pertinencia propter defectum portacionis seu reposicionis huiusmodi aut alias qualitercumque per negligenciam alicuius capellanorum predictorum furari asportari deperdi consumi vel deteriorari, quod tunc infra quadraginta dies post huiusmodi furacionem asportacionem deperdicionem consumpcionem vel deterioracionem de propriis bonis et expensis et porcione sua satisfaciet cantarie predicte ille cuius culpa vel negligencia huiusmodi foracio asportacio deperdicio consumpcio vel deterioracio facta fuerit eisdem; et si infra quadraginta dies huiusmodi non satisfecerint seu non satisfecerit cantarie predicte ille cuius culpa vel negligencia huiusmodi furacio asportacio deperdicio consumpcio vel deterioracio facta fuerit ut prefertur pro eisdem, a dicte cantaria ipso facto sint privati et ammoti seu sit privatus et ammotus. DE REPARACIONIBUS ET EMENDACIONIBUS VESTIMENTORULM. Volumus insuper statuimus et ordinamus quod capellani cantarie predicti ad reparacionem et emendacionem dictorum librorum vestimentorum et aliorum ornamentorum cantarie predicte et in futurum eidem cantarie qualitercumque pertinenciis de bonis predicte cantarie singulis annis imperpetuum quadraginta denarios habebunt et recipient, et si huiusmodi summa quadraginta denariorum ad reparacionem et emendacionem huiusmodi faciendas non sufficient, quod tunc ijdem capellani de propriis porcionibus suis et expensis huiusmodi reparacionem et emendacionem librorum vestimentorum et aliorum ornamentorum cantarie predicte ad altare spectantium compleant et perimpleant cum effectu; et si contingat in futurum aliquem librum calicem vestem ornamentum seu vestimentum quodcumque cantarie predicte furari asportare deperdi consumi vel deteriorari absque predictorum capellanorum aut alicuius eorundem culpa defectu seu negligencia sive usu temporis vel vetustate consumi lacerari aut deformari, ita quod amplius congrue reparari seu reformari nec ad cultum divini faciendum eisdem honeste deservire valeat, quod tunc juxta ad et per supervisionem consilium et consensum fundatorum cantarie predicte dum vixerint et post mortem fundatorum predictorum per supervisionem patronorum cantarie huiusmodi pro tempore existentium et de bonis cantarie predicte alius liber calis vestis ornamentum seu vestimentum quodcumque ad cultum divinum in dicta cantaria necessaria de novo quam cito poterit ematur et ordinetur et ad cultum divinum in dicta cantaria faciendum traditur et conservetur. DE NON CELEBRANDO MISSAM IN ALIO LOCO QUAM IN ECCLESIA DE ECCLES. Ac insuper volumus statuimus et ordinamus quod si aliquis dictorum duorum capellanorum et eorum successorum seu aliorum capellanarum per eosdem pro tempore conductorum et conducendorum dum presentes fuerint infra parochiam de Eccles predictam in alio loco quam in ecclesia sive capella predicta missam celebraverit quocumque quisito colore, ipsum tunc a dicta cantaria ipso facto ordinamus esse privatum et ammotum, loco cuius sic privati et ammoti volumus et ordinamus alium capellanum idoneum in dicta cantaria canonice intitulari juxta formam superius annotatam; et capellani cantarie predicte illud idem facient observari per capellanos per eos conductos et conducendos et unus ipsorum capellanorum cantarie predicte tempore admissionis seu recepcionis eorundem capellanorum conductorum et conducendorum ab ipsis conductam et conducendum huiusmodi ad observacionem premissorum juramentum recipiat corporale. DE PROCESSIONIBUS INTERESSENDIS. Item volumus statuimus et ordinamus quod iidem capellani cantarie predicte et alii capellani eciam per eosdem conducti et conducendi dum presentes fuerint ut prefertur infra parochiam de Eccles predictam singulis diebus dominicalibus et festivis duplicibus ac principalibus in processionibus et aliisque diebus quibuscumque in processionibus infra dictam parochiam de Eccles faciendum processionaliter debite et honeste superpelliciis induti intersint procedant et progrediantur. DE INTERESSENDIS HORIS CANONICIS CUM NOTA CELEBRATIS INFRA ECCLESIAM DE ECCLES. Ac capellani cantarie predicte et alii per eos conducti et conducendi omnes et singuli dum presentes fuerint infra parochiam predictam ut premittitur horis canonicis vidiicet matutinis missis et vesperis ac aliis infra dictam ecclesiam cum nota celebratis superpelliciis inducti intersint cum debita intencione et devocione ut decet, in choro juxta eorum scienciam diligenter cantando desideria negligencia et confabulacionibus quibuscumque postpositis et omissis quousque hore canonice huiusmodi fuerint plenarie complete. QUOD MISSA DE REQUEM CUM NOTA CELEBRETUR DIE MERCURII QUALIBET SEPTIMANA DURANTE VITA EPISCOPI FUNDATORIS. Item volumus statuimus et ordinamus quod singulis perpetuis annis durante vita nostri Willelmi episcopi predicti die Mercurii in qualibet septimana unus dictorum capellanorum missam de requiem cum nota si commode fieri poterit, alioquin sine nota, celebravabit in ecclesia sive capella predicta pro animabus certarum aliarum personarum inferius nominatorum ac omnium benefactorum dicte cantarie et omnium fidelium defunctorum, nisi duplex festum in ipso die Mercurii evenerit vel aliquod legitimum impedimentum obstiterit, et tunc missam de Requiem celebrabit proximo die sequenti si duplex festum non fuerit, et quod post mortem nostri Willelmi episcopi unus eciam dictorum capellanorum die Mercurii in qualibet septimana singulis annis huiusmodi missam de Requiem cum nota si commode fieri poterit, alioquin sine nota, celebrabit in ecclesia sive capella predicta pro anima nostri Willelmi episcopi et pro animabus certarum personarum inferius nominatarum ac omnium benefactorum dicte cantarie et omnium fidelium defunctorum ut prefertur, nisi aliquod duplex festum ipso die evenerit vel aliquod aliud legitimum impedimentum obstiterit, et tunc missam de Requiem celebrabit proximo die sequente si duplex festum non fuerit. DE MISSA DE REQUIEM CELEBRANDA POST MORTEM CUM CERTIS ORACIONIBUS. Ac insuper volumus statuimus et ordinamus quod post mortem nostri Willelmi episcopi uterque duorum capellanorum predictorum et eorum successores ac alii quicumque per eosdem conducti et conducendi dicant imperpetuum singulis diebus in missa sua pro anima nostri dicti Willelmi episcopi specialem oracionem cum secreto et postcommunione in forma sequente, videlicet: DEUS qui inter apostolicos sacerdotes familum nostrum Willelmum pontificali fecisti dignitate censeri presta quis ut quorum vicem ad horam gerebat in terris eorum perpetuo consortio letet in celis per dominum. Item secretum offerimus tibi domine oblacionem nostre servitutis pro anima famuli tui pontificis supplicantes ut cum presulibus apostolice dignitatis quorum est executus officium habere intreatur sempiterne beatitudinis porcionem per dominum. Item postcommunio proficiat quis domine anime famuli tui pontificis divina celebracio misterii ut quem in terris huius numeris dispensatorem esse fecisti inter electos antistes cum jubeas communicari per dominum. Ordinamus eciam et statuimus quod dicti capellani eorumque successores prefate cantarie capellani et alii per eosdem conducti et conducendi quicumque singulis perpetuis futuris annis diem obitus nostri Willelmi episcopi quo die ab hac luce migraverimus teneant et devote continuent ac plenum servicium morturorom videlicet PLACEBO et DIRIGE cum novem leccionibus quocumque tempore anni contigerit ac commendacionem et missam de requiem simul in capella per nos Willelmum episcopum de novo constructa in predicta parochia de Eccles pro anima nostri Willelmi episcopi perdicant, nisi aliquod duplex festum ipso die evenerit vel aliquod aliud impedimentum obstiterit, et tunc missam de Requiem celebrabunt proximo die sequente si duplex festum non fuerit. DE FORMA TENENDA ET CONTINUANDA DIES OBITUUM FUNDATORUM ET ALIORUM. Eciam volumus ordinamus et statuimus quod dicti capellani eorumque successores prefate cantarie capellani et alii quicumque per eosdem conducti et conducendi singulis perpetuis futuris annis diem obitus Johannis patris mei et Johanne matris mee in dominicali proximo ante festum nativitatis beate Marie Virginis, et diem obitus Margerie sororis mee nuper uxoris Johannis Byron militis primo die Julii, ac eciam diem obitus Roberti Bothe militis, diem obitus Rogeri Bothe fratrum nostri episcopi, diem obitus Nicholai Byron filii Johannis Byron militis, diem obitus Willelmi Bothe filii Roberti Bothe militis, diesque obituum nostrorum Johannis Byron militis Ricardi Bothe Laurencii Bothe clerici et Seth Worsley, videlicet diebus quibus ab hac luce migraverint et migraverimus, teneant et devote continuent ac plenum servicium mortuorum, videlicet PLACEBO et DIRIGE cum novem leccionibus quocumque tempore anni contigerit ac COMMENDACIONEM ET MISSAM DE REQUIEM simul in capella predicta pro animabus omnium et singulorum predictorum ac nostram singulis perpetuis futuris annis perdicant, nisi aliquod duplex festum in huiusmodi die dominicali prescripta seu aliquo die obituum dictarum personarum evenerit vel aliud legitimum impedimentum obstiterit, et tunc missam de Requiem celebrabunt proximo die sequente si duplex festum non fuerit. Et si aliquis dictorum capellanorum aliquo dierum huiusmodi obituum a dicta capella tempore celebracionis huiusmodi servicii obituum predictorum cessante legitimo impedimento absens fuerit, ipsum sic absente tociens quociens sic absens fuerit in sex denarios ipso facto mulcari. Volumus quod sex denarios sex diversis pauperibus pro anima ejus cuius obitus huiusmodi die celebraturi volumus et ordinamus realiter persolvi. DE CERTA SUMMA PECUNIE DISTRIBUENDE DIE ANNIVERSARII EPISCOPI FUNDATORIS. Volumus quoque insuper ordinamus et statuimus singulis perpetuis futuris annis die anniversarii nostri prefati Willelmi episcopi in dicta capella solempniter faciendi celebrandi et tenendi triginta solidos monete Anglicane pro proventibus dicte cantarie per capellanos dicte cantarie et hoc in quolibet die anniversarii nostri prefati Willelmi episcopi distribuendos in hunc modum, videlicet vicario dicte ecclesie de Eccles sex denarios et cuilibet dictorum duorum capellanorum et aliorum per eosdem pro tempore conductorum et conducendorum cantarie predicte sex denarios, et cuicumque alii capellano presente in huiusmodi die anniversarii nostri predicti Willelmi episcopi quatuor denarios, et clerico parochiali dicte ecclesie de Eccles quatuor denarios et quatuor clericis superpelliciis indutis cantantibus in huiusmodi die anniversarii nostri octavo denarios, videlicet cuilibet dictorum clericorum duos denarios et pro oblacionibus faciendis ad missam in huiusmodi die anniversarii nostri Willelmi episcopi viginti denarios diversis hominibus parochie de Eccles predicte distribuendos, videlicet uni hominum primo offerenti unum denarium et aliis hominibus offerentibus, videlicet duobus vel quatuor unum denarium pro huiusmodi oblacionibus faciendis, quouque predicta summa viginti denariorum totaliter compleatur et offeratur, et quod tunc totum residuum dicte summe viginti denariorum et triginta solidorum quod superfuerit inter pauperes in dicto die anniversarii nostri parentes, videlicet cuilibet pauperi ibidem presenti unus denarius distribuatur et persolvatur. DE SUMMA PECUNIE DISTRIBUENDE DIE ANNIVERSARII JOHANNIS BOTHE ET UXORIS EJUS. Item ordinamus volumusque et statuimus quod singulis annis futuris imperpetuum in predicto die dominicali primo ante festum nativitatis beate Marie Virginis cessante aliquo legitimo impedimento ut superius prescribitur et ordinatur quando dies anniversarii Johannis patris mei et Johanne matris mee teneri et fieri ac celebrari contigerit decem solidi monete anglicane de proventibus dicte cantarie per capellanos dicte cantarie in quolibet die anniversarii patris et matris meorum predictorum superius limitati et assignati distribuantur et persolvantur, videlicet vicario de Eccles qui pro tempore fuerit sex denarii et cuilibet dictorum capellanorum et aliorum per eosdem pro tempore conducti et conducendi cantarie huiusmodi sex denarii, et cuicumque alio capellano presenti in huiusmodi die anniversarii patris et matris meorum predictorum quatuor denarii, et clerico parochiali dicte ecclesie de Eccles quatuor denarii et quatuor clericis superpelliciis indutis cantantibus in huiusmodi die anniversarii patris et matris meorum predicti Willelmi episcopi octo denarii, videlicet cuilibet clericorum duo denarii tantum et pro oblacionibus faciendis ad missam in huiusmodi die anniversarii dictorum patris et matris meorum Willelmi episcopi predicti viginti denarii diversis hominibus parochie de Eccles predicte distribuendi, videlicet uni hominum primo offerenti unum denarium et aliis hominibus offerentibus, videlicet duobus vel quatuor unum denarium pro huiusmodi oblacionibus faciendis, quousque predicta summa viginti denariorum totaliter compleatur et offeratur; et si aliquid residuum dicte summe viginiti denariorum huiusmodi decem solidorum superfuerit, illud inter pauperes in huiusmodi die anniversarii presentes, videlicet cuilibet pauperi ibidem presenti unus denarius distribuatur et persolvatur. DE STIPENDIO CAPELLANIS LIMITATIS. Item volumus statuimus et ordinamus quod uterque dictorum duorum capellanorum cantarie predicte singulis perpetuis futuris annis pro suo stipendio et salario decem marcas monete anglicance ad quatuor anni terminos per equales porciones habeat et percipiat, et quod de ipsis decem marcas sic percipiendis ut prefertur ordinatum contentatur. DE INHABITACIONE CAPELLANORUM ET PRO EIS ORDINATA. Et quod dicti duo capellani eorumque successores prefate cantarie capellani et alii per eosdem conducti et conducendi quecumque in quadam domo cum certis cameris in quadam area dicte cantarie juxta cimiterium ecclesie de Eccles predicte pro mansionibus capellanorum huiusmodi ordinata limitata et assignata per nos Willelmum episcopum predictum et de bonis nostris noviter et de novo construendis et edificandis ac pro inhabitacionibus dictorum capellanorum ordinandi limitandi et assignandi simul cohabitent maneant et pernoctent. QUOD CAPELLANI EXTRA CANTARIAM NON PER NOCTABANT ET DE HORIS CUSTODIENDIS IN NOCTIBUS ANNUATIM DIVERSIS TUM TEMPORIBUS ANNI. Et postquam huiusmodi domus mansiones seu camere dicte cantarie in area predicta fuerint racionabiliter et competenter edificate et constructe, nullus tunc dictorum duorum capellanorum prefate cantarie seu aliorum per eosdem pro tempore conductorum et conducendorum dum presentes fuerint infra parochiam de Eccles predictam extra dictam cantariam sint pernoctabit, et quod capellani huiusmodi non sint extra mansionem eorum propriam cantarie predicte a festo sancti Michaelis archangeli usque in festum Pasche post horam octavam per veram estimacionem et a festo Pasche usque in festum sancte Michaelis archangeli post horam novenam per veram estimacionem, nisi causa racionabilis id exposcat quod raro et non frequento volumus exerceri, et quod tunc tum extra fuerint sint in comitavi honesta et cum personis honestis ac conversacionis honeste. QUOD CAPELLANI NON SINT VERBOSI ET RIXOSI DE PENA DELINQUINCIE. Ordinamus insuper volumus et statuimus quod dicti capellani cantarie predicte eorumque successores et alii quicumque per eosdem pro tempore conducti et conducendi ubique et presertim in dicta cantaria bene et honeste ac pacifice se habeant mutuo atque gerant, et siquis ipsorum capellanorum omnium et singulorum predictorum cum suo concapellano verbosus vel contumeliosus fuerint seu rixas aut verba opprobria sive contumeliosa quoquo modo inter se seminaverit, tociens quociens sic fecerit et de hoc alii concapellano et vicario de Eccles predicto pro tempore existente consteterit ipsum in duodecim denarios ipso facto de porcione sue propria mulcari et tantum de salario sive porcione sua huiusmodi defalcari et puniri volumus, quos duodecim denarios dicto vicario et huiusmodi concapellano predicto realiter persolvi eciam volumus et ordinamus. DE PENA CAPELLANORUN UTLAGATUR ET PUBLICE CONCUBINAS TENENTIBUS. Item volumus statuimus et ordinamus quod cum aliquis dictorum duorum capellanorum cantarie predicte super aliquo crimine fornicacionis seu adulterii coram judice ecclesiastico vel pro aliqua felonia coram judice seculari fuerit convictus vel de seu pro prodicione aut felonia utlagatus vel concubinam seu concubinas publice habuerit vel detinuerit, quod extunc ipse capellanus sic convictus vel utlagatus aut concubinam seu concubinas publice habens vel tenens, ipso facto a cantaria predicta sic privatus et ammotus. Locus cuius sic privatus et ammotus volumus et ordinamus alium capellanum idoneum juxta effectum et formam presentis ordinacionis nostre in dicta cantaria canonice intitulari. DE NOMINIBUS IN QUADAM TABULA INTITULANDIS. Ordinamus insuper et statuimus quod nomen dicti domini regis Henrici sexti ac nomen et cognomen nostri dicti Willelmi episcopi et nomina et cognomina Johannis Bothe et Johanne nuper uxoris sue parentum nostri Willelmi episcopi predicti, ac eciam nomina et cognomina nostrum Johannis Byron militis, Ricardi Bothe, Laurencii Bothe clerici et Seth Worsley, ac nomina et cognomina Thome Bothe militis, Roberti Bothe militis, Johannis Bothe, Rogeri Bothe filiorum dicti Johannis Bothe, ac nomina et cognomina Margerie nuper uxoris Johannis Byron militis, Elizabeth nuper uxoris Edwardi Wever militis, Katerine nuper uxoris Thome Radcliff militis, Johanne nuper uxoris Thome Sothworth armigeri, et Alicie uxoris Roberti Clyfton armigeri filiarum predicti Johannis Bothe, ac nomina et cognomina Dulcie uxoris Roberti Bothe militis, Ricardi Byron, Nicholai Byron filiorum Johannis Byron militis, Willelmi Bothe filii Roberti Bothe militis, Thome Bothe filii Thome Bothe militis, Roberti Bothe filii eiusdem Thome, Roberti Longley armigeri et Thome Longley filii predicti Roberti, in una tabula decenti et honesta inscribantur et intitulentur. Et quod ipsa tabula super altari in dicta capella ponatur publice et collocetur, ut singulis diebus capellani cantarie predicte pro salubri statu dicti domini nostri regis Henrici sexti ac pro salubri statu nostri Willelmi episcopi et pro salubri statu omnium et singulorum superius nominatorum dum vixerint, et pro animabus ipsius domini nostri regis et nostri Willelmi episcopi cum ab hac luce migraverimus et pro animabus omnium et singulorum superius nominatorum cum ab hac luce migraverint, et pro animabus omnium et singulorum superius nominatorum qui jam viam universe carnis ingressi sunt, et pro animabus omnium benefactorum dicte cantarie ac pro animabus omnium fidelium defunctorum in eorum capellanorum missis deum specialiter deprecentur, et ipsos in specie habeant cotide in eo missis et aliis oracionibus devoti recommendatos, et quod dicti capellani omnes et singuli in singulis eorum missis in ecclesia sive capella predicta post offertorium misse antequam laverint manus vertant se ad populum et excitent populum ut orent pro omnibus et singulis benefactoribus dicte cantarie tam vivis quam defunctis, ac postea dicat capellanus sic celebrans pro defunctis psalmum de Profundis cum versiculis et oracionibus consuetis, et postea dicat sacerdos missam celebrans anime eorum et omnium fidelium defunctorum 'per misericordiam Jesu Christi in pace requiescant'. Et postea lavet manus more solito et ulterius in missa procedet. DE ORDINACIONE UNIUS CISTE ET DE CUSTODIA EIUSDEM. Insuper volumus ordinamus et statuimus quod de bonis nostris Willelmi episcopi predicti sit una cista bona et fortis in qua omnia munimenta cantarie antedicte et summa quadraginta librarum pecunie per nos dicte cantarie ordinata et major summa pecunie, si majorem summam pecunie per nos dicte cantarie ordinarii contingat, ponatur et conserventur, ipsamque cistam sub tribus clavibus et firmis feris firmari volumus et ordinamus, quarumquidem clavium unam senior capellanus dictorum duorum capellanorum cantarie predicte, secundus vero capellanus in ipsorum capellanorum secundum clavem, terciam vero clavem vicarius dicte ecclesie de Eccles qui pro tempore fuerit restent et fideliter conservent, sic quod nunquam de unus ipsorum duorum capellanorum huiusmodi tres claves simul gerat aut custodiat, dictamque cistam sic ut prefertur feratam in abbathia de Whalley Coventrensis et Lichfeldensis diocesis poni et collocari volumus et ordinamus. Et

quod omnia et singula munimenta ac jocalia aliaque bona quecumque dicte
cantarie pertinencia et spectanta in uno libro conscribantur quem librum sic
conscriptum in dicta cista una cum munimentis originalibus dicte cantarie poni et
conservari volumus et ibidem remanere, exceptis temporibus oportunis quibus
ijdem capellani cantarie predicte necesse habeant pro utilitate et commodo ipsius
cantarie munimenta huiusmodi ostendere aliis et exhibere. DE BONIS
IMMOBILIBUS NON ALIENDIS ET QUOD FRUCTUS NON DIMITTANTUR AD
FIRMAM ULTRA TERMINUM. Item volumus statuimus et ordinamus quod bona
immobilia dicte cantarie, videlicet redditus terre tenementa servicia pensiones
annuitates decime oblaciones proventus et emolumenta sive fuerint spiritualia sive
temporalia eiusdem cantarie vel capellanis dicte cantarie vel capellanis dicte
cantarie et eorum successoribus data vel imposterum danda adquisita impetrata
vel adquirenda seu aliqua parcella eorundem, nullo modo per capellanos dicte
cantarie vel successores suos seu per aliquem alienentur nec ad firmam dimittantur
alicui persone seu personis ultra terminum tercium annorum et hoc pro firma
racionabili. Et si capellani cantarie predicte seu aliquis eorundem contrarium
fecerint seu fecerit a dicta cantaria ipso facto sint privati et ammoti seu privatus et
ammotus. DE BONIS MOBILIBUS NON ALIENDIS ET DE PENA CONTRAVENCIUM.
Item statuimus volumus et ordinamus quod thesaurius pecunie cantarie cuiquam
sub quibuscumque securitate aut colore seu titulo non mutetur, et quod bona
mobilia dicte cantarie ordinata sive spectanta quecumque per capellanos dicte
cantarie vel eorum successores non alienentur nec impignorentur sine causa
legitima et urgente necessitate et hoc cum consensu concordia et assensu dictorum
capellanorum et vicarii eiusdem ecclesie de Eccles predicte ac cum avisamento et
consilio patronorum eiusdem cantarie pro tempore existencium. Et si in
contrarium fecerint vel eorum aliquis fecerit, ipson tunc seu ipsum mutacionem
impignoracionem et alienacionem huiusmodi facientes seu facientem a dicta
cantaria ipso facto ordinamus esse privatos et ammotos ac privatum et ammotum,
ac alios capellanos seu alium capellanum in dicta cantaria canonice intitulari juxta
formam superius annotatam. DE ORDINACIONE REDDITUARII SIVE RECEPTORIS
ET QUOD SIT EJUS OFFICARIUS. Ordinus quoque volumus et statuimus quod de
dictis duobus capellanis singulis perpetuis futuris annis unus eorum successive sit
reddituarius et receptor prefate cantarie qui reddituarius et receptor fructus
redditus et proventus quoscumque prefate cantarie provenientes et proventuros
per sufficientem deputatum suum de bonis dicte cantarie ad hoc conductum et
conducendum pro quo ipse reddituarius respondere tenebitur diligenter petat
colligat et recipiat, sic quod idem reddituarius et receptor cantarie predicte resideat
in eadem cantaria predicta juxta formam fundacionis et ordinacionis nostre
superius et inferius ordinatam, ac idem reddituarius et receptor cantarie predicte
qui pro tempore fuerit fructus et proventus dicte cantarie ad et in usum
commodum et utilitatem eiusdem cantarie ut superius et inferius per nos
ordinatum conservet et convertat ac expensas necessarias in reparacionibus
capelle sancte Katerine in ecclesia parochiali de Eccles et nove capelle noviter per
nos constructa ac tenementorum domorumque et aliorum locorum
quorumcumque eiusdem cantarie agnoscat supportet et persolvat. Insuper
volumus ordinamus et statuimus quod idem reddituarius et receptor expensas
necessarias in reparacionibus librorum vestimentorum et aliorum ornamentorum
prefate cantarie et in futurum eidem cantarie qualitercumque spectanctium de
fructibus dicte cantarie juxta et secundum formam et effectum fundacionis et

ordinacionis nostrarum superius et inferius conscripta debite persolvat, necnon idem reddituarius et receptor cantarie predicte expensas necessarias vini panisque et cere in dictis capellis deservituris ac certorum onerum in fundacione et ordinacione dicte cantarie superius et inferius specificatis et eidem cantarie spectancium in futurum contingencium cum fructibus ut prefertur et proventibus eiusdem cantarie juxta formam fundacionis et ordinacionis nostre superius et inferius descripte debit subeat et persolvat cum effectum. DE COMPUTO REDDENDO SINGULIS ANNIS. Volumus insuper ordinamus et statuimus quod idem reddituarius et receptor singulis perpetuis futuris annis coram concapellano et vicario predicte ecclesie de Eccles qui pro tempore fuerit plenum et fidelem computum de omnibus et singulis suis receptis collectis solutis et expensis factis atque et super omniam sua administracione in officio reddituarii et receptoris predicta facta atque de arreragiis et nominabus dibitorum et stauris et aliis rebus quibuscumque dicte cantarie spectantibus et remanentibus citra festum natalis domini in scriptis ostendere reddere et facere ac plene computare teneatur, et siquid residuum per reddituarium et receptorem collectum ultra expensis illius anni debite superfuerit illud ad usum et commodum dicte cantarie juxta formam ordinacionis nostre superius et inferius factam et imposterum per nos faciendum conservetur. Et si reddituarius et receptor predictus in premissis ut prefertur limitatis negligens vel remissus fuerit, ipsum tunc in viginti solidos de salario suo ipso facto defalcari et puniri. Ordinamus quos viginti solidos ad usum et commodum cantarie predicte converti et disponi eciam ordinamus per presentes. Et si reddituarius et receptor huiusmodi per triginta dies post quodlibet festum natalis domini immediate sequentes in premissis ut prefertur faciendis negligens vel remissus fuerit, ipsum extunc capellanum reddituarium et receptorem a dicta cantaria ipso facto ordinamus esse privatum et ammotum, loco cuius sic privatus et ammotus volumus et ordinamus alium capellanum in dicta cantaria canonice intitulari juxta formam superius annotatam. DE ABSENCIA REDDITUARIL A DICTI CANTARIA. Et idem reddituarius et receptor de consensu semper et scientia dicti capallani regimen et gubernacionem omnium reddituum et proventuum quorumcumque dicte cantarie habeat et exerceat, et ad supervidendum regimen et gubernacionem huiusmodi habeat si necesse triginta dies quolibet anno simul vel successive capiendos, sed non ultra triginta dies nisi ex consensu et avisamento concapellani sui vicarii de Eccles predicte et patronorum dicte cantarie qui pro tempore fuerint, mansionesque domos edificia tenementa et loca quecumque dicte cantaria spectantia capellamque sancte Katerine in dicta ecclesia parochiali de Eccles ac ad novam capellam per nos dictum Willelmum noviter constructam congrue et sufficienter reparari et emendari faciat de bonis cantarie predicte, ac visum racionem et computum plenum et fidelem de premissis in officio suo idem reddituarius et receptor ut prefertur terminis superius limitatis ostendat et reddat, juretque idem reddituarius et receptor in assumpcione officii sui coram dictis concapellanos et vicario de Eccles predicto pro tempore existentibus ad sancta dei evangelia per ipsum corporale tacta quod erit fidelis in officio reddituarii et receptoris predicto sub hac forma verborum: Ego, N, capellanus perpetuus cantarie perpetue sancte Katerine in ecclesia parochiali beate Marie virginis de Eccles in reddituarium et receptorem ipsius cantarie assumptus, juro et hac sancti dei evangelia per me corporaliter tacta quod officium reddituarii et receptoris huiusmodi quamdiu in ipso officio permansurus bene et fideliter juxta formam et effectum statutorum et orainacionem dicte cantarie huiusmodi officium reddituarii et receptoris tangencium exercebo in eadem cantaria in omnibus fidelis ero, sicut me deus adjuret et hec sancta dei evangelia. DE SUMMA XL LIBRARUM PER FUNDATOREM ORDINATA CANTARIE. Item volumus statuimus et ordinamus quod summa quadraginti librarum pecunie per nos dicte cantarie ordinata et major summa pecunie, si major summa pecunie per nos dicte cantarie ordinari contingat, in et ad usum utilitatem et incrementum eiusdem cantarie in huiusmodi communi cista predicta eciam ponatur et integraliter conservetur et nullo modo diminuatur nisi sub forma superius et inferius descripta, quamquidem pecunia de proventibus dicta cantarie provenientem ultra summam quadraginta librarum prescriptarum et majorem summam pecunie superius specificate prefati duo capellani dicte cantarie ad invencionem capellani et capellanorum idoneorum qui missas et alia divina officia in ecclesia parochiali de Eccles predicta et nullo alio loco infra parochiam de Eccles predictam, prout ipsi duo capellani cantarie predicte tenentur juxta fundacionem huiusmodi cantarie in omnibus per nos factam, debite celebrabunt et observabunt fideliter, et integre disponant distribuant et persolvant de anno in annum prout huiusmodi residuum in quantitate sic extenderit, quod quilibet eorundem capellanorum per ipsos duos capellanos conductorum pro stipendio suo sive salario septem marcas monete anglicane annuatim recipiat et non ultra, si pro tali summa conduci poterit durante incremento huiusmodi ultra summam quadraginta librarum suprascriptarum et majorem summam pecunie superius specificatam, quiquidem summa quadraginta librarum et major summa pecunie superius specificata inter ipsos duo capellanos cantarie predicte vel alios per ipsos sic conductos vel conducendos minime distribuatur expendatur aut dividuatur sed plene et integre ad et in sustentacionem et stabilimentum cantarie et capellarum predictarum atque reparacionem et emendacionem earundem cum necesse fuerit et ad defensionem jurum et proventuum eiusdem cantarie bene et fideliter custodiatur et conservetur. Item volumus et statuimus quod quociens contigerit in futurum dictam summam quadraginta librarum et majoren summam superius specificatam vel aliquam partem circa reparacionem emendacionem et sustentacionem cantarie et capellarum predictarum vel ad defensionem jurum et proventuum eiusdem cantarie ut prefertur expendi persolvi seu in aliquo minui, volumus et ordinamus quod tunc per eosdem duos capellanos dicte cantarie quam cicius fieri poterit absque aliqua fraude seu decepcione dicta summa quadraginta librarum vel major summa superius specificata ad et in dictam cistam commune de residuis proventuum dicte cantarie plenarie redintegretur reponatur et restaureter, et quod dicta summa quadraginta librarum et major summa superius specificata per nos ut premittitur dicte cantarie ordinatorum ad alium usum quam ut premittitur nullo modo per capellanos huiusmodi alienetur distribuatur seu expendatur nec alicui sub modo forma causa seu colore quibuscumque mutuetur seu impignoretur, et si in contrarium fecerint vel aliquis eorum fecerit, ipsos tunc seu ipsum a dicta cantaria ipso facto ordinamus esse privatos seu privatum ammotos seu ammotum, loco quorum seu cuius sic privatorum seu privati et ammotorum seu ammoti volumus et ordinamus alios seu alium capellanos seu capellanum in dicta cantaria canonice intitulari juxta formam superius descriptam. DE ALIA SUMMA XL LIBRARUM DICTE CANTARIE PER FUNDATORUM ORDINATA. Volumus statuimus et ordinamus quod capellani dicte cantarie de Eccles predicte ex nostra dotacione et ordinacione habeant quadraginta libras legalis monete anglie de bonis nostri Willelmi episcopi predicti ultra summam quadraginta librarum superius specificatam, de qua summa se exhibere et sustentare ac alia onera eidem cantarie incumbencia supportare singulis annis valeant quosque fructus redditus et proventus eiusdem cantarie recipere colligere et habere poterint, et quamquidem summam quadraginta librarum in alia decenti et forti cista sumptibus nostris fienda poni et conservari volumus sub tribus clavibus ferandum et clavendum, quarum unam senior capellanus dicte cantarie secundum alter capellanus eiusdem cantarie ac tercium vicarius de Eccles predictus qui pro tempore fuerit habeat gerat et portet, et quod cista predicta infra dictam cantariam quamcito edificata fuerit seu in alio loco securo per nos imposterum ordinandum ponatur dimittatur et custodiatur, ita quod de fructibus redditus et proventibus dicte cantarie postquam collecta fuerunt predicta summa quadraginta librarum restauretur et redintegretur quamcito comode poterit, et quod huiusmodi restauracio et redintegracio fiat ut prefertur singulis annis quociens predicta summa quadraginta librarum pro sustentacione capellanorum et omnibus supportandi vel alia justa causa dictos capellanos in aliquo fuerit diminuata. Et si contrarium fecerint capellani predicti seu eorum aliquis fecerit ipsos tunc seu ipsum a dicta cantaria ipso facto ordinamus esse privatos seu privatum, ammotos seu ammotum, loco quorum seu ejus sic privatorum vel privati alium seu alios capellanum seu capellanos in dicta cantaria volumus canonice intitulari juxta formam suprascriptam. Et ne capellani cantarie predicte ignoranciam pretendere valeant omnium et singulorum premissorum, volumus statuimus et ordinamus quod dictas ordinaciones et statuta perpetuis futuris annis bis in anno inter ipsos capellanos quoscumque dicte cantarie et coram eis perlegantur publice recitentur. Volumus insuper statuimus et ordinamus nos Willelmus Bothe episcopus Coventrensis et Lichfeldensis Johannes Byron miles Ricardus Bothe Laurencius Bothe clericus et Seth Worsley supradicti quod premissa omnia et singula per nos ut prefertur acta facta gesta statuta et ordinata ceteraque per nos imposterum ordinanda quecumque per dictos duos capellanos eorumque successores quoscumque dicte cantarie capellanos perpetuis futuris temporibus plene et fideliter observentur quatinus facultates bonorum cantarie predicte sufficere valeant in hac parte. Et quia non humanum est sed divinum omnia prospicere et providere ... sepe contingat quod illud quod ab initio perturbatur prodesse, postea experimento minus utile reperitur, idcirco facultatem et potestatem omnia et singula per nos ut prefertur statuta et ordinata interpretendi declarandi minuendi subtrahendi mutandi eisdemque addendi eademque corrigendi commutandi augendi suppliendi emendandi et reformandi nobis Willelmo Bothe episcopo Coventrensi et Lichfeldensi Johanni Byron militi Ricardo Bothe Laurencio Bothe clerico et Seth Worsley antedictis aut duobus nostrum reservamus per presentes. In quorum omnium et singulorum premissorum fidem et testimonium sigilla nostra presentibus apposuimus. Datum apud Clayton vicesimo octavo die mensis Julii anno domini millesimo quadragentesimo quinquagesimo et regni regis Henrici sexti post conquestum Anglie vicesimo octavo.

315. [Fos 95–104] Foundation by William Bothe, archbishop of York, Nicholas Byron, Robert Clyfton, Richard Bothe and Seth Worsley of a perpetual chantry for two chaplains in the parish church of Eccles, Lancashire, for the good estate of King Henry VI and the archbishop while they live, and for their souls after death, and for the souls of certain other persons nominated by the founders, and for the souls of all the faithful departed. The chaplains and their successors are to be enabled to take lands, tenements, rents, services and other possessions from any persons, and to do so by the name of 'the chaplains of the chantry of Jesus and the Blessed Virgin Mary' in the parish church of Eccles, and to be capable of impleading and of being impleaded by others by that name. The royal licence, tested by King Henry VI at Coventry on 1 December 1459 concedes to the founders the advowson of the parish church of Beetham (*Bethom, Bethum*), Westmorland, and the founders give to three or more of their number the said advowson to hold to the said chaplains for ever. The founders make statutes for the chantry. The archbishop shall appoint suitable persons to the chaplaincies while he lives and after his death the right of presentation shall pass to the co-founders, who shall present suitable persons to the bishop of the diocese, or to his vicar general, or, sede vacante, to the keeper of the spiritualities. Chaplains shall take a corporal oath on their admission and the vicar, or his vicar general, or sede vacante, the keeper of the spiritualities, shall address letters of induction to the vicar of Eccles. This form of induction shall be sufficient in itself. After the death of the archbishop and the co-founders the right of presentation is vested in Sir Robert Both and Nicholas Byron and their lawful male heirs, who shall present successively within six weeks of any vacancy. Should either fail to present within the six weeks then the right of presentation will devolve on the other and should he fail to present then the right of presentation shall pass to the bishop of the diocese, or his vicar general, or, sede vacante, the keeper of the spiritualities. In the event of Sir Robert Bothe and Nicholas Byron dying without lawful male heirs the right of presentation shall pass to the heirs and assigns of the archbishop, who shall present a suitable person within six weeks of a vacancy, and should they fail to so present then the right of presentation will devolve on the bishop of the diocese, or his vicar general, or, sede vacante, the keeper of the spiritualities. Continuous absence from the chantry of more than thirty days in any year without permission of the archbishop, the acceptance by the chaplains of any other benefice incompatible with the chantry, and failure to reside, and the penalty for breaches of these conditions are all as in **314**. The requirement that the chaplains shall daily observe all the hours, according to the use of Sarum, and say mass for the dead, that is, PLACEBO and DIRIGE, with the LESSONS and COMMENDATION, for the souls of King Henry VI and the archbishop while they live, and for the souls of certain other persons nominated, and to celebrate the mass DE HORA on festivals, are also as in **314**. After the celebration of mass the chaplains shall remove the vestments, books, chalices and other ornaments of the chantry, which are to be carefully preserved and kept in the vicarage house. Should the chaplains neglect to put away the vestments, books, chalices and other ornaments in the manner prescribed above then the vicar of Eccles will do so and will receive the sum of 40d for his labour, which sum is to be deducted from the salary of the negligent chaplains. Articles stolen or otherwise lost through the failure of the chaplains to observe the above directions shall be replaced within forty days at the expense of him whose negligence was at fault, and failure to do so will result in deprivation, as in **314**. Articles lost or destroyed or worn out through no fault of the chaplains will be replaced from the profits of the chantry, as in **314**. The chaplains are forbidden to celebrate mass elsewhere than in the parish church of Eccles under pain of deprivation. On Sundays and principal and double festivals the chaplains and any chaplain or chaplains hired by them, are always to walk in procession in the parish of Eccles with other priests wearing their surplices, and in canonical hours they shall celebrate with note, devoutly and with skill, within the choir of the said church of Eccles.

VOLUMUS STATUIMUS ORDINAMUS et DECERNIMUS quod qualibet septimana singulis annis in futuris post matutinas in dicta ecclesia parochiali de Eccles decantatas et finitas quolibet die dominico cito post horam octavam per estimacionem seu saltem post adventum plurimorum parochianorum ad dictam ecclesiam parochialem de Eccles confluencium una missa de gloriosissimo nomine Jhesu Christi devote celebretur eciam cum sequentia in dicta missa dicti consueta usque ad Septuagesimam et tunc loco huiusmodi sequentie a Septuagesima usque ad festum Pasche cum tractu in eadem missa pro tempore huiusmodi dicti consueto devote celebretur missa predicta in dicta ecclesia parochiali de Eccles per unum dictorum duorum capellanorum cantarie Jhesu et beate Marie Virginis de Eccles predicte seu saltem per alium capellanum quecumque deputandum et subrogandum loco sui. Et quod quolibet die Jovis qualibet septimana imperpetuum eadem missa de gloriosissimo nomine Jhesu devote celebretur cum sequentia et tractu in eadem missa pro temporibus ut prefertur ordinatis diu quod consuetis presertim circa horam novenam in eadem ecclesia parochiali de Eccles per alterum dictorum duorum capellanorum cantarie Jhesu et beate Marie Virginis de Eccles predicte seu per alium capellanum quecumque deputandum et subrogandum vice sua ut premittitur volumus eciam statuimus et ordinamus per presentes. ITEM volumus statuimus et ordinamus quod singulis perpetuis futuris annis durante vita nostri Willelmus archiepiscopi predicti die Mercurii in qualibet septimana unus dictorum capellanorum missam de Requiem cum nota si comode fieri poterit alioquin sive nota celebrabit in ecclesia sive capella predicta pro animabus certarum aliarum personarum inferius nominatorum ac omnium benefactorum dicte cantarie et omnium fidelium defunctorum nisi duplex festum in ipso die Mercurii evenerit vel aliquod legitimum impedimentum obstiterit et tunc missam de Requiem celebrabit proximo die sequenti si duplex festum non fuerit. Et quod post mortem nostri prefati Willelmi archiepiscopi unus eciam dictorum capellanorum die Mercurii in qualibet septimana singulis annis huiusmodi missam de Requiem cum nota si comode fieri poterit alioquin sine nota celebrabit in ecclesia sive capella predicta pro anima nostri Willelmi archiepiscopi et pro animabus certarum personarum inferius nominatarum ac omnium benefactorum dicto cantarie et omnium fidelium defunctorum ut prefertur nisi aliquod duplex festum ipso die evenerit vel aliquod aliud legitimum impedimentum obstiterit et tunc missam de Requiem celebrabit proximo die sequenti si duplex festum non fuerit. Ac insuper volumus statuimus et ordinamus quod post mortem nostri Willelmi archiepiscopi uterque capellanorum predictorum et eorum successores ac alii quicumque per eosdem conducti et conducendi dicant imperpetuum singulis diebus in missa sua pro anima nostri dicti Willelmi archiepiscopi specialem oracionem cum Secreto et Postcommunio in forma sequenti, videlicet: CONCEDE quesumus Domine Deus noster ut anima famuli Tui Willelmi pontificis cuius commemoracionem speciali devocione agimus et pro qua exorare jussi et debitores sumus, atque animae omnium parentum consanguineorum et familiarium suorum cunctorumque fidelium in funeribus sanctorum Tuorum requiesant moxque et mortuis recusitate Tibi placeant in regione vivorum per Dominum nostrum et cetera. Cum Secreto et Postcommunione subsequentibus videlicet: HEC munera quesumus Domine que oculis Tue majestatis offerimus animae famuli Tui Willelmi pontificis cuius commemoracionem speciali devocione agimus pro qua exorare jussi et debitores sumus atque animabus omnium parentum consanguineorum et familiarium suorum cunctorum que fidelium salvataria esse concede ut Tua pietate vinculis horrende mortis exute eterne beatudinis mercantur esse participes per Dominum et cetera. DEUS qui inestimibili misericordia animas mortalium ab angustiis transfferre ad requiem propiciare supplicacionibus nostris pro anima famuli Tui Willelmi pontificis cuius commemoracionem speciali devocione agimus et pro quo exorare jussi et debitores sumus atque pro animabus omnium parentum consanguineorum et familiarium suorum fidelium ut eas paradiso restituens in Tua censeas sorte justorum per Dominum et cetera. Ordinamus eciam et statuimus quod dicti capellani eorumque successores prefate cantarie capellani et alii per eosdem conducti et conducendi quicumque singulis futuris annis diem obitus nostri Willelmi archiepiscopi quo die ab hac luce migraverimus teneant et devote continuent ac plenum servicium mortuorum videlicet PLACEBO et DIRIGE cum NOVEM LECCIONIBUS quocumque tempore anui contigerit ac COMMENDACIONEM et MISSAM de REQUIEM simul in capella per nos Willelmum archiepiscopum de novo constructa in predicta parochia de Eccles pro anima nostri Willelmi archiepiscopi perdicant nisi aliquod duplex festum ipso die evenerit vel aliquod aliud legitimum impedimentum obstiterit; Et tunc missam de Requiem celebrabunt primo die sequenti si duplex festum non fuerit.

The anniversaries of the following persons are to be observed in the chantry with due solemnity for ever: John Bothe and Joan Bothe, mother and father of the archbishop, on the Sunday before the feast of the birth of the Blessed Virgin Mary; Margery, sister of the archbishop, formerly wife of Sir John Byron, on 1 June; Sir Robert Bothe and Roger Bothe, Brs of the archbishop; Nicholas Byron, son of Sir John Byron, William Bothe, son of Sir Robert Bothe, Sir John Byron, Robert Clyfton, Richard Bothe, Laurence Bothe and Seth Worsley on the anniversaries of their deaths. On the anniversary of the archbishop, which is to be observed with due solemnity for ever, the sum of 30s is to be distributed in alms, as in **314**. On the anniversary of John Bothe and Joan Bothe, parents of the archbishop, to be celebrated on the Sunday before the feast of the birth of the Blessed Virgin Mary, the sum of 10s is to be distributed in alms in the manner prescribed in **314**.

VOLUMUS tamen ac tenore presencium decernimus statuimus et ordinamus quod dicti capellani cantarie Jhesu et beate Marie Virginis in ecclesia parochiali de Eccles predicte sint contributores una cum capellanis cantarie sancte Katerine in eadem ecclesia singulis perpetuis futuris annis ad solucionem omnium et singulorum summarum predictarum pro et in diebus anniversariis nostri Willelmi archiepiscopi ac patris et matris nostris superius in fundacione cantarie sancte Katerine predicte conscriptarum et limitatarum et solvi assignatarum Necnon iidem capellani dicte cantarie Jhesu et beate Marie Virginis medietatem summarum huiusmodi solvant annuatim de fructibus et proventibus dicte cantarie Jhesu et beate Marie Virginis in ecclesia parochiali de Eccles ad eadem onera perimplendi pro et in diebus anniversariis nostri Willelmi archiepiscopi ac patris et matris nostrorum superius limitat expressata et ordinata ad que iidem capellani cantarie sancte Katerine de Eccles nostris priori fundacione et ordinacione eiusdem tenentur et obligantur prout supra plenius conscribitur et recitatur. Et

cum nos eciam alias in fundacione et creacione dicte cantarie sancte Katerine in
ecclesia parochiali de Eccles inter cetera statutorum eiusdem ordinaverimus et
statuerimus quod capellani cantarie sancte Katerine in ecclesia parochiali de
Eccles quandam domum cum certis cameris in quadam area juxta cimiteriam
dicte ecclesia de Eccles pro mansionibus capellanorum dicte cantarie sancte
Katerine ac pro aliis capellanis per nos prefatum archiepiscopum in dicta ecclesia
ordinatis et ordinandis per nos Willelmum archiepiscopum predictum de bonis
nostris noviter et de novo construendi et edificandi pro inhabitacione pro
capellanis cantarie sancte Katerine ac pro aliis capellaniis per nos prefatum
archiepiscopum in dicta ecclesia ordinatis et ordinandis ac capellani sancte
Katerine in dicta ecclesia parochiali de Eccles ac eciam novam capellam per nos
dictum Willelmum archiepiscopum noviter constructa congrue et sufficienter
facient construent reparabunt et emendabunt de bonis cantarie sancte Katerine
predicte iidem quod capellani cantarie sancte Katerine predicte expensas
necessarias in reparacionibus librorum vestimentorum et aliorum ornamentorum
prefate cantarie et in futurum eidem qualitercumque spectancium et pertinencium
de fructibus et proventibus dicte cantarie sancte Katerine juxta et secundum
formam et effectum fundacionis et ordinacionis cantarie predicte debite persolvant
prout in dicta fundacione inter cetera statutorum eiusdem cantarie sancte
Katerine plenius continetur. VOLUMUS tamen ac statuimus et ordinamus quod
dicti capellani cantarie Jhesu et beate Marie Virginis in dicta ecclesia parochiali de
Eccles sint contributores una cum capellanis cantarie sancte Katerine in eadem
ecclesia de Eccles singulis perpetuis futuris annis ad solucionem omnium
expensarum necessarium in contribucionibus et reparacionibus capelle sancte
Katerine in ecclesia parochiali de Eccles predicte et nove capelle ibidem per nos
noviter constructe ac cuiusdam domus cum certis cameris in quadam area juxta
cimiterium dicte ecclesie de Eccles pro mansionibus capellanorum dicte cantarie
sancte Katerine et capellanorum dicte cantarie Jhesu et beate Marie Virginis ac
pro capellanis per nos prefatum archiepiscopum ordinatis et ordinandis de bonis
nostris noviter de novo construendi et edificandi pro inhabitacionibus huiusmodi
capellanorum in quibus iidem capellani utriusque cantarie predictarum
cantariarum in futurum inhabitabunt necnon idem capellani dicte cantarie
predictarum cantariarum in futurum inhabitabunt necnon idem capellani dicte
cantarie Jhesu et beate Marie Virginis sint contributores una cum capellanis
cantarie sancte Katerine predicte singulis futuris annis ad solucionem expensarum
necessarium in reparacionibus librorum vestimentorum et aliorum ornamentorum prefate cantarie sancte Katerine ac eciam cantarie Jhesu et beate Marie
Virginis et utriusque cantariarum predictarum qualitercumque spectancium et
pertinencium ac medietatem omnium expensarum necessariarum in et pro
reparacionibus capelle sancte Katerine in dicta ecclesia parochiali de Eccles et
nove capelle ibidem per nos noviter constructe et cuiusdam domus cum certis
cameris eidem cantarie ut prefertur assignate pro mansionibus capellanorum
utriusque cantarie cantariarum predictarum ac eciam medietatem omnium
expensarum necessariarum equaliter cum capellanis dicte cantarie sancte
Katerine in et pro reparacionibus librorum vestimentorum et aliorum
ornamentorum prefate cantarie sancte Katerine ac cantarie Jhesu et beate Marie
Virginis et utriusque cantariarum predictarum in dicta ecclesia parochiali de
Eccles qualitercumque in futurum spectancium et pertinencium persolvant

imperpetuum de fructibus et proventibus cantarie Jhesu et beate Marie Virginis antedicte.

The salary of the chaplains is assigned at 10 marks p.a. payable in four equal portions. They should stay in their house at night. They shall not be outside their house after the hour of 8 from Michaelmas to Easter, and after the hour of 9 from Easter to Michaelmas. They are required to associate only with persons of good reputation, and to conduct themselves religiously, honestly and peaceably and never use opprobrious words to each other or to the chaplains of the chantry of St Katherine, or act contumaciously to other chaplains under pain of a fine of 12d for each offence to be levied by the vicar of Eccles from the offender's salary. Should any chaplain be impeached and convicted by law for treason or felony or be outlawed by a judge in a secular court, or for fornication or adultery before the church, or keep a concubine or concubines publicly, he will be deprived. All the above are as in **314**. The provision of a tablet, bearing the names of King Henry VI and the archbishop, John Bothe and Joan Bothe, parents of the archbishop, and the names of Nicholas Byron, Robert Clyfton, Richard Bothe and Seth Worsley, also Laurence Bothe, bishop of Durham, Sir John Byron, Sir Thomas Bothe, Sir Robert Bothe, John Bothe and Roger Bothe, sons of the aforesaid John Bothe, also Margery, late wife of Sir John Byron, Elizabeth, late wife of Sir Edward Wever, Katherine, late wife of Sir Thomas Radclyff, Joan late wife of Thomas Sotheworth esq., and Alice, late wife of Robert Clyfton esq., daughters of the aforesaid John Bothe, also Dulcie, wife of Sir Robert Bothe, Richard Byron, son of Sir John Byron, William Bothe, son of Sir Thomas Bothe, Thomas Bothe, son of Sir Thomas Bothe, Robert Bothe, son of Thomas Bothe, Robert Longley esq. and Thomas Longley his son, is provided for. The tablet is to be suspended above the altar in the chantry so that the chaplains may see it and pray daily for the souls of those named thereon, as in **314**. The provision of the sum of £40, the custody of the chest, the preservation of property, the office of receiver, his duties, his absences from the chantry, and the form of oath on admission, the provision of a second sum of £40, and the custody of the chest, all as in **314**.

VOLUMUS insuper decernimus statuimus et ordinamus quod postquam semel aliqua camera infra mansionem ordinata pro capellanis cantarie Jhesu et beate Marie Virginis et cantarie sancte Katerine in ecclesia parochiali de Eccles predicte assignata et limitata fuerit aliqui capellanorum cantariarum predictarum per nos Willelmum archiepiscopum predictum dum vixerimus vel post mortem nostri prefati Willelmi archiepiscopi per dictum Nicholaum Byron Robertum Clyfton Ricardum Bothe et Seth Worsley seu per aliquem eorundem quod extunc quocienscumque contigerit in futurum aliquem capellanorum dictarum duarum cantariarum Jhesu et beate Marie Virgini et sancte Katerine in dicta ecclesia parochiali de Eccles obire cedere privari seu aliquo modo ammoveri volumus tunc et ordinamus quod capellanus proximo succedens huiusmodi capellanum mortuum privatum vel ammotum postquam legitime ad capellaniam huiusmodi fieri prefertur vacantem presentatus institutus admissus et inductus fuerit habebit et occupabet cameram infra mansionem predictam quamdiu capellanus fuerit huiusmodi capellanie quam cameram capellanus proximus ejus predeccessor huiusmodi et occupavit. Et si contingat in futurum aliquam discordiam rixam sive dissensionem aut contencionem fore seu generari inter capellanos dictarum cantariarum Jhesu et beate Marie Virginis ac sancte Katerine in dicta ecclesia parochiali de Eccles pro cameris infra mansionem predictam habendis et occupandis tunc volumus et ordinamus quod huiusmodi discordia rixa sive dessencio aut contencio omnio ordineur funatur terminetur et sopiatur per nos Willelmum archiepiscopum predictam dum vixerimus et post mortem nostri prefati Willelmi archiepiscopi per supervisionem et discreccionem fundatorum vel patronorum cantariarum huiusmodi pro tempore existencium. Ac insuper volumus statuimus decernimus et ordinamus quod quamcito mansio pro capellanis cantarie Jhesu et beate Marie Virginis et cantarie sancte Katerine in dicta ecclesia parochiali de Eccles erecta et edificata fuerit quod tunc capellani dictarum duarum cantariarum communas suas in simul ponant in et pro esculentis et poculentis suis cotidianis et quod infra mansionem predictam sint commensales et quando commedunt infra mansionem predictam tunc cessante legitimo impedimento insimul comedant in aula mansionis antedicte vel in parlur infra mansionem huiusmodi si imposterum parlur ibidem ordinari et edificari contigerit. Et si capellani cantariarum predictarum seu aliquis eorundem contrarium fecerit seu fecerint cessante legitimo impedimento ut prefertur a dictis duabus cantariis ipso facto sint privati et ammoti seu privatus et ammotus.

The provision that the statutes be read twice annually and the reservation by the founders to amend them – as in **314**. Dated under the seals of the founders on 6 May 1460 at the manor of Scrooby.[223]

316. [Fo. 105] 12 August 1447. Commission to John, bishop of *Insulensis*,[224] as suffragan; during pleasure.

COMMISSIO PRO EPISCOPO SUFFRAGANEO. Willelmus, permissione divina Coventrensis et Lichfeldensis episcopus, venerabili in Christo patri domino Johanni dei gracia Insulensi episcopo salutem et fraternam in domino caritatem. Ad benedicendum altaria superaltaria calices vestimenta campanas ac alia ornamenta quecumque, et si jus exigerit propter defectum eorum et abusum eadem suspendendum ac crisma et oleum sacrum conficiendum, puerosque in fronte crismandum; primamque tonsuram clericalem personis idoneis conferendum ac eciam minores et majores ordines (temporibus tamen debitis et a jure statutis) celebrandum vobis plenariam potestatem in et super premissis omnibus et singulis vice et auctoritate nostris per nostras civitates et diocesi tenore presencium licenciam concedimus specialem quamdiu nobis placuerit tantum modo duratur'. In cuius rei testimonium sigillum nostrum fecimus hiis apponi. Datum in manerio nostro de Heywode duodecimo die mensis Augusti anno domini millesimo quadringentesimo quadragesimo septimo et nostre consecracionis anno primo.[225]

---

223 The remainder of this folio is blank.
224 See note 30.
225 In space between commission and the first list of orders: 'Nomina illorum qui ordinati sunt accoliti'.

317.[226]   General orders in the prebendal church of Eccleshall on 23 September 1447 by John, bishop of *Insulensis*, by authority of William, bishop of Coventry and Lichfield.

[col. a]

ORDINES GENERALES CELEBRATI IN ECCLESIA PREBENDALI DE ECCLESHALE DIE SABBATI QUATUOR TEMPORUM VIDELICET VICESIMO TERCIO DIE MENSIS SEPTEMBRIS ANNO DOMINI MILLESIMO CCCCMO QUADRAGESIMO SEPTIMO PER REVERENDUM PATREM DOMINUM JOHANNEM DEI GRACIA INSULENSEM EPISCOPUM VIGORE ET AUCTORITATE DICTI REVERENDI PATRIS DOMINI WILLELMI DEI GRACIA COVENTRENSIS ET LICHFELDENSIS EPISCOPI SUPRADICTI ET COMMISSIONIS SUE PREDICTE.

ACCOLITI SECULARES

Thomas Bury	Thomas Engless
Willelmus Kente	Thomas Sharpe
Ricardus Coteler	Willelmus Hyll

Religiosus: Frater Thomas Wasname de conventu fratrum minorum, Cestrie

SUBDIACONI SECULARES

Magister Rogerus Shireshagh ad titulum domus [de] Derley ad omnes
Rogerus Baguley ad titulum domus de Whalley ad omnes
Thomas Hertishorne ad titulum prioratus de Repyngdon
Johannes Bonsale ad titulum domus de Derley ad omnes
Johannes Mychell ad titulum domus hospitalis sancti Egidii Salop ad omnes
[col. b] Johannes Cholmley ad titulum de Derley
Raginaldus Pynder ad titulum de Rupe
Ricardus Strangulford ad titulum domus de Derley
Ricardus Bury ad titulum domus de Whalley ad omnes

RELIGIOSI

Frater Robertus Chilwell canonicus de Derley

DIACONI SECULARES

Johannes Marleston ad titulum domus de Combermer
Willelmus Garard Lincolniensis diocesis per litteras dimissorias ad titulum hospitalis sancti Johanni baptisti Coventr'
Ricardus Deyne ad titulum domus de Dalaw ad omnes
Willelmus Orme ad titulum domus de Pollesworth
Johannes Jecok ad titulum domus de Osney ad omnes
Johannes Harrymon ad titulum domus de Tuttebur'
Ricardus Howson ad titulum domus de Novo Loco in Shyrewode ad omnes sacros ordines
Thomas Rowley ad titulum domus de Hyllton

---

226 In the following lists, the separate columns are where appropriate identified as 'col. a' and 'col. b'.

RELIGIOSI
Fratres Johannes Loughtborow ⎫
Johannes Assheburn   ⎬ canonici domus de Derley
Robertus Stafford   ⎭

PRESBITERI SECULARES
Robertus Walker ad titulum domus de Holand
[Fo. 105v, col. a] Robertus Whitlawe ad titulum domini Johannis Boteller militis et baronis de Weryngton
Johannes Stopford ad titulum domus de Hyllton
Thomas Prestbury ad titulum domus de Dieuleucres
Robertus Smalwode at titulum de Osney
Rogerus Wilkyn ad titulum domus de Bradwell Lincolniensis diocesis
Thomas Legh ad titulum prioratus sancti Thome martiris juxta Stafford ad omnes sacros
Jacobus Wilson ad titulum prioratus de Landa
Johannes Herewey ad titulum collegii sancti Bartholomei de Tonge ad omnes sacros ordines
Willelmus Messager ad titulum domus sancti Egidii de Northwico Norwiciensis diocesis ad omnes
Ricardus Sadeler ad titulum domus de Osney ad omnes
Johannes Boteler ad titulum domus de Chirbury
Johannes Balme ad titulum domus de Blida
Thomas Whalley alias Walley ad titulum prioratus sancti Thome martiris juxta Stafford
Ricardus Cokke ad titulum domus de Haghmond
Henricus Whatford alias Watford ad titulum domus sancte Anne juxta Coventrensem ad omnes

RELIGIOSI
Fratres Johannes Mendis fratrum minorum Cestrie
Gerardus Uden ordinis minorum de conventu Salopie
Nicholaus Rolleston canonicus de Repyngdon

318. [Fo. 105v] General orders in Lichfield cathedral on 23 December 1447 by John, bishop of *Insulensis*[227]

ACOLYTES

John Burdon	Humphrey Burton
Richard Okes	John Holte
John Batemon	Richard Wolfall
Mr Richard Stokton	John Michelson
John Lench	Richard Wode

---

[227] See note 30.

RELIGIOUS

Brs   Henry Bonnay, minor of Lichfield
      Tedericus de Trunania, minor of Lichfield

SUBDEACONS

Thomas Mody, t. Darley
Robert Fowke, t. the nuns of Derby to all orders
William Cottrell, t. Darley, to all orders
John Linton, t. Baswich by Stafford
Thomas Bateson, t. Darley, to all orders
Henry Smyth, t. Darley, to all orders
William Leyton, t. Haughmond

RELIGIOUS

Brs   Robert Neuport ⎱ monks of Hulton
      Robert Chester ⎰

SECULAR DEACONS.

William Lightwode, t. Rocester, to all orders
Bonsale, Baguley,[228] Stranggulford (cf. Strangulford), Shireshagh, Cholmley, Pynder, Bury, Mychell, as in 317

RELIGIOUS

Brs John Englond ⎱ monks of the convent of Salop
    Thomas Mynte ⎰
John Asslow, O.F.M.

SECULAR PRIESTS

John Twys, t. the nuns of Derby, for all orders.
William Lincroft, t. the hospital of the Holy Trinity, Bridgnorth (*Bruggenorth*), for all orders.
Deyne, Orme, Harrymon, Rowley, Garard, Jecok, Marleston, as in **317**

RELIGIOUS

Br. Thomas Walton, monk of Croxden

319.   [Fo. 105v] General orders in Lichfield cathedral on 16 February 1447/8 by John, bishop of *Insulensis*.[229]

[Fo. 106r, col. a]
ACOLYTES

John Dykson	John Gilbert
John Lache	William Caldewall
Robert White	Robert Waley
Nicholas Broke	Ralph Wadyngton
Henry Herdmon	

---

[228] Here called George.
[229] See note 30.

SECULAR SUBDEACONS
John Marresse, t. Dale, to all orders
Richard Wolfall, t. Burscough, to all orders
Gilbert Horcyll, t. Whalley, to all orders
John Pert, t. Upholland, to all orders
Robert Speke, t. Upholland, to all orders
Humphrey Burghton, t. Baswich, to all sacred orders
John Holte, t. Trentham, to all sacred orders
Richard Brereley, t. Darley, to all orders
John Wodecoke, t. Whalley, to all orders
William Colyns, t. Osney, to all orders
Richard Cutteler, t. the priory of St George, Church Gresley, to all orders
John Pavy, t. the hospital of St John the baptist, Coventry, to all sacred orders
William Wryght (Lincoln dioc., by l.d.), t. Studley, to all orders
John Burdon (Durham dioc., by l.d.), t. Launde, to all orders
William Andrew, t. Ranton
Mr Richard Stokton, t. Arnold Savage

RELIGIOUS.
Friars Henry Bonna
   Tedericus de Trunania } O.F.M., Lichfield

SECULAR DEACONS
Fowke, Bateson, Smyth, Cotterell (cf. Cottrell), Lynton (cf. Linton), Leyton, as in **318**

RELIGIOUS.
Br. John Toppyng, monk of Upholland

SECULAR PRIESTS
Baguley,[230] Stranggulford (cf. Strangulford), Shireshagh, Bury, Pynder, as in **317**

RELIGIOUS.
Englond, Mynd (cf. Mynte), as in **318**

320. [Fo. 106] Special orders in the parish church of Whitchurch (*Whitechurch*), Salop, on 9 March 1447/8, by John, bishop of *Insulensis*.[231]

SECULAR SUBDEACONS
John Lache, t. Whalley, to all orders
John Cowper, t. Combermere

SECULAR DEACONS
Burdon, Bourghton (cf. Burghton), Holte, Andrew, as in **319**

[230] Here called George.
[231] See note 30.

321. General orders in Lichfield cathedral on 18 May 1448 by John, bishop of *Insulensis*.

ACOLYTES

Richard Wasse	Ralph Vowdray
Richard Bythewater	Thomas Janyns
John Bullok	John Cortell
Thomas Barow	Richard Seffton
William Bragges	Roger Heth [Fo. 106v]
John Hulme	

SECULAR SUBDEACONS

Ralph Wadyngton, t. Sawley (*Salley*), to all orders
Richard Orme, t. Upholland, to all orders
William Kente, t. Darley, to all orders
William Taillour (Lincoln dioc., by l.d.), t. Chacombe, to all orders
John Freman, t. Farewell (*Farewall*), to all orders
John Boteller, t. Upholland, to all orders
Henry Herdmon, t. John Botiller knight and baron of Warrington (*Weryngton*)
John Gylbert, t. Burton upon Trent
Gilbert Croston, t. Breadsall Park (*Bredsalle Parke*)
William Beke, t. Farewell, to all orders

RELIGIOUS

Br. John Endesor, canon of Rocester

SECULAR DEACONS

Robert White, t. Buildwas, to all orders
Mody, as in **318**
Wolfall, Pertt (cf. Pert), Brereley, Speke, Pavy, Stokton,[232] Colyns, Horcyll, Cutteler, Wodecok (cf. Wodecoke), as in **319**
Cowper, as in **320**.

RELIGIOUS.

Br. Henry Hunkull, O.F.M., Lichfield
Br. Thomas Feld, monk of Burton upon Trent
Br. John Stow, monk of Evesham
Neuport,[233] Chester, as in **318**

SECULAR PRIESTS

John Pereson, t. Icketon (*Iklyngton*), for all orders
Hugh Padyham, t. Whalley
Howson, Bonsale, Cholmley, as in **317**
Fowkes (cf. Fowke), Smyth, Lynton (cf. Linton), Cotterell
(cf. Cottrell), Lightwode, Leyton, as in **318**

---

232 The donor of his title here called esquire.
233 Here called William.

Burdon, Bourghton (cf. Burghton), Holte, Wryght,[234] as in **319**
Lache, as in **320**

RELIGIOUS
Br. Stephen Mosse, canon of Stone
Br. John Shireley, monk of Burton upon Trent
Br. John Midelton, canon of Dale
Br. William Sydeley, monk of Evesham
Br. William Kelmestow, canon of Maxstoke
Toppynge (cf. Toppyng), as in **319**

322. [Fo. 106v] General orders in the principal chapel of the manor of Haywood on 21 September 1448 by William, bishop of Coventry and Lichfield.

ACOLYTES

John Hextall	John Robert
Geoffrey Somner	William Cowper

SECULAR SUBDEACONS
Richard Seffton, t. John Botiller knight and baron of Warrington, to all orders
Mr Wistan Brown, t. St Anne by Coventry
John Rasse, t. Chirbury (Hereford dioc., by l.d.) to all orders
William Aaron, t. Chirbury (*Chirbery*), to all orders
Roger Ardern, t. Combermere

RELIGIOUS
Br. William Glossop, monk of Dieuleucres

SECULAR DEACONS
Marresse (Norwich dioc., by l.d.), as in **319**
Wadyngton, Herdmon, Fremon (cf. Freman), Orme, Kente, Gylbert, Beke, Croston, Botiller (cf. Boteller), Taillour, as in **321**

RELIGIOUS
Friar William Redyngton, O.F.M., Bridgnorth[235]
Friar Michael Lutsonbroke, O.F.M., Salop
Endesor, as in **321**

SECULAR PRIESTS
Bateson, as in **318**
Wulfall (cf. Wolfall), Horcyll, Wodekoc (cf. Wodecoke, Wodecok), Pavy, Pertt (cf. Pert), Speke, Brereley, Colyns, Cutteler, Stokton,[236] as in **319**
Cowper, as in **320**
White, as in **321**

---

[234] Here said to be of York diocese.
[235] Said to be of Coventry (see **330**).
[236] Donor of title here called esquire.

RELIGIOUS
Br. Thomas Ludlow, canon of Haughmond
Br. Richard Coll, monk of Salop
Br. Richard Condor ⎱ monks of Salop
  Edward Ruton ⎰
Neuport, Chester, as in **318**

323. [Fo. 107] Item memorandum quod anno domini millesimo CCCC^{mo} quadragesimo octavo, terciodecimo die mensis Octobris, fratres Thomas Holam canonicus sancti Thome martiris juxta Stafford' et Willelmus Stoywall in accolitum per reverendum in Christo patrem dominum W., dei gracia Coventrensem et Lichfeldensem episcopum, ex gracia speciali, in capella principali manerii sui de Heywode ejusdem patris diocesis canonice extiterint ordinati, etc.

324. General orders in Lichfield cathedral on 2 December 1448 by John, bishop *Insulensis*.[237]

SECULAR ACOLYTES
Randal Tildesley	Adam Alikoc
Thomas Merbury	John Smyth
David Mortymer	William Haryson
Richard Glover	Thomas Knyghtley
James Fissher	John Fray
Richard Bawmford	Edward Darneton

RELIGIOUS
Friar Richard Higate, O.F.M., Lichfield, to all orders

SECULAR SUBDEACONS
Richard Wasse, t. Darley, to all orders
Roger Heth (Canterbury dioc, by l.d.), t. Dieuleucres, to all orders
Henry Kynnerton, t. Halesowen, to all orders
William Wever, t. St Anne by Coventry
Robert Leyot, t. the nuns of Chester, to all orders

RELIGIOUS
Br. Walter Lichefeld, monk of Coventry, to all orders
Br. John Stratford, O.Carm., Coventry, to all orders
Br. John Eccleshale, O.S.A., Repton
Friar John Wade, O.F.M., Lichfield

SECULAR DEACONS
William Welles, t. St Anne by Coventry, to all orders Ardern, Seffton, Brown,[238] as in **322**

---

[237] See note 30.
[238] Also entitled M.A.

RELIGIOUS
[Fo. 107v]
Friar John Moselak, O.F.M., Lichfield

SECULAR PRIESTS.
Marresse (Norwich dioc., by l.d.), as in **319**
Wadyngton, Botiller (cf. Boteller), Beke, Orme, Taillour, Croston, Freman, Herdemon (cf. Herdmon), as in **321**

RELIGIOUS.
Br. Henry Charnok, O.F.M., Lichfield
Br. John Brown, O.Carm., Coventry

325. [Fo. 107v] General orders in Lichfield cathedral on 8 March 1448/9 by John, bishop of *Insulensis*.[239]

ACOLYTES.

John Chestre	Thomas Spycer
William Strynger	John Shermon (all orders)
William Taillour	Nicholas Wilson

SECULAR SUBDEACONS.
John Fraye, t. Sandwell (*Sanwall*), to all orders
Robert Balshagh, t. Upholland, to all orders
Ralph Vawdray, t. the nuns of Farewell
William Haddeley, t. the hospital of the Holy Trinity, Bridgnorth, to all orders
Richard Pykeryng, t. Norton, to all orders
William de Hill, t. Church Gresley, to all orders
John Batemans, t. Osney, to all orders
Thomas Wynturton, t. Darley, to all orders
Thomas Knyghtley, t. Lilleshall, to all orders
Thomas Clayton, t. Thurgarton, to all orders
William Bukley (York dioc., by l.d.), t. Garendon, dioc. Lincoln, to all orders
John Hexstall, t. Croxden, to all orders
William Hapsford, t. St Anne by Coventry
Thomas Janyns, t. Haughmond, to all orders
Geoffrey Somnour, t. Vale Royal, to all orders
William Harryson, t. Dieuleucres
John Bullokhorne, t. Church Gresley
Thomas Hankynlowe, t. Combermere
Ranulf Tildesley, t. Whalley
Adam Alikoc, t. Dieuleucres, to all orders
Henry Lapley, t. Thelsford, to all orders
Richard Okus, t. Polesworth, to all orders
Thomas Coke (York dioc., by l.d.), t. Thelsford, to all orders
John Lench, t. the hospital of St John the baptist, Warwick, to all orders

[239] See note 30.

Thomas Merbury, B.A., t. Farewell, to all orders
Thomas Sharpe, t. Darley, to all orders

SECULAR DEACONS
Richard Mareys, t. the abbot and convent of Alcester (*Alincestr'*)
Aaron, as in **322**
Heth, Wasse, Kynnarton (cf. Kynnerton), Wever, Leyot, as in **324**

[Fo. 107v] RELIGIOUS
Glossop, as in **322**
Eccleshale, as in **324**

SECULAR PRIESTS
Richard Heth (Worcester dioc., by l.d.), t. Maxstoke, to all orders
Andrewe (cf. Andrew), as in **319**
Ardern, Brown,[240] Seffton, as in **322**
Wellys (cf. Welles), as in **324**

RELIGIOUS
Br. Eneas de Hibernia, O.F.M., Salop
Br. William Sonky, O.S.A., Repton

326. [Fo. 108] Special orders in the principal chapel of the manor of Haywood on 12 April 1449 by W[illiam], bishop of Coventry and Lichfield.

SECULAR SUBDEACONS
John Beesty, t. Thomas de Pulle[241] esq., and Thomas Pulle, his son and heir
Ranulf Mandeley, t. the nuns of Chester
Thomas Hardyng, t. Farewell
John Venables, illegitimate, by apostolic dispensation, t. Lilleshall
John Moreton, t. Baswich by Stafford, for all orders
William Stonywall, t. Baswich by Stafford, for all orders

SECULAR DEACONS
Merbury, Vawdray, Haddeley, as in **325**

327. General orders in Lichfield cathedral on 7 June 1449 by John, bishop *Insulensis*.[242]

SECULAR ACOLYTES

Richard Graunger	William Bretherton
John Wright	William Brow
Thomas Bate	John Akermon
Christopher Clompton	John Kynge

---

240 Given degree of M.A.
241 Surname given as Pule in **327**.
242 See note 30.

John Smyth	James Nayler
Geoffrey Denthor	Walter Wasteley
John Davy	John Goghe

RELIGIOUS
Br. William Kynasey, canon of Wombridge
Br. John Norton, monk of Burton upon Trent

SECULAR SUBDEACONS
Richard Baumforth, t. Whalley
James Fissher, t. Whalley, to all orders
William Newbrige, t. Sandwell
Oliver Lye, t. Lilleshall, to all orders
James Hodeleston (York dioc., by l.d.), t. Whalley, to all orders
Thomas Merton, t. Baswich by Stafford, to all orders
Roger Davys, t. Lilleshall, to all orders
John Skaylehorn, t. Dieuleucres
William Taillour, t. Beauchief, to all orders
John Richeforth (Lincoln dioc., by l.d.), t. Markby
Thomas Ryle, t. Farewell, to all orders

RELIGIOUS
Brs Robert Fygon ⎫
   Robert Wilkys ⎬ canons of Lilleshall
   William Elarton ⎭
Br. John Malefeld, canon of Darley
Br. Henry Eggebaston, canon of Halesowen
Friar Thadeus Clerici, O.P., Warwick, to all orders

SECULAR DEACONS
John Sadeler (exempt jurisdiction of Evesham), t. nuns of Cook Hill
Richard Duyre (Worcester dioc., by l.d.), t. Sulby, to all orders
Fraye, Somnour, Balshagh, Harryson, Hexstall, Clayton,[243] Janyns, Batemans, Pykering (cf. Pykeryng), Alikoc (cf. Alicok), Lappeley (cf. Lapley), Knyghtley, de Hill, Tildesley, Wynturton, Sharpe, Okus, Bullokhorne, Hankelowe (cf. Hankynlowe), as in **325**
Beesty, Mandeley, Venables, Moreton, Stonywall, Hardyng, as in **326**

RELIGIOUS
Br. Robert Chilwell, canon of Darley
Friar Peter Hert, O.P., Warwick, to all orders
Friar Roger de Campo, O.F.M., Stafford

SECULAR PRIESTS
William Dyer (Worcester dioc. by l.d.), t. Alcester, to all orders
Mody, as in **318**

---

[243] Here called Richard.

Gilbert (cf. Gylbert), as in **321**
Aaron, as in **322**
Leyot, Wasse, Kinnarton (cf. Kinnerton), as in **324** Merbury, Vawdray, Bukley,
Cooke (cf. Coke),[244] Haddeley, Lench, as in **325**

RELIGIOUS
Br. William Chichester, monk of Coventry
Br. John Westbury, canon of Haughmond
Loghburogh (cf. Loughtborow), Assheburn, as in **317** Fyld (cf. Feld), as in **321**

328. [Fo. 108v] General orders in Lichfield cathedral on 20 September 1449 by
John, bishop of *Insulensis.*[245]

SECULAR ACOLYTES

Nicholas Bryne	William Waturfall
Thomas de Pole	Thomas Hunt
William Ferrour	Thomas Stacy
John de Millynton	Laurence Typpynge
Thomas Smyth	Gilbert Marsden
William Northale	John Baker
Henry Russell	John Porter

RELIGIOUS
Br. Robert Newman, O.Carm., Coventry
Friar Richard Martyn, O.F.M., Lichfield
Br. Peter Wybbe, O.F.M., Lichfield
Brs John Notyngham } canons of Dale
    Nicholas Trentham }

SECULAR SUBDEACONS
William Bretherton, t. Upholland, to all orders
William Caldewall, t. Trentham, to all orders
John Hanerey (exempt jurisdiction Evesham, by l.d.), t. nuns of Cook Hill (*Kokhill*),
dioc. Worcester, to all orders
Thomas Whitakris (York dioc;), t. St Anne by Coventry, O.Carth., to all orders
James Nailer, t. Upholland, to all orders
Richard Worthyngton, t. Whalley, to all orders
Richard Porter, t. Trentham, to all orders
Edward Darneton (Durham dioc., by l.d.), t. St Anne by Coventry, O.Carth., to all
orders
Thomas Barowgh, t. Ulverscroft
Thomas Wilkus (Hereford dioc., by l.d.), t. Thelsford (*Talesforde*), to all orders
Richard Robynson, t. Whalley, to all orders
Richard Glover, t. Whalley, to all orders

[244] Title given in full, as provided by Robert Bolton, minister of the house of St Radegund,
Thelsford, for all orders.
[245] See note 30.

Richard Spicer, t. the hospital of St John the baptist, Coventry, to all orders
John Fissher (Worcester dioc; l.d.), t. the hospital of St Oswald in the suburbs of the
city of Worcester,   to all orders
[Fo. 109r] John Baker, t. Croxden, to all orders
Walter Westeley, t. Arbury

RELIGIOUS
Br. William Kynarsey, canon of Wombridge, to all orders
Br. John Stretforde, O.Carm., Coventry
Br. Henry Asshe ⎫
Br. Thomas Sutton ⎭ canons of Repton
Friar Peter de Colonia, O.F.M., Bridgnorth

SECULAR DEACONS
Hapssforde (cf. Hapsford), as in **325**
Fissher, Merton, Lye, Hodelston (cf. Hodeleston), Tailleour (cf. Taillour),
Skaylehorn, Davys, Newbrigge (cf. Newbrige), Richeforth, Ryle, as in **327**

RELIGIOUS
Br. John Kyngeswode, monk of Stoneleigh
Wade, Stretforde (cf. Stratford), as in **324**

SECULAR PRIESTS
Robert Cowell (York dioc., by l.d.), t. Bolton in Craven
Oliver Blakewall, t. Barnwell
Hankelowe (cf. Hankynlowe), Tildesley, Knyghtley, Somnour, Hill (cf. de Hill),
Bollokhorde (cf. Bullokhorne), Alicok (cf. Alikoc), Pikerynge (cf. Pykeryng),
Hexstall, Lappeley (cf. Lapley), Wynturton, Janyns, Okes (cf. Okus), Sharpe,
Batemans, as in **325**
Moreton, Mandeley, Brescy (cf. Beesty), Venables, Hardynge (cf. Hardyng), as in
326
Sadeler, Duyre,[246] as in **327**

RELIGIOUS
Br. John Aldewerke of Dale, to all orders
Ednesover (cf. Endesor), as in **321**
Hert, as in **327**

329. [Fo. 109v] General orders in Lichfield cathedral on 20 December 1449 by
John, bishop of *Insulensis*.[247]

SECULAR ACOLYTES.
John Eyre   John Taillour
Richard Walkeden   Henry Merell

---

[246] Described as of the exempt jurisdiction of Evesham, diocese of Worcester, by letters
dimissory.
[247] See note 30.

Walter Grene	Henry Lande
William Thomson	John Harmon
Robert Momsell	Thomas Hikyns
John Bloxwich	William Partrich to all orders

SECULAR SUBDEACONS.
Thomas Phippes, M.A. (Worcester dioc., by l.d.), t. St Mary, Osney
William Braggis, t. Farewell
Thomas Pole, t. Darley, to all orders
William Bromelle (York dioc., by l.d.), t. St Anne by Coventry, O.Carth.
Laurence Tippynge, t. Whalley
William Waturwall, t. Dodford
[Fo. 109v] William Thurston, t. St Anne by Coventry
Richard Morres, t. St John the baptist, Coventry, to all orders
Thomas Smyth, t. Henry Bulde esq., to all orders
Hugh Brown, t. Arbury, to all orders
Thomas Englisshe, t. Farewell
John Leghes, t. Whalley, to all orders
John Peynter, t. Haughmond, to all orders
John Tiler, t. Wombridge, to all orders
Thomas Stacy, t. Baswich by Stafford

RELIGIOUS
Friar Richard Martyn ⎫
Friar Albert Werpage ⎬ O.F.M., Lichfield
Br. Thomas Holam, canon of Stafford, St Thomas
Br. John Shrovesbury, monk of Wenlock

[Fo. 109v] SECULAR DEACONS
Richard ap Jankyn (St David's dioc., by l.d.), t. *Nerth land*, to all orders
Baumforde (cf. Baumforth), as in **327**
Glover, Caldewall, Porter, Wilkis (cf. Wilkus), Westley (cf. Westeley), Fissher, Hanerey, Whitakers (cf. Whitakris), Barowgh, Bretherton, Darneton, Spicer, Baker, as in **328**

RELIGIOUS
Friar William Middelton, O.F.M., Lichfield
Friar [Hugh][248] Okalan, O.E.S.A., Atherstone
Kynarsey, as in **328**

SECULAR PRIESTS.
John Jonys, B.A. (Worcester dioc., by l.d.), t. Bruern, Lincoln diocese
Thomas Smyth (York dioc., by l.d.), t. Bruern
Clayton,[249] Balshagh, as in **325**
Stonywall, as in **326**

---

248 Christian name omitted here, but given in **330**.
249 Called Richard here.

Fissher, Skailehorn (cf. Skaylehorn), Newbrygge (cf. Newbrige), Davys, Lye, Tailliour (cf. Taillour), Richeford (cf. Richeforth), Rile (cf. Ryle), Hodelston (cf. Hodeleston), Merton, as in **327**

RELIGIOUS
Friar Denis Lavyn, O.E.S.A., Atherstone
Friar John Canter, O.F.M., Lichfield

330. [Fo. 109v] General orders in Lichfield cathedral on 28 February 1449/50, by John, bishop *Insulensis*.[250]

SECULAR ACOLYTES

Alexander Newton
William Skynner
Richard Burgis (Exeter dioc.)
Oliver Langton
Richard Heye

John Smyth
William Roke
William Bassett
Robert Overton
Alexander Cleyveley

RELIGIOUS
Friar William Berfom, O.F.M., Lichfield
Br. John Notyngham ⎫
Br. Robert Shelford ⎬ monks of Lenton

SECULAR SUBDEACONS
William Whitley, t. Buildwas
John Porter, t. Farewell
Thomas Pole, t. Darley
Thomas Hoptun, t. Haughmond
Thomas Bury, B.A., t. Osney
John Pensell, t. the nuns of Chester, to all orders [Fo. 110]
William Stryngar, B.A., t. Osney
William Coke, t. the hospital of St John the Baptist, Coventry
Henry Land, t. the hospital of St John the Baptist, Northampton
John Perkyn, t. St Anne (O.Carth.), by Coventry
Ralph Sompnour, t. Vale Royal
Hugh Adames, t. the hospital of St James, Bridgnorth
Henry Webster, t. Upholland, to all orders
John Fowlus (Worcester dioc., by l.d.), t. Alcester
Thomas Spycer, t. Croxton
Thomas Hyckyns (Worcester dioc., by l.d.), t. Cook Hill
Thomas Bradley, t. the nuns of Chester
Nicholas Bryn, t. Birkenhead, to all orders
Thomas Hunt, t. Burscough, to all orders
William Grenehull, t. the hospital of St James, Coventry
Richard Steven (Worcester dioc., by l.d.), t. Halesowen
Laurence Broxhop, t. Upholland

[250] See note 30.

RELIGIOUS
Friar John Makeblyth, O.F.M., Lichfield
Br. Nicholas Trentham } monks of Dale
Br. John Notyngham }
Br. Richard Merston, canon of Stone

SECULAR DEACONS
Robynson, Nayler (cf. Nailer), Worthyngton, Darreton (cf. Darneton, as in **328** Tiler, Waturfall (cf. Waturwall), Smyth, Bromle (cf. Bromelle), Englysshe (cf. Englisshe), Thurston, Morres, Bragges (cf. Braggis), Leghes, Peynter, Stacy, Brown, as in **329**

RELIGIOUS
Elarton, Fygon, Welkis (cf. Wilkys), as in **327** Martyn, Holom (cf. Holam), Merbagh (cf. Werpage), as in 329

SECULAR PRIESTS
Porter, Caldewall, Barowgh, Whitakurs (cf. Whitakris, Whitakers), Wilkys (cf. Wilkis, Wilkus), Baker, as in **329**

RELIGIOUS
Friar William Redyngton, O.F.M., Coventry (cf. Redyngton, O.F.M. Bridgnorth,) as in **322**
Br. John Drax, monk of Lenton
Kynasey (cf. Kynarsey), as in **328**
Middulborgh (cf. Middelton), Okelan (cf. Okalan), as in **329**

331. [Fo. 110–v] General orders in Lichfield cathedral on 30 May 1450 by John, bishop of *Insulensis*.[251]

ACOLYTES SECULAR
Elias Rider, of Co. Lancaster
Humphrey Mille
John Chatburn, to all orders
Henry Wodehowse
John Walker
John Ursewike
William Ruttur
Thomas Diche
William Ridware
John Alysse

RELIGIOUS
Br. John Seyntemond, O.Carm., Coventry
Friar Richard Spenser, O.F.M., Lichfield
Br. William Bretherton, monk of Beauchief
Friar William Elburch, O.F.M., Salop

SECULAR SUBDEACONS
Henry Russell, t. Polesworth
William Tomsun, t. Halesowen [Fo. 110v]

[251] See note 30.

Robert Mawnsell, t. Halesowen, to all orders
William Gryme, t. Cook Hill (Worcester dioc.)
John Shermon, t. Haughmond, to all orders
William Barker, t. Feeley, to all orders
Walter Grene, t. Polesworth, to all orders
John Hermon, t. Haughmond, to all orders
Thomas Andrewes (Worcester dioc., by l.d.), t. Halesowen, to all orders
Thomas Meolis, LL.B., t. John Stanley esqre;
John Baker, t. Stoneleigh, to all orders
Henry Merell (Worcester dioc., by l.d.), t. Thelsford, to all orders
Robert Knoll, t. Upholland, to all orders
Richard Hey, t. St John the Baptist and John the Evangelist, Leicester

RELIGIOUS
Br. John Samon, O.Carm., Coventry
Br. Robert Wise, O.S.A., Stone
Br. Richard Higate ⎱ monks of Combe
Br. John Banks ⎰
Br. John Corbeke, monk of Beauchief
Br. John Hamsterley, canon of Kenilworth
Br. John Allerwas, monk of Hilton
Br. John Pygot, canon of Maxstoke

SECULAR DEACONS
John Robyns, t. St Anne, Coventry
Elias Ingram, 'exempt' jurisdictionis de Evesham' (Worcester dioc., by l.d.), t. Wraxall, to all orders
Thomas Carson, t. Burscough, to all orders
John Ewike (Lincoln dioc.; l.d.), t. Cook Hill, to all orders
Stryngar, Bury, Bruyn (cf. Bryn), Parkyn, Whiteley (cf. Whitley), Hopton (cf. Hoptun), Broxhope (cf. Broxhop), Land, Hunt, Sompnour, Bradley (cf. Bradeley), Webester, Adames, as in **330**

RELIGIOUS
Notyngham, Trentham, Merston, as in **330**

SECULAR PRIESTS
Porter, Bretherton, Glover, Robynson, Worthyngton, Nayler (cf. Nailer), as in **328**
Waturfall (cf. Waturwall), Tiler, Leghes, Bromele (cf. Bromle, Bromelle), Pole, Smyth, Peynter, Brown, Stacy, as in **329**
Fowlus, Hickyns (cf. Hyckyns), Steven, Pensell, Coke, as in **330**

RELIGIOUS
Stretford (cf. Stretforde, Stratford), Kyngeswode, as in **328**
Holom (cf. Holam), as in **329**

332. [Fo. 111] Memorandum quod prefatus reverendus in Christo pater Willelmus Coventrensis et Lichfeldensis episcopus decimo die mensis Augusti anno domini millesimo CCCC^{mo} quinquagesimo in capella manerii de Claiton dicti patris diocese Willelmum Brand Johannem Whalley Robertum Batemon et Johannem Wadyngton ex gracia in ordinem accoliti ordinaverit.

333.   General orders in Lichfield cathedral on 19 September 1450 by John, bishop *Insulensis*.[252]

SECULAR ACOLYTES

William Whithed ⎫ Isti fuerint ordinati in capella
Alexander Defele ⎬ manerii de Claiton per Willelmum
John Mathewe   ⎭ Coventrensem et Lichfeldensem episcopum ut supra
Nicholas Stonywall   Thomas Astley
John Osbarne   Hugh Byker
Hugh Lathom   John Albod
Robert Russell   John Abraham
Ralph Faireclogh

RELIGIOUS
Br. Richard Assheby, monk of Burton upon Trent

SECULAR SUBDEACONS
Elias Rider, t. Whalley
Alexander Cleyveley, t. Whalley
John Chatbourn, t. Whalley
Memorandum quod isti tres superscripti extiterint ordinati subdiaconi per reverendum patrem Willelmum Coventrensem et Lichfeldensem episcopum in capella manerii predicti die supradicto et eciam quod fratres Henricus Haghmond et Willelmus Wode monachi de Whalley ordinati fuerint subdiaconi loco die et anno domini supradictis per Willelmum episcopum antedictum.
Humphrey Mille, t. the hospital of St John, Bridgnorth
William Ridware, t. the nuns of Nuneaton, to all orders
Alexander Newton, t. Upholland, to all orders
Richard Hyne, t. Polesworth, to all orders
Henry Lynacre, t. Jervaulx (York dioc.)
Henry Wodehowse, t. the hospital of St John, Leicester
William Cowper, t. Somerewall
Roger Breyn, t. Cymmer, to all orders
Edward Curtaise, t. the hospital of the Holy Trinity, Bridgnorth
William Amot, t. Upholland, to all orders
Thomas Kendale, t. Upholland, to all orders
William Wynton, t. Baswich by Stafford
William Brampton, 'jurisdiccionis exempt' de Evesham', t. Alcester, to all orders
Richard Kempe, t. St Frideswide, Oxford
William Partriche, t. Farewell
William Ferrour, t. the nuns of Chester
John Thomelynson, t. the nuns of Chester
Richard Stonywall, t. Farewell

[252] See note 30.

RELIGIOUS
Br. Henry Bramond ⎫ subdeacons by William, bishop of
  monks of Whalley who ⎬ Coventry and Lichfield, in the
  were ordained Br. William Wode ⎭ chapel of the manor of Clayton
Friar William Elbruch, O.F.M.
Br. John Norton, monk of Burton upon Trent
Br. William Bretherton, canon of Beauchief

SECULAR DEACONS
Reginald Kyssyn (St Asaph dioc.; l.d.), t. John Hanmer esqre, to all orders
Shermon, Hey, Mawnsell, Tomsun, Grene, Barker, Andrewes, Gryne (l.d.),
Hermon, Baker, Knolle, Meolis, as in **331**

RELIGIOUS
Friar Peter de Rupa, O.F.M.
Br. John Newerke, O.S.A.
Asshe, Sutton, as in **328** [Fo. 111v]
Carbrek (cf. Corbeke), Wise, as in **331**
Br. Miles Bradford ⎫ monks of Whalley who were
Br. John Walton ⎪ ordained in the chapel of
Br. James Lawe ⎬ Clayton by William, bishop
Br. Laurence Grenhilton ⎪ of Coventry and Lichfield
Br. Thomas Hunt ⎭

334. [Fos 111v–112] General orders in Lichfield cathedral on 19 December
1450 by John, bishop of *Insulensis*.[253]

SECULAR ACOLYTES
Richard Rugge   Henry Chryme
Richard Golosur   William Bolton

RELIGIOUS
Br. William Coventry to all orders

SECULAR SUBDEACONS
William Brande, t. Whalley
Humphrey Faryngton, t. Farewell
George Parlour, t. Wigmore, to all orders
William Turnour, t. Upholland
William Bekett, t. Lenton
William Wildy, t. St Frideswide, Oxford
John Mathewson, t. Lenton
John Abbot (Worcester dioc., by l.d.), t. Bordesley
Ralph Assheton, t. Richard Assheton esqre, of Assheton
John Jenkynson, t. the nuns of Chester, to all orders
Gilbert Mersden, t. Burton upon Trent

[253] See note 30.

RELIGIOUS
Br. Thomas Trowbrugge, monk of Coventry
Brs William Chirke
   William Peris ⎫ canons of Haughmond
   Thomas Sompnour ⎭
Br. John Glowcester, monk of Combe
Br. Richard Assheby, monk of Burton upon Trent
Br. Alexander Burton, Canon of Trentham

SECULAR DEACONS
Geoffrey Dabbdor (St Asaph dioc., by l.d.), t. Strata Marcella, to all orders
Curteyse (cf. Curteise), Kempe, Ridware, Newton, Rider, Thomlynson (cf.
Thomelynson), Mille, Brayn (cf. Breyn), Kendale, Wodehowse, Hyne, Lynacre,
Ferrour, Amot, Stonywall, Wynton, Cleyveley, Patrich (cf. Partriche), as in **333**

RELIGIOUS
Br. Thomas Warwik, monk of Combe
Eggebaston, as in **327**
Shelforde (cf. Shelford), Notyngham, as in **330** Bretherton, Norton, as in **333**

SECULAR PRIESTS
Robert Crompe, Worcester dioc., by l.d.), t. Wombridge, to all orders
John Glade (Lincoln dioc., by l.d.), t. St John, Leicester, to all orders
Hey, Thomson (cf. Tomsun), Mawnsell, Andrews (cf. Andrewes), Knoll (cf.
Knolle), Russell, Shermon, Gryme, Grene, Hermon, Meolis, Baker (Worcester
dioc., by l.d.), as in **331**

RELIGIOUS
Br. Richard Botiller, monk of Evesham
Wise, Corbrugge (cf. Corbeke, Carbrek), as in **331** Newerke, as in **333**

335. [Fo. 112] Memorandum quod Robertus Stacy et Radulphus Davenport
ordinati fuerint accoliti per Insulem episcopum in ecclesia prebendali de
Eccleshale videlicet XIX° die Martii videlicet die sancti Patricii. [*sic*]

336. General orders in the prebendal church of Eccleshall on 20 March 1451 by
John, bishop *Insulensis*.[254]

ACOLYTES
John Cowper   Thomas Symond
John Averell   Richard Broke
William Grendon   John Owynsen
William Bradbury

SECULAR SUBDEACONS
Hugh Gartside, M.A., t. the hospital of St John the Baptist, Coventry, to all orders

[254] See note 30.

Thomas Melton (Rochester dioc., by l.d.), t. Combermere, to all orders
Mr Richard Fresby, M.A., t. St Anne by Coventry O.Carth.
Richard Gildon, t. the hospital of the Holy Trinity, Bridgnorth
John Holme (York dioc., by l.d.), t. Farewell
William Bolton, t. Whalley, to all orders
Richard Owyns, t. the hospital of St James the apostle, Bridgnorth
William Browe, t. Merevale
Thomas Typpe (Lincoln dioc., by l.d.), t. the priory of the Holy Sepulchre, Warwick, to all orders
Robert Stacy, t. Trentham
John Hopton (Hereford dioc., by l.d.), t. the hospital of St John the Baptist, Ludlow
William Whitehede, t. Whalley

RELIGIOUS
Friar Malachius Henly, O.P., Warwick

SECULAR DEACONS
Richard Geffray (Hereford dioc., by l.d.), t. the dean and chapter of Hereford cathedral
Brampton (l.d.) as in **333**
Brande, Mathewson, Faryngton, Beket (cf. Bekett), Wildy, Mersden, Jenkynson, Turnour, Abbott (cf. Abbot), Parlour, as in **334**

RELIGIOUS
Hampsterley (cf. Hamsterley), Pygot, as in **331**
Burton, Cherke (cf. Chirke), Sompnour, Peris, as in **334**

SECULAR PRIESTS
Wever, as in **324**
Partrych (cf. Partrich, Partriche), Newton, Stonywall, Cleyveley, Kempe, Wodehowse, Rider, Mille, Kendale, Amott (cf. Amot), Brayn (cf. Breyn), Hyne, Curteyse (cf. Curteise), Lynacre, FerrTour, Thomlynson (cf. Thomelynson), as in **333**
Dewddor (cf. Dabbdor), as in **334**

RELIGIOUS
Br. Richard Mershton, canon of Kenilworth
Friar John Symond, O.F.M., Coventry
Br. Robert Fitzjohn, canon of Lilleshall
Br. William Alen, canon of Lilleshall
Br. Robert Wilkes, canon of Lilleshall
Friar Ralph Otur, O.P., Newcastle under Lyme

337.   [Fo. 112v] Special orders in the prebendal church of Eccleshall on 10 April 1451 by John, bishop of *Insulensis*.[255]

---

[255] See note 30.

SECULAR DEACONS
Frysby (cf. Fresby), Browe, Bolton, Holme, Typpe, Melton, as in **336**

RELIGIOUS
Friar William Olbrech, O.F.M., Salop
Friar Malachius, O.P., Warwick (cf. Henly), as in **336**

SECULAR PRIESTS
Brande, Mersden, as in **334**
Peter de Berdesley, rector of Trusley, t. his benefice

RELIGIOUS
Friar Thomas Lynall, O.E.S.A., Stafford

338. [Fos 112v–113] General orders in the prebendal church of Eccleshall on 19
June 1451 by John, bishop of *Insulensis*.[256]

SECULAR ACOLYTES

John Braillesford	Henry Burton
Robert Amery	Roger Dukworth
John Yoxhale	Simon Pope
Robert Gropenhale	Thomas Waters
Thomas Apulton	

Memorandum that Robert Lynay and James Smethehurst were
ordained acolytes by the reverend father, the bishop of *Insulensis*, on 18 June 1451
in the prebendal church of Eccleshall.

RELIGIOUS
Br. Thomas Longdon, monk of Tutbury

SECULAR SUBDEACONS
William Wirrall, t. Norton
Thomas Symonde, t. Polesworth
John Alis, t. Merevale
Richard Walkeden, t. Farewell
Thomas Barker, t. Baswich by Stafford
Thomas Bolton, t. Burscough
James Smethehurst, t. Whalley
Edmund Taillour, t. Bordesley
John Heywarde, t. Nuneaton
John Curtell, t. St Anne by Coventry
Oliver de Langton, rector of Wigan, t. his benefice

[256] See note 30.

RELIGIOUS
Br. William Castell ⎫
Br. John Penkill   ⎬ monks of Hulton
Br. Alexander Sekon, monk of Coventry

SECULAR DEACONS
Assheton, as in **334**
Whitehede, Owyne, Gildon, as in **336**

RELIGIOUS
Br. Thomas Whytyngton, monk of Combe
Alderwa (cf. Allerwas), as in **331**
Glowcester, Trentbrugge (cf. Trowbrugge), as in **334**

SECULAR PRIESTS
Barker, as in **331**
Wildy, Beket (cf. Bekett), Albode (cf. Abbot), Turnour, Parlour, Jenkynson, as in
334
Browe, Holme, Bolton, Melton, as in **336**

RELIGIOUS
Friar Geoffrey Pulton, O.E.S.A., convent of Salop
Br. Robert Shawe, canon of Kenilworth
Samon, Hamsterley, as in **331**
Warwik, as in **334**
Henly, as in **336**

339. [Fo. 113] General orders in the prebendal church of Eccleshall on 18
September 1451 by John, bishop of *Insulensis.*[257]

SECULAR ACOLYTES

Richard Calaw   Nicholas Webbe
Christopher Houghton   George Bastwell
John Swyneshede   John Addow
Nicholas Bybby   Thomas Brome
Thomas Bradley   Thomas Meere
William Clerke

RELIGIOUS
Friar John Danyell, O.F.M., Lichfield

SECULAR SUBDEACONS
William Forster, t. Lilleshall, to all orders
John Cowper, t. Polesworth, to all orders
John Mulyngton, t. Norton, to all orders
John Hakyrman (Worcester dioc., by l.d.), t. Thelsford

[257] See note 30.

John Yoxhale, t. Farewell, to all orders
John Drayton, t. Halesowen

RELIGIOUS
Br. William Hoton, monk of Dieuleucres
Br. John Bury ⎤
Br. Thomas Longdon ⎦ monks of Tutbury
Br. John Yerdley, canon of Kenilworth

SECULAR DEACONS
Thomas Lawe, t. Whalley
de Langton, Smethehurste (cf. Smethehurst), Wirrall, Walkden (cf. Walkeden),
Symond (cf. Symonde), Bolton, Heywarde, Barker, Alis, Taillour, Curtell, as in
338

RELIGIOUS
Haghmond (cf. Bramond), Wode, as in **333**

SECULAR PRIESTS

pycer (cf. Spicer), as in **328**
Brampton, as in **333**
Whitehede, Gildon, Owyne, as in **336**

RELIGIOUS
Merton (cf. Martyn), as in **329**
Chirke, as in **334**

340. [Fo. 113v] General orders in Lichfield cathedral on 18 December 1451 by
John, bishop of *Insulensis*.[258]

SECULAR ACOLYTES

John Bedford   Richard Martyn
Richard Veysyn, B.A.   Richard Derby
Thomas Warde   Nicholas Brown
John Jeffrey   Thomas Countour
Hugh Whitehede   Richard Batemon
Thomas Grypton

RELIGIOUS
Friars John Barly ⎤
   Thomas Poorson ⎬ O.F.M., Lichfield
William Evesham) ⎦

---

[258] See note 30.

SECULAR SUBDEACONS
William Grendon, t. Tutbury
Roger Dukworth, t. Whalley
John Swyneshed, t. Baswich by Stafford, to all orders George Bastewisell, t. Whalley
John Eyre, t. Beauchief
Nicholas Webbe, t. Ranton
William Evys, t. Upholland
John Braydesale, t. Dale
Thomas Wattus, t. the Holy Sepulchre, Warwick
Richard Broke, t. Clattercote
John Scotte, t. St Anne by Coventry, O.Carth.,
John Robertson, t. the hospital of Ss John the Evangelist and John the Baptist, Leices

RELIGIOUS
Br. John Bassyngton, canon of Rocester
Br. Richard Whityngton ⎫ monks of Merevale
Br. Richard Bordesley ⎭
Friar Richard Spenser ⎫ O.F.M., Lichfield
Friar Ludovic Wycom ⎭

SECULAR DEACONS
William Plughwright (Lincoln dioc., by l.d.), t. Shap, to all orders
Yoxhale, Drayton, Mulyngton, Cowper, Hakirman (cf. Hakyrman), Forster, as in **339**

RELIGIOUS
Bury, Longdon, de Hoton (cf. Hoton), as in **339**

SECULAR PRIESTS
Christopher Bradeford of Bradford (York dioc., by l.d.), t. Cockersand, to all orders
Assheton, as in **334**
Typpe, as in **336**
de Langton, Curtell, Wirall, Walkeden, Taillour, Bolton, Smetherhurst, Alis, Heyward (cf. Heywarde), Symonde, as in **338**

RELIGIOUS.
Sutton, as in **328**

341. General orders in Lichfield cathedral on 4 March 1452 by John, bishop *Insulensis*.[259]

SECULAR ACOLYTES

Henry Yonge	Thurstan Shurrok
Christopher Clerk	Richard Dowmbell

[259] See note 30.

Richard Arnycok
John Grenehull
John May
Thomas Stewynson

Thomas Wilcok (all orders) [Fo. 114]
William Smolte
John Maystres

RELIGIOUS
Friar Richard Parker, O.F.M., Lichfield

SECULAR SUBDEACONS
Thomas Brome, t. Garendon
Richard Veysyn, B.A., t. St Frideswide, Oxford
Ralph Chirton, t. the nuns of Chester
William Fleccher, t. the nuns of Chester, to all orders
Simon Pope (Worcester dioc., by l.d.), t. Cook Hill
John Molle, t. Great Malvern
William Berford of Rokby, t. Pipewell
Thomas Maire, t. Dale
Henry de Burton, t. John Botiller knight and baron of Warrington
Richard Derby, t. Repton
Thomas Warde, t. Combermere
John Walker, t. Halesowen
William Clerke, t. Polesworth

RELIGIOUS
Friars John Barly
  Richard Coventry } O.F.M., Lichfield
Brs Nicholas Pencrech
  John Bromsgrove } monks of Stoneleigh

SECULAR DEACONS
John Osbern (Lincoln dioc., by l.d.), t. hospital of St John, Coventry
Evis (cf. Evys), Bastewysell (cf. Bastewisell), Eire (cf. Eyre), Grendon, Webbe, Dukeworth (cf. Dukworth), Broke, Skotte (cf. Scotte), Wattus, Robertson, as in **340**

RELIGIOUS
Malefeld, as in **327**
Yerdeley (cf. Yerdley), as in **339**
Brasyngton (cf. Bassyngton), as in **340**

SECULAR PRIESTS
Barker, as in **338**
Cowper, Forster, Mulyngton, Drayton, Yoxhale, as in **339**
Plughtwryght, as in **340**

RELIGIOUS
Stafford, as in **317**
Trentham, Notyngham, as in **330**

342. [Fo. 114] Special orders in the prebendal church of Colwich on 25 March 1452 by John, bishop of *Insulensis*.[260]

ACOLYTE
Simon Peynter

SECULAR SUBDEACONS
Robert Dounville, t. Norton
John Bate, t. Darley
Thurstan Shurrok, t. Burscough
Henry Yonge, t. Whalley

SECULAR DEACONS
Fleccher, Veysyn, Mair (cf. Maire), Derby, as in **341**

SECULAR PRIESTS
Lawe, as in **339**
Grendon, Dukworth, Bastwisell (cf. Bastewisell), as in **340**

343. [Fo. 114v] Special orders in the chapel of the manor of Haywood on 8 April 1452 by William, bishop of Coventry and Lichfield.

SECULAR SUBDEACONS
William Dounne, t. the nuns of Chester, to all orders
Hugh Lathum, t. Burscough

SECULAR DEACONS
Chirton, as in **341**
Shorrok, Bate, Yonge, Dounville, as in **342**

SECULAR PRIESTS
Ridware, as in **333**
Mair (cf. Maire), Veysyn, as in **341**

344. [Fos 114v–115] General orders in Lichfield cathedral on 3 June 1452 by John, bishop of *Insulensis*.[261]

SECULAR ACOLYTES
Nicholas Foxe   Charles Dethik
Richard Nelsthorp   Thomas Jaye
Roger Bowett   Maurice Spicer
John Honey   William Molynton
Christopher Howe

---

[260] See note 30.
[261] See note 30.

RELIGIOUS
Br. James Lichefelde of Stoneleigh

SECULAR SUBDEACONS
Thomas Stokport, t. Dieuleucres
Richard Enkeston, t. Burscough
John Holme, t. Burscough
Christopher Crompton, t. Whalley
Richard Arnecok, t. Nuneaton
Christopher Houghton, t. Beauchief
Thomas Brodehurst, t. Welbeck
Richard Calaw, t. Norton
John Thorley, t. Dieuleucres
Nicholas Dykson, t. Lenton
John Smyth, 'exempt' jurisdictionis de Evesham', t. Cook Hill, by l.d.
Robert Lynay, t. Upholland
John Wryght, t. Baswich by Stafford
Richard Jordan (Worcester dioc., by l.d.), t. Halesowen
Richard Smyth (Worcester dioc., by l.d.), t. the nuns of Wiston
John Ursewike, t. Farewell
Nicholas Thomson, t. Ranton
John Clerke, t. the hospital of St John, Leicester
Mr John Bedon, M.A., t. St Anne by Coventry to all orders
John Grene, B.A., t. Buildwas
John de Bede, t. Dieuleucres
William Fissher, t. Great Malvern

RELIGIOUS
William Coventry, monk of Burton upon Trent

SECULAR DEACONS
Robert Walter (Llandaff dioc., by l.d.), t. Chepstow
Mr William Asser, rector of the parish church of Tarporley
Swyneshed, as in **340**
Bedford (cf. Berford), Brome, Warde, Nolle, Pope, Clerk, Burton (cf. de Burton), as in **341**
Dounne, Lathum, as in **343**

RELIGIOUS
Assheby, as in **334**
Berdesley (cf. Bordesley), Whytyngton (cf. Whityngton), as in **340**
Coventry, Pencrich (cf. Pencrech), Bromsgrove (cf. Bromsgrowe), as in **341**

SECULAR PRIESTS
Hakirman (cf. Hakyrman), as in **339**
Evis (cf. Evys), Webbe, Broke, Scotte, Wattis (cf. Wattus), Eyre, Robertson, as in **340**
Chirton, Derby, as in **341**
Bate, Yonge, Dounville, as in **342**

RELIGIOUS
Br. John Zargla, canon of Kenilworth
Allerwas (cf. Alderwas), as in **331**
Whoton (cf. Hoton), as in **339**
Brassyngton (cf. Bassyngton), as in **340**.
Br. John Hamsterley, canon of Kenilworth
Br. John Allerwas, monk of Hilton
Br. John Pygot, canon of Maxstoke

SECULAR DEACONS
John Robyns, t. St Anne, Coventry
Elias Ingram, 'exempt' jurisdictionis de Evesham' (Worcester dioc., by l.d.), t. Wraxall, to all orders
Thomas Carson, t. Burscough, to all orders
John Ewike (Lincoln dioc; l.d.), t. Cook Hill, to all orders
Stryngar, Bury, Bruyn (cf. Bryn), Parkyn, Whiteley (cf. Whitley), Hopton (cf. Hoptun), Broxhope (cf. Broxhop), Land, Hunt, Sompnour, Bradley (cf. Bradeley), Webester, Adames, as in **330**

RELIGIOUS
Notyngham, Trentham, Merston, as in **330**

SECULAR PRIESTS
Porter, Bretherton, Glover, Robynson, Worthyngton, Nayler (cf. Nailer), as in **328**
Waturfall (cf. Waturwall), Tiler, Leghes, Bromele (cf. Bromle, Bromelle), Pole, Smyth, Peynter, Brown, Stacy, as in **329**
Fowlus, Hickyns (cf. Hyckyns), Steven, Pensell, Coke, as in **330**

RELIGIOUS
Stretford (cf. Stretforde, Stratford), Kyngeswode, as in **328**
Holom (cf. Holam), as in **329**

APPENDIX

The Itinerary of William Bothe 1447–1452

1447

2 May[1]	Croydon	Lambeth Palace, Register of John Stafford, fo. 26v.
9 July	London, St Paul's	BL, Cotton MS Vesp. E. xvi, fo. 346; *Registrum Sacrum Anglicanum*, p. 89; **10**
13 July	London	**187**
28 July	London	**188**
4 August	Coleshill	**12**
6 August	Haywood	**13**
12 August	Haywood	**316**
14 August	Haywood	**312**
18 August	Coventry	**14, 15**
20 September	Wilmslow	**189**
28 September	Haywood	**72**
2 October	Lichfield	**312**
3 October	Lichfield	**16**
11 October	Lichfield	**11, 277**
12 October	Lichfield	**73**
13 October	Kenilworth	**74**
11 November	Strand, London	**190**
16 December	Strand, London	**281**
1448		
3 January	Hackney, London	**76**
13 January	Strand, London	**160**
19 January	Strand, London	**127**
25 January	Hackney, London	**90**
8 February	Strand, London	**130**
14 February	Hackney, London	**161**
18 February	Strand, London	**92**
19 March	Strand, London	**19**
12 April	Strand, London	**162**
6 May	Strand, London	**20**
18 May	Beaudesert	**79**
25 May	Beaudesert	**191**
28 May	Haywood	**88**

---

[1] This date is clearly an error: for a discussion of the more likely date of profession see introduction, p. xvi.

3 June	Haywood	**21**
4 June	Haywood	**22**
7 June	Haywood	**83, 229**
12 June	Haywood	**230**
15 June	Lichfield	**276**
4 July	Haywood	**84**
10 July	Haywood	**228, 287**
15 July	Haywood	**131, 232**
20 August	Eccleshall	**85**
22 August	Eccleshall	**23**
31 August	Eccleshall	**86**
5 September	Eccleshall	**192**
13 September	Haywood	**163**
20 September	Haywood	**87, 132**
21 September	Haywood	**133, 322**
25 September	Haywood	**287**
26 September	Haywood	**164**
1 October	Haywood	**281**
2 October	Haywood	**282**
5 October	Haywood	**193**
13 October	Haywood	**323**
18 October	Haywood	**286**
22 November	Strand, London	**194, 227**
21 December	Strand, London	**233**
1449		
16 January	Hackney, London	**24, 234**
17 January	Hackney, London	**195**
23 January	Hackney, London	**89**
25 January	Hackney, London	**90**
1 February	Hackney, London	**165, 166**
5 February	Strand, London	**25**
6 February	Strand, London	**91**
12 February	Westminster	Anne Curry, ed., 'Henry VI: Parliament of February 1449, Text and Translation', in *The Parliament Rolls of Medieval England*, Appendix no. 1
18 February	Strand, London	**92**
25 February	Hackney, London	**26**
7 March	Strand, London	**93, 196**
8 March	Strand, London	**235**
18 March	Strand, London	**27, 167, 236**
24 March	Strand, London	**28**
28 March	Strand, London	**29**
10 April	Haywood	**30**
12 April	Haywood	**326**
14 April	Haywood	**94**

17 April	Haywood	**31, 288**
26 April	Haywood	**197**
27 April	Haywood	**237, 238**
28 April	Haywood	**198**
29 April	Haywood	**32, 135, 239**
17 May	Beaudesert	**134**
10 July	Haywood	**287**
15 July	Eccleshall	**169**
17 July	Hackney, London	**95**
31 July	Haywood	**168**
4 August	Haywood	**33**
13 August	Haywood	**34**
16 August	Haywood	**199**
22 August	Haywood	**96, 241**
25 August	Stone	**35**
26 August	Haywood	**36**
20 September	Haywood	**245**
1 October	Haywood	**37**
2 October	Haywood	**38**
14 October	Eccleshall	**243**
15 October	Eccleshall	**39**
16 October	Haywood	**136**
20 October	Haywood	**289**
22 October	Haywood	**244**
29 October	Haywood	**137**
30 October	Haywood	**279**
1 November	Haywood	**97**
6 November	Westminster	Anne Curry, ed., 'Henry VI: Parliament of November 1449, Text and Translation', in *The Parliament Rolls of Medieval England*, no. 1
12 November	Strand, London	**98**
22 November	Strand, London	**99, 200**
23 November	Strand, London	**201**
5 December	Strand, London	**248**
9 December	Strand, London	**40, 41**
20 December	Strand, London	**247**
1450		
23 January	St Paul's London	**138**
26 January	London	**42**
29 January	London	**280**
31 January	Westminster	*CPR* 1447–52, p. 194
4 February	Strand, London	**139**
20 February	Strand, London	**44, 249**
3 March	Strand, London	**100, 171**
4 March	Strand, London	**172**

17 March	Westminster	Anne Curry, ed., 'Henry VI: Parliament of November 1449, Text and Translation', in *The Parliament Rolls of Medieval England*, no. 50
15 April	Haywood	**45**
18 April	Sawley	**140**
22 April	Leicester	**101**
24 April	Leicester	**250, 251**
25 April	Leicester	**46**
30 April	Leicester	**306**
6 May	Leicester	**141**
22 May	Leicester	**173**
23 May	Leicester	**174**
30 May	Leicester	**252**
6 June	Leicester	**253**
7 June	Leicester	**202**
16 June	Eccleshall	**203**
26 June	Clayton	**254**
17 July	Prescot	**204**
18 July	Prescot	**142**
26 July	Clayton	**205**
28 July	Clayton	**314**
30 July	Clayton	**102**
1 August	Clayton	**207, 208**
7 August	Eccleshall	**258**
10 August	Clayton	**332**
29 August	Clayton	**47**
5 September	Clayton	**206**
23 October	Clayton	**175**
28 October	Clayton	**143**
29 October	Bollin	**48**
1 November	Lichfield	**103, 144, 260**
20 November	Strand, London	**49, 50**
14 December	Strand, London	**104**
30 December	Eccleshall	**105, 106**
1451		
2 January	Eccleshall	**209**
5 January	Eccleshall	**308**
12 January	Eccleshall	**55**
21 January	Eccleshall	**145**
22 January	Eccleshall	**51**
24 January	Eccleshall	**146**
5 February	Eccleshall	**52, 53, 54**
15 February	Eccleshall	**210**
16 February	Eccleshall	**55**
19 February	Eccleshall	**211**

20 February	Eccleshall	**261**
23 February	Eccleshall	**176**
24 February	Eccleshall	**56**
17 March	Eccleshall	**283**
19 March	Eccleshall	**57**
20 March	Eccleshall	**212**
21 March	Eccleshall	**147**
27 March	Eccleshall	**148, 262**
19 April	Haywood	**149**
1 May	Eccleshall	**285**
5 May	Eccleshall	**264, 265**
18 May	Eccleshall	**62, 213**
5 June	Eccleshall	**263, 267, 269**
7 June	Eccleshall	**214**
8 July	Eccleshall	**107**
21 July	Haywood	**108**
30 July	Haywood	**293**
31 July	Haywood	**58, 59, 109, 215, 293**
2 August	Haywood	**150**
3 August	Haywood	**110**
9 August	Haywood	**151**
17 August	Haywood	**152**
18 August	Haywood	**216**
20 August	Haywood	**267**
21 August	Haywood	**111**
9 September	Eccleshall	**153**
11 September	Eccleshall	**177**
12 September	Eccleshall	**60**
18 September	Eccleshall	**268**
23 September	Eccleshall	**178**
9 October	Eccleshall	**112, 154, 179**
10 October	Eccleshall	**113**
24 October	Eccleshall	**155**
29 October	Eccleshall	**61, 156**
31 October	Eccleshall	**62**
2 November	Eccleshall	**217, 295**
3 November	Eccleshall	**114**
6 November	Eccleshall	**180**
8 November	Eccleshall	**218**
15 November	Eccleshall	**219**
18 November	Eccleshall	**115**
26 November	Eccleshall	**220, 296**
2 December	Eccleshall	**63**
3 December	Eccleshall	**116, 271**
4 December	Eccleshall	**272**
20 December	Eccleshall	**157**
22 December	Eccleshall	**117**

1452

23 January	Daventry	**294**
1 February	Strand, London	**64, 181**
15 February	Coventry	**65**
16 February	Lichfield	**66**
26 February	Haywood	**182**
28 February	Haywood	**67**
15 March	Haywood	**297**
1 April	Haywood	**68**
3 April	Haywood	**69, 183**
7 April	Haywood	**298**
8 April	Haywood	**343**
17 April	Haywood	**158**
18 April	Haywood	**119**
20 April	Haywood	**120**
21 April	Haywood	**184, 221, 307**
24 April	Haywood	**121, 122, 123**
25 April	Haywood	**185**
2 May	Daventry	**299**
12 May	Strand	**159**
21 May	Strand	**221**
21 June	Strand	**124**
28 June	Haywood	**70**
3 July	Haywood	**222**
8 July	Haywood	**223, 305**
15 July	Haywood	**303**
18 July	Haywood	**125**
19 July	Haywood	**186**
9 August	Haywood	**224**
19 August	Haywood	**126**
24 August	Haywood	**225, 304**
26 August	Coventry	**71**

INDEX OF PEOPLE AND PLACES

Walter, 329, 331, 333, 334
Grenehull, Thomas, 341
   William, 330
Greseley, Sir John, 72, 117
Grey, Lady Joan, 20
   mr William, prebendary of Longdon, 78, 312
Gropenhale, *see* Grappenhall
Gropenhale, Robert, 338
Grosvenor, Robert le, 195
Grotwich, *see* Gratwich
Grove, Richard, vicar of Aston by
   Birmingham, 35, 242
Gruffis, John Ap, rector of Christleton, 213
Gryme, William, 331, 333, 334
Grypton, Thomas, 340
Gylbert, *see* Gilbert
Gylowe, William, rector of Thurstaston, 190

Hackney, *see* London
Haddeley, William, 325–7
Haddon, William, vicar of Great
   Packington, 54
Hagmond, Haggemond, *see* Haughmond
Hagmond, Bramond, Henry, 333, 339
Hakirman, Hakyrman, John, 339, 340, 344
Halesowen, Halesowyn, Halesowyne
   (Worcs), Premonstratensian abbey,
   80, 324, 325, 327, 330, 331, 333,
   334, 339–41, 344
Hall, James, vicar of Leigh, 210, 212
Halshale, Henry, 296
Halughton, *see* Haughton
Halyngbury, John, vicar of Eccleshall, 246, 259
Hampstereley, Hamsteley, Hamsterley,
   John, 331, 336, 338
Hampton (Warw), 248, 255
Hamstall Ridware, Rydware (Staffs),
   church, 248, 255
Hamsteley, Hamsterley, *see* Hampstereley
Hancok, Richard, rector of Aldridge, 76
Handesworth, *see* Handsworth
Handsworth, Handesworth (Warw),
   church, vicar of, *see* Leytwharte,
   alias Lovelady, John
Hanery, John, 328, 329
Hankelowe, Hankynlowe, Thomas, 325, 327, 328
Hanneley, Robert, 73
Hansacre, prebendary of, *see* Heywode, mr
   Thomas

Hapsforde, Hapsford, William, 325, 328
Haraway, Hereway, John, 9, 246, 265, 267, 269, 317
Harcourt, Richard, 92
   William, 92
Hardborough Magna, Herdeburgh
   (Warw), church, 248
   rector of, *see* Stodeley, John; Wadilove,
   Richard
Hardynge, Hardyng, Thomas, 326–8
Harnage, Christopher, 296
Harper, Joan, 280
Harrymon, John, 317–18
Harryson, Humphrey, vicar of Alstonfield,
   vicar of Biddulph, 85, 306
Hartington, Hertyngton (Derbys), church,
   248, 255
Hartshorne, Hertishorn (Derbys), church,
   248, 255
Hatherton, Richard, 258
Hatton, Thomas de, 231
Haughmond, Haggemond, Haghmond,
   Haghmonde, Hagmond (Salop),
   Augustinian abbey, 171, 180,
   317–19, 321, 322, 325, 327–31,
   333, 334, 336, 339
Haughton, Halughton (Staffs), church, 248
   rector of, *see* Alkyn, William
Hawkyn, Richard, vicar of Madeley, 126
Hawkys, Thomas, vicar of Wombourn, 96, 241
Hawson, Richard, chaplain of chantry at
   Chesterfield, 9, 149
Hawte Hukenall, *see* Ault Hucknall
Haywood, Heywod, Heywode, Heywood
   (Staffs), xvii, 12, 13, 21, 22, 30–4,
   36–8, 45, 58, 59, 67–70, 72, 121–3,
   125, 126, 131–3, 135–7, 150–2,
   158, 163, 164, 168, 182–6, 193,
   197–9, 215, 216, 222–5, 228, 232,
   237–9, 241, 242, 244, 245, 267,
   276, 278, 282, 286–9, 193, 197,
   198, 303–5, 307, 312, 323, 326,
   343, Appx pp. 157–62
Henley, Br Malachius, 336–8
Henry IV, king of England, xiii, xv
Henry V, king of England, 279
Henry VI, king of England, xv, 79, 90, 91,
   99, 164, 314, 315
Henshagh, Ralph, 246, 258, 269
Henwood, Henwode (Warw), Benedictine
   priory, 333, 334
Hepp, *see* Shap
Herdeburgh, *see* Hardborough Magna

INDEX OF SUBJECTS

oath (*cont.*)
   absolution by bishop from illegal oath,
      100
obedience, reserved in exchange, *see*
      permutation
obits, in a chantry, 314, 315
official of archdeacon, induction by
      archdeaconry vacant, 195
   certificates by, 226, 229, 230
oratory, in a mansion, 247, 305, 307
   marriage in, 247, 305
orders, general, 317–19, 321, 322, 324,
      325, 327–31, 333–6, 338, 340, 341,
      344
   special, 320, 323, 326, 332, 337, 339,
      342, 343
   exemplification of, 313
   and see dimissory, letters; dispensation
ordinations, xxviii, 317–44

papal letters, *see* bulls
patronage, litigation in King's Bench
      concerning, 129
   pro hac vice, 73, 90, 94, 103, 119, 206
patrons, bishop as patron, *see* collation
   king as patron, 79, 91, 99, 165
   queen as patron, 73, 89
   lay patrons, 4, 7, 18, 19, 20, 24, 25, 29..
      33. 38, 39, 42, 45, 47, 49, 59, 65,
      72, 75, 76, 81, 82, 83, 86, 90, 94,
      103, 107, 109, 110, 116, 117–19,
      128, 136, 141, 143, 149–52, 156,
      162, 163, 168–70, 172, 187–9, 191,
      200, 202, 206, 209–11, 214, 218,
      223, 224
   religious as patrons, 12, 13, 14, 16, 17,
      21, 23, 24, 26, 31, 34, 35, 37, 41,
      50, 51–4, 56–8, 60, 61, 63, 66–8,
      71, 77, 85, 96, 101, 102, 111, 115,
      120, 123, 125–7, 130–2, 137, 138,
      140, 144, 146, 153–5, 157, 161,
      164, 166, 167, 171, 175, 177, 178,
      180, 182–5, 190, 194, 196, 201,
      203–5, 213, 215, 216, 222
   others, 3, 30, 78, 84, 122, 133, 145, 148,
      158–60, 193
pension, to archdeacons, 178–81, 283, 303
   absolution from unlawful oath to pay,
      100
   to the bishop, 279, 280, 281, 283, 303
   to a cathedral, 167, 209, 278
   to former incumbents, 227, 234, 236,
      241, 242, 249, 254, 260–2, 270,
      271, 275

   to poor parishioners, 278–81, 283, 303
Peter's pence, 237
pluralism, declaration concerning, 277
prayers, form prescribed for use in a
      chantry, 314, 315
prebends, *see under individual names*
prebendaries, *see under* Lichfield, canons of,
      and under individual names
presentation, *see* patronage
priories, *see under individual names*
prison, *see* gaol
prisoner, *see* clerks, criminous
probate, jurisdiction in, 237
proctors, of archdeacon, 281
   of abbot and convent, 280
   of dean and chapter of a cathedral, 281
   of a college, 281
   of a prior and convent, 281, 283, 303
   of a vicar general, 280
   of the clergy, 20, 39, 45, 61, 63, 70, 71,
      78, 118, 135, 149, 161, 166, 167,
      169, 171, 172, 176, 186, 198
provision, of a prior by the bishop, 97
   of a prioress, 121, 199
purgation, *see* clerks, criminous

rebellion, xxiii–xxiv
rectory, moiety of, 188, 191
   presentation to, 4, 15, 18, 19, 25, 29, 33,
      39, 47, 49, 64, 65, 72, 73, 76,
      79, 81–3, 86, 89, 90, 94, 100, 103,
      107, 109, 110, 116–19, 133, 134,
      136, 137, 143, 145, 147, 148, 150,
      151, 152, 156–9, 162, 163, 167–70,
      177, 182, 187–92, 195, 198, 200,
      202, 205, 206, 209–11, 213, 215,
      216, 223
register, of bishop, xxi–xxiv
   of papal vicar general, 313
   of vicar general, xxii
registrar, *see under individual names*
religious houses, as appropriators, 279, 280,
      283, 303
   commissions to confirm election of heads
      of, 62, 74, 217
   dispensation to religious to hold benefice,
      referred to, 43, 187
   as patrons, see patrons
   quashing of election of priories, 199
   statutes for a priory following visitation,
      285
   and see under names of individual houses
resignation, *see* vacancy
robbery, by criminous clerks, 267–9